DATE DUE

~~NOV 1 1 2004~~		
~~DEC 0 1 2004~~ 𝒞		
MAR 1 5 2005		
MAR 2 9 2005		
JUN - 3 2005		
~~MAR 1 0 2007~~		
MAY - 4 2007		

Demco

Also by Bernard Lugan

Histoire de l'Afrique du Sud [The History of South Africa]

Afrique: Histoire à l'Endroit [Africa: Its History Set Right]

Afrique, Bilan de la Décolonisation
[Africa: The Legacy of Decolonization]

Histoire de la Louisiane Française (1682-1804)
[History of French Louisiana, 1682-1804]

Afrique: de la Colonisation Philanthropique
à la Recolonisation Humanitaire; [Africa: From Philanthropic
Colonization to Humanitarian Re-Colonization]

Ces Français qui Ont Fait l'Afrique du Sud
[The Frenchmen Who Built South Africa]

Histoire du Rwanda [History of Rwanda]

La Guerre des Boers (1899-1902) [The Boer War, 1899-1902]

Histoire du Maroc des Origines à nos Jours
[History of Morocco from Its Origins to the Present]

Atlas Historique de l'Afrique des Origines à nos Jours
[Historical Atlas of Africa from Its Origins to the Present]

Histoire de l'Egypte des Origines à nos Jours
[History of Egypt from Its Origins to the Present]

Robert de Kersauson: le Dernier Commando Boer
[Robert de Kersauson: The Last Boer Commando]

Villebois-Mareuil, le La Fayette de l'Afrique du Sud
[Villebois-Mareuil: South Africa's Lafayette]

Cette Afrique qui Était Allemande
[The Africa that Was German]

AFRICAN LEGACY
Solutions for a Community in Crisis

Bernard Lugan

Carnot USA Books
22 West 19th Street, 5th Floor
New York, NY 10011

First edition
Originally published as *God Bless Africa: Contre la mort programée du Continent noir*
Translated and adapted by Tom Clegg, Carnot Editions, Chatou, France

Cover design by Priya Kale
Book design by Sharon Lewis
Printed in the United States of America

Library of Congress Cataloguing-in-Publication Data

Lugan, Bernard, 1946 -
African Legacy: Solutions for a Community in Crisis
1. Decolonization—Africa, 2. Afro centrism, 3. Africa—Economic condition, 1960,
4. Africa—Colonization, History, 5. Africa—Colonial influence, 6. Africa—Social conditions, 1960. I. Title.

DT31 .L85 2003   960 21
ISBN 1-59209-035-4 (hardcover)

Published by:

Carnot USA Books, Inc.
22 West 19th Street, 5th Floor
New York, NY 10011
www.carnotbooks.com

212-255-6505
Email: sales@carnot.fr

If you don't know where you're going,
turn around and look where you've come from.

Senegalese proverb

Table of Contents

List of Maps

Foreword

Thirty-two years spent in Africa as a professor of history, an archeologist, a journalist, and a simple traveler, as well as teaching at the University of Lyon and at the French military academy, have guided my reflections and allowed me to write this book which is intended to revolutionize the approach that industrialized nations are taking to Africa. My reflections give evidence, and have led to the conclusion, that Africa's problems have been diagnosed incorrectly. They also provide alternative solutions. At the outset, let's take a look at the present situation:

— Today, one out of three Africans is experiencing famine, and the Africa of 2003 is poorer than the Africa of 1970.

— Africa's share of international trade keeps dropping; it declined six percent in 1980 and two percent in 2003.

Africa represents less than two percent of the United States' foreign trade, two percent of that of the United Kingdom, one percent of Germany's and Japan's and four percent of France's. Since 1960, all forms of development have been used. None of them has worked.

— "Politically correct African," imposed in the United States by the Afrocentric lobby and in Europe by the historical school of European culpability prevents us from designating the real causes of these failures and leads to an error in diagnosis.

Causes of the Wrong Diagnosis

If both Europeans and Americans alike have misdiagnosed the roots of Africa's problems, we must ask ourselves why. Here are some of the reasons I have identified:

First and foremost, the belief Europeans have that they once plundered Africa feeds on their culpability syndrome.

Secondly, the electoral weight of African-American citizens prevents Americans from taking a realistic approach to Africa. For example, during his visit to Senegal in 2003, President G.W. Bush thought he had to acknowledge the legend of the island of Gorée, and so he arranged to be photographed in the well-known "House of Slaves." This is a badly misnamed landmark since it could never been used as a slave center, not having been built until 1783 when no more slave trading was taking place in this part of Africa (see pp 61-63). But Bush's actions demonstrate how much politicians will manipulate history in order to get the Afro-American vote.

African-Americans have an idealized vision of the African continent and a perception of the white world based on resentment. They cling to Martin Bernal's myth of Afro-centrism in *Black Athena*. This vision is critical since it conditions the entire American approach to the African continent while challenging the philosophical basis on which the USA was built.

The most fundamental principle of the United States of America is the importance of the individual. European migrants who landed in New York wanted to melt into the American nation through enterprise, thrift, and hard work. Individual achievement was proposed as a model.

Such values, while implemented by Europeans, traumatized the African-American community which was isolated and abandoned to marginalization. Later, as African-Americans realized the electoral weight that they could muster in America's bi-partisan system, they transformed their demands for integration into a philosophy of resentment. The latter yielded "affirmative action" and "politically correct" speech. So that certain communities could elevate themselves artificially, their members were favored to facilitate their access to levels of schooling they could not reach through open competition.

As practiced by America, "Trade, not Aid" attempts to apply the same idea to the entire continent. In June 1997, President Clinton defined a specific policy for the black continent, coined as "a new partnership for growth in Africa." Its goal was to try and make sub-Saharan countries participate in the world economy.

The chosen solution consisted in artificially stimulating Africa's exports. The method was akin to "affirmative action" as it is practiced in American universities. But the root problem of Sub-Saharan Africa is not economic; it is, above all, political and constitutional.

My Proposals

First, I propose letting the people who constitute the prime engine of Africa rediscover the dynamism they lost through colonization, instead of using affirmative action which only leads to pushing the least competent to the forefront. While competition, even confrontation, is the engine of history, democracy founded on the "one man, one vote" principle has favored the most numerous but not necessarily the most capable.

Secondly, the post-colonial states, which are built inside artificial borders, are nothing but empty legal shells that do not coincide with the flesh-and-blood countries at the root of human societies. But they do exist, and, since it is not foreseeable, at this stage, to redraw Africa's boundaries, the priority is to find an institutional means that will allow political change so that the most numerous tribe may not necessarily wield all political power.

Thirdly, the societies of the northern hemisphere are individualistic, and their constitutional bases are built on common convictions and political programs that transcend cultural and social differences. Such a notion is foreign to Africa, where societies are traditionally communal, hierarchical and where voting is ethnic. The concept of "nation" is not the same in America as it is in Africa since, in one case the social order rests upon the individual, and, in the other, upon the group as a whole.

The solution to this contradiction must be found in a system where representation would go to groups and not to individuals. But in order to do this, it is of paramount importance to repudiate the western system based on the principle of "one man, one vote."

This would constitute a veritable revolution in the eyes of the Americans and Europeans but also of those Africans who thought they could get an eternal rest because of the advantages of a dominant demographics.

In conclusion, let us be realistic and let us cease to think that Africans are white men with black skin. Drowning sub-Saharan Africa under a flood of grants and aid will not achieve anything. Let us meditate over this African proverb: "Rain does not wash away the zebra's stripes." Africa does indeed have a powerful personality as well as a powerful history. Africa is not a continent in its infancy. The only true problem is that our individualistic philosophy not only is foreign to her but, worse still, is killing her slowly.

Introduction

Inventory of a Stricken Africa

Seen from the shores of Europe or North America, black Africa, meaning the portion of the continent that begins at the southern edge of the Sahara desert, is a devastated land, abandoned to its famines, its wars, its epidemics, its political, economic, and social disasters.

This vision is simplistic, because Africa as a geographical object is composed of a myriad of realities as removed from one another as the Balkans are from Sweden, and as much by their languages as by social habits. The local situations are contrasted and often very different. It is difficult to compare the landlocked countries with those with coastlines, the oil-producing countries with agricultural ones, or those that have succeeded in diversifying their productions with those which rely wholly on one or two products and whose economies are dependent on variations in world prices. Nevertheless, this tragic vision, still remains globally true.

In the 1950s, Asia was the part of the world in distress. It suffered terrible famines and underwent bloody upheavals: the civil war in China, the partition of India and Pakistan, the conflicts in Korea and Indochina, the turmoil in Bangladesh, etc., while the Dark Continent was experiencing peace, undergoing industrialization locally, and developing by giant steps. But all that was in "colonial times," under white imperialism.

Today, Asia seems to have pulled itself out of the abyss while Africa has tumbled into it. As opposed to what happened in Asia, the African standard of

Map I: Principal Areas of Tension in 2002

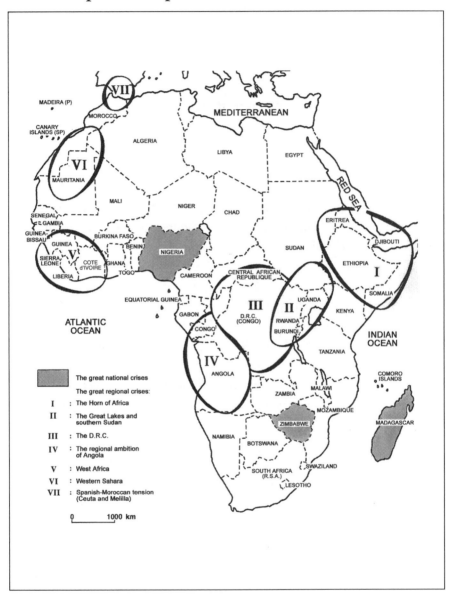

The great national crises

The great regional crises:

I : The Horn of Africa

II : The Great Lakes and southern Sudan

III : The D.R.C.

IV : The regional ambition of Angola

V : West Africa

VI : Western Sahara

VII : Spanish-Moroccan tension (Ceuta and Melilla)

0   1000 km

living has not stopped falling over the last half century. The percentage of the African population living beneath the "poverty level" established by the United Nations – one dollar a day or less per person – was 47 percent in 2002. This figure has not changed since the 1990s, and, while one might be "reassured" at least by its stability, this stability means that, taking into account the demographic expansion, the number of poor people has increased considerably. In its 2002 report, the United Nations Development Program (UNDP) even indicated that sub-Saharan Africa was five percent poorer than in 1990.

We will examine the conflicts in Africa and their roots at greater length later. For the moment, we will limit ourselves to the painful observation that, due to numerous national and regional crises, Africa is being plundered and raped. The current upheavals in Côte d'Ivoire, which involve states beyond its borders (Guinea, Liberia, Burkina Faso) should not cause us to forget the continent's other conflicts. The wars, both civil and cross-border, of the "Kongo[1] bloc," have not been resolved and similarly extend beyond the limits of the Democratic Republic of the Congo (DRC). The genocide in the Great Lakes area (Uganda, Burundi, Rwanda) has not put an end to clashes in this region. The Horn of Africa (southern Sudan, Ethiopia, Eritrea, Djibouti, and Somalia) has been left to itself following the disaster of the American operation, Restore Hope, which was even broadcast live by CNN. The coronation of a new king in Morocco has not resolved the very profound dispute with Algeria over the question of Western Sahara, and even the ancient tension between Spain and Morocco over the former's enclaves, Ceuta and Melilla, has been revived.

If there are multiple African crises that notably present important regional differences, they often appear to be humanitarian and nutritional tragedies stemming from excessive, not to say suicidal, population growth.

Today, as a result of the changes introduced by "colonial" medicine, the African population has been increasing on average by about three percent each year, which means a doubling of the population every 20 years. Among the sectors affected has been the power supply. In 1970, 200 million Africans did not have access to electricity. By 2002, that figure had grown to 500 million, even

---

[1] The names of the clans, ethnic groups, and tribes are indexed at the end of this volume.

though thousands of kilometers of lines had been stretched over the land and connected to power plants in the 30 years intervening.

In addition, the soaring population has produced an irreversible destruction of the natural environment, despite the fact that it is the major source of food. On the ground, with each passing year, the expanding deserts of sub-Saharan Africa and the impoverishment of the equatorial rain forests is visible to the naked eye, without the aid of any sort of measuring instrument.

Behavioral patterns have also not adapted to the major new factor of overpopulation, and Africans continue to function according to the criteria of traditional societies, dating back prior to colonization when they could make use of the inexhaustible resources of the environment. An example? Less than 10 percent of the wood cut down on the continent involve timber operations for export, which would provide an important source of foreign currency. Because eight out of ten Africans still eat food cooked over wood or charcoal fires, 85 percent of the cuttings are used purely for cooking. The remainder is used in local construction.

The net effect is that births are outstripping the infrastructure. This undeniable fact is most dramatically illustrated by the question of agricultural resources. Between 1960 and the present, African agricultural production increased by 45 percent. This is a remarkable result, even if it was achieved more through cultivating new land than by technical improvements. But, in the same period, the population rose by more than 110 percent. The food situation is thus hopeless. In these conditions, it is impossible for African states to ensure a minimal subsistence for their people.

In 1960, Africa was self-sufficient and exported foodstuffs. In 1980, it imported 11 million tons of food. By 1995, it needed 45 million tons. And by 2002, 30 African countries were experiencing a permanent food crisis. A dozen of them, notably in southern and eastern Africa, were on the edge of famine. In all, taking one year with the next, between 150 and 200 million Africans are undernourished and tens of millions survive only thanks to international food aid.

Map II: The Great African Barriers

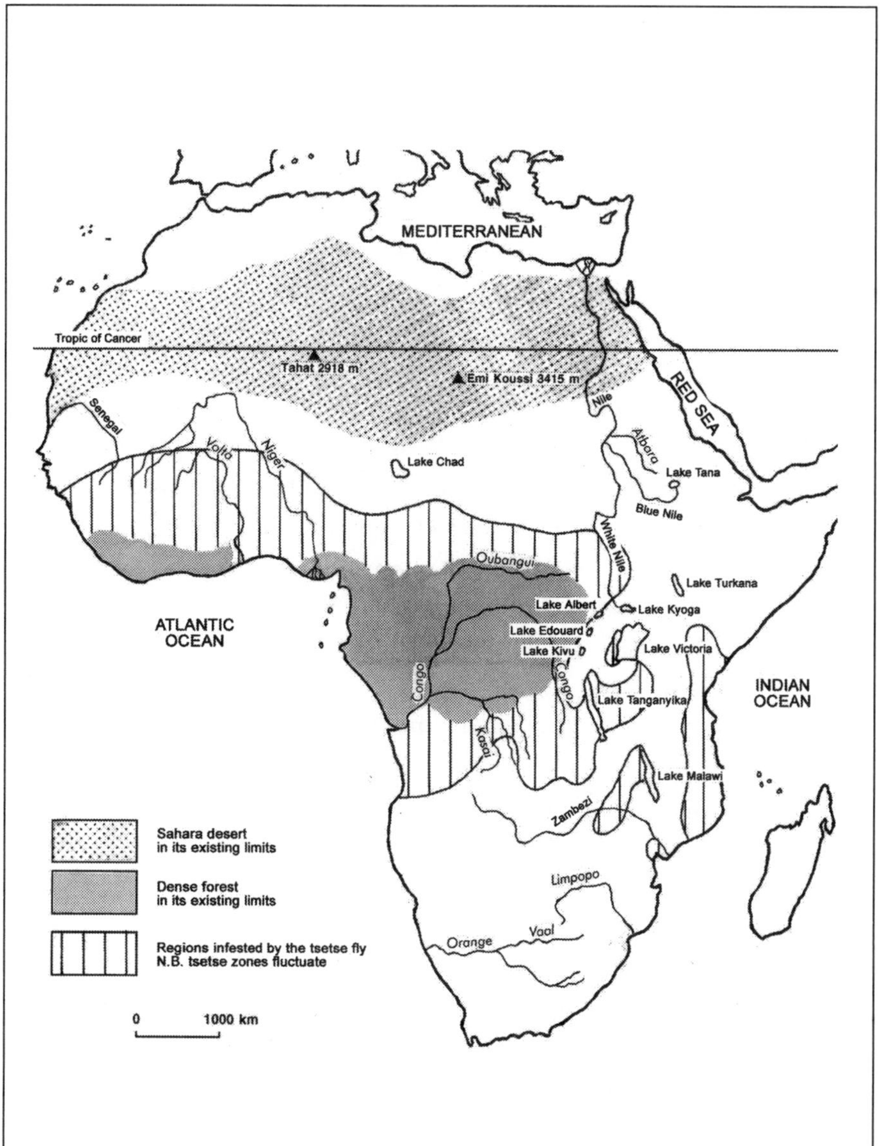
MEDITERRANEAN
Tropic of Cancer
Tahat 2918 m
Emi Koussi 3415 m
Nile
RED SEA
Senegal
Volta
Niger
Lake Chad
Atbara
Lake Tana
Blue Nile
White Nile
Oubangui
Lake Turkana
Lake Albert
Lake Kyoga
ATLANTIC
OCEAN
Lake Edouard
Lake Kivu
Lake Victoria
Congo
Congo
Lake Tanganyika
INDIAN
OCEAN
Kasai
Lake Malawi
Zambezi
Limpopo
Orange
Vaal
Sahara desert
in its existing limits
Dense forest
in its existing limits
Regions infested by the tsetse fly
N.B. tsetse zones fluctuate
0
1000 km

Does the continent at least play some economic role? Alas, the answer is clearly negative. The situation might change if major reforms were carried out, but in the immediate future, it would be futile to bet on an economic takeoff south of the Sahara.

The most important new development of the 1990s was the end of the rivalry between the Eastern and Western blocs, marking the conclusion of what the English historian Eric Hobsbawm called, the "short 20th century."[1] This conclusion has sunk the African continent even further into a deep hole. As the Cape route – around the Cape of Good Hope, at the continent's southern point – is no longer threatened by Soviet submarines, and control of the mineral deposits of central and southern Africa is no longer essential to Western economies, Africa has ceased to be a strategic and economic factor. As a result, those who courted its favors yesterday have today turned their backs on it.

The Gross National Product (GNP) of sub-Saharan Africa (excluding the Republic of South Africa[2] [RSA]) is equivalent to half of Ohio's, and represents half a percentage point of the world's combined GNPs (1/200). California's output is seven times larger than that of sub-Saharan Africa excluding the RSA; New York's is more than four times larger. As for the United Kingdom, with its 61 million inhabitants, its GNP is 10 times that of sub-Saharan Africa and its 600 million people.

In 2001, oil produced by 11 countries in the zone comprised half of all African exports. Yet, in spite of the oil boom, Africa's share in world trade has steadily shrunk: in 1980, it dropped to 5.9 percent, in 1996 to 2.3 percent, and in 2002 to two percent. Moreover, these figures refer to the continent as a whole. Taken together, the 46 countries of sub-Saharan Africa account for less than 1/300 of world trade.

For six of the continent's principal products (cacao, coffee, cotton, wood, sugar, and copper), the fall in production since 1960 has been between 22 and 38 percent. Even more serious, Africa's share in the export of these products has collapsed. Africa has little by little been supplanted by Asia and South America in domains where, up until recently, it had provided essential foreign currency

---

[1] E. Hobsbawm, *Age of Extremes,* London, 1995.
[2] Its economy is not at all comparable with the rest of the continent.

earnings. In 1960, Africa accounted for 73 percent of world trade in vegetable oils. That figure had dropped to 27 percent in 1990, and it is less than 10 percent today. Peanut oil exports were 60 percent African in 1960 but only about 20 percent today. Have oleaginous plants lost ground due to changes in our mode of consumption? Not at all. The fall is solely African in origin. While Africa continues to lose market share, Asia has been steadily gaining.

African Share in the Foreign Trade of the Five Largest Economic Powers

	Exports	Imports
France	5.3%	4.3%
Great Britain	3.2%	2.1%
Germany	2%	2.2%
United States	1%	2%
Japan	1%	1%

Let's see how this has impacted U.S.-African trade. Despite speeches and declarations of good intent, the economic importance to Washington of the African continent in its entirety is ridiculously small. Taken as a whole, Africa sells only $28 billion worth of goods and services to the U.S., and sub-Saharan Africa, excluding the RSA, barely crosses the $5 billion threshold. Of these, over two-thirds are comprised of oil and natural gas, and they represent less than 1/400 of the United States' imports. Taken as a whole, Africa purchases roughly $10 billion worth of goods and services from the United States, well below one percent of the latter's sales; and sub-Saharan Africa, represents less than 1/300 of America's exports.

Other than Nigeria, the Republic of South Africa, and secondarily Algeria, American trade with the rest of the continent amounts to practically nothing compared to the total.

The same applies to trade between Europe and Africa, even if, due to historical links, Africa has a somewhat greater economic "weight" on the continent. In the case of France, Africa represents approximately 4.5 percent of total foreign

African Suppliers of the United States

Nigeria	3.4%
Angola	12%
Algeria	9.6%
Gabon	8%
Rest of Africa	18%

African Customers of the United States

Egypt	33.3%
Republic of South Africa	30%
Algeria	8.7%
Nigeria	7.2%
Morocco	5.25%
Rest of Africa	14.75%

trade, about $21 billion per year, of which about $11 billion are imports, and $10 billion are exports. Half of these involve flows with Morocco, Algeria, and Tunisia. Sub-Saharan Africa represents only slightly over one percent of France's trade.

Following independence, most of the countries comprising French West Africa (Afrique Occidentale Française – AOF), and French Equatorial Africa (Afrique Equatoriale Française – AEF), adhered to the African Financial Community (Communauté Financière Africaine – CFA), which established parity between French francs and CFA francs in order to ensure the monetary stability of these countries, while facilitating trade both amongst the member countries and with the former colonial power. Thirty years later, in the 1990s, the share of the CFA region within total foreign trade by France was less than one percent Morocco alone is a more important trade partner for France than the entire "favored" CFA zone.

As for French investments in Africa, they represent only 1.8 percent of total overseas investments. This small percentage is concentrated in nine countries: Nigeria, Egypt, Algeria, Angola, Gabon, Tunisia, Zimbabwe, the South African Republic, and lastly, Morocco. These nine countries together account for 81 percent of total French investment in the continent. Among them, only Gabon belongs to the CFA zone.

We find the same tendencies in the case of Great Britain. Africa represents on average two percent of all its imports and three percent of all exports. These weak commercial flows essentially involve a small number of countries such as the South African Republic (35 percent), Nigeria (25 percent), Zimbabwe, and Kenya. As opposed to France, Great Britain did not maintain any currency peg with Africa after its colonies became independent. Either way, trade and investment flows remain negligible.

The situation is even more clear-cut in the case of Germany, whose colonial history ended with its defeat in 1918 and the Treaty of Versailles. Beyond certain well-defined sectors of economic interest, Berlin simply does not have any African economic policy. In 2000, the African continent represented only two percent of all German exports and less than two percent of total imports, Trade exists essentially with the two geographical extremities of Africa: in the north, with Morocco, Algeria, Tunisia, Libya, Egypt, and in the south, with the South African Republic. The rest of the continent does not matter to Germany.

As for Japan, Africa is neither a trading partner nor a real outlet for its finished goods. It is merely a supplier of raw materials and has represented on average only one percent of total Japanese foreign trade since 1996. Most of this trade is conducted with three countries: the South African Republic, Nigeria, and Liberia. The mention of Liberia appears odd, but less so once one learns that trade relations between this country and Japan are fictitious. They involve ships "sold" to Liberia in order to sail under a flag-of-convenience. Ninety percent of all Japanese investments in the continent in fact consist of the registration of Japanese ships in Liberia, which does not benefit the African economy at all.

The painful reality is that 40 African countries depend solely on "international solidarity," as one calls it these days. In other words, they depend on charity. To put it bluntly, if the peasants of Africa disappeared from the face of the Earth tomorrow, Wall Street would not even raise an eyebrow. At least if it were only the peasants, because, of course, oil is another matter.

As we have seen, the principal export, and the only one growing on the continent, is petroleum. Could this oil save Africa?

In 1997, 11 African countries produced oil. By 2002, there were 15. Today, the African continent as a whole holds 8-10 percent of known reserves and on average provides about 11 percent of world production. In ten years, African oil production has risen by more than 40 percent, compared to slightly under 20 percent on the other producing continents. The trend in the medium and long term is therefore very favorable to Africa. The inventory of its proven reserves shows an increase of over 25 percent in the last 10 years, a remarkable figure when one compares it to the world average of 15 percent. Africa will thus continue to see its share increase and its production will easily exceed 10 million barrels per day in 2005 as opposed to eight million barrels today.

American oil policy in Africa has been evolving for several years. As the biggest world oil importer, with 494 million tons of crude oil in 2000, the United States has tried, since the 1970s, to reduce its dependence on the Persian Gulf. The Americans have diversified by turning to other suppliers including Africa; notably Nigeria, Gabon, and Angola. Two-thirds of America's imports originating in Africa now involve crude oil, mainly from Nigeria, which constitutes 13 percent of American supplies. Angola also possesses immense oil fields offshore and is becoming a major supplier of the United States. Thus, in a single year, between June 2001 and June 2002, the quantity of Angolan petroleum exported to the United States rose by nearly 60 percent.

All this has led to the emergence of new oil-producing countries. Discoveries of oil have multiplied. The most promising finds have been made in deep waters offshore where surveys have only just begun. Very encouraging results are expected in the coming years all along the coast of the Gulf of Guinea. But discoveries have also been made inland. In Algeria they have increased the country's reserves by a third, while in the Sudan and Chad, they will change the local economic situation.

One can thus legitimately ask the question: will oil, on its own, be enough to raise Africa out of its slump? Will it have a carry-on effect for the continent's stricken economies?

It would be excessively optimistic to answer "yes" to this question. The examples from the past have hardly been encouraging. In Algeria, Angola, or Nigeria, the oil windfalls, have, at best, only slowed the catastrophe. At worst, the focus on oil alone has destroyed once flourishing agricultural sectors, as in Algeria and Nigeria. Everywhere, the exploitation of oil fields has caused waste and even, ironically, fuel scarcities. And above all, it has increased corruption in an exponential fashion.

Can the new oil-producing countries avoid making the same errors as those preceding them? Not under its existing political and social conditions.

Africa also suffers from serious sanitary crises, resulting from the deeply dilapidated state of its health system and evident in the troubling problems associated with large-scale epidemics. According to some projections, AIDS alone could turn the whole African demographic question upside down.

The only "reliable" figures on the extent of AIDS come from southern Africa and lead one to fear a cataclysm within the populations and, notably, among the elite. As far as a true measurement, we can only provide estimates based on the extrapolation of this fragmentary data, and it is risky to try to construct a scientific analysis founded on such projections, since the worst case is not always certain.

However, according to the figures of the Joint United Nations Program on HIV/AIDS (UNAIDS), over 30 million individuals, or 70 percent of the world's HIV-positive population live in Africa. In 2001, 2.2 million Africans died of AIDS. Each year, hundreds of thousands of babies are born with the virus, and nearly 10 percent of HIV-positive Africans are children. The number of "AIDS orphans" is considerable, as 25 million adults have died since the illness first appeared.

(. . .) and in the countries where infection is very widespread, the AIDS virus is killing teachers faster than they can be trained.[1]

According to the report by UNAIDS,[2] "the epidemic is still in its early

---

[1] World Bank, Fourteenth International Conference on AIDS, Barcelona, 7-12.
[2] Preamble to the Fourteenth International Conference on AIDS, Barcelona, July 2002.

stages" while the international community is gambling on an assumed stabilization of the disease due to the loss of the categories most exposed to the virus, a projection refuted by the continuing strong progression in the worst infected countries.

Another crisis, but not the least, is that of "brain drain." Large numbers of African graduates emigrate, deserting their continent where they are nevertheless indispensable, in order to work in the developed industrialized countries where they constitute a surplus. According to French Minister of the Interior Nicolas Sarkozy,[1] "There are more Beninese doctors practicing in France than in Benin."[2] This example eloquently illustrates the policy of desertion by African elites. European countries support this in the name of an open-door policy even though the consequences are deadly for Africa. In short, France has no shortage of doctors, while, in Benin, hundreds of patients die due to the lack of medical practitioners. The result is almost a new form of the slave trade, as its graduates who are the most valuable children of Africa and the only people equipped to undertake its reconstruction, are picked off.

In addition to the brain drain, there is a problem with the massive migration of unskilled populations to host countries. This creates tensions and conflicts that will affect Europeans' perceptions of Africa in future decades. Independent Africa has never accepted responsibility for this sorry state of affairs. In its eyes, the blame lies squarely with the colonial nations.

In October 2001, when the New Partnership for Africa's Development (NEPAD) was born, it seemed as though Africa was finally giving up such accusatory incantations. The initiative was universally hailed as a sign of a new spirit of African awareness, and a new determination that the continent's future should no longer rely on international aid. The creation of NEPAD even seemed to mean that Africa had at last decided to carry out a realistic examination of the causes of its failures, that it had resolved to take charge of itself, and that it would stop asking the outside world for solutions to its problems.

But, despite these laudable intentions, Senegal, one of the principal instigators behind NEPAD, published a document[3] which constitutes a perfect

---

[1] All the named persons cited are indexed at the end of this volume.
[2] Declaration broadcast on 100 *Minutes to Win*, on the Francez channel 12/9/02.
[3] Senegal's Vice Presidency, Le NEPAD Expliqué [NEPAD Explained], Dakar, 2002.

summary of what has contributed to the continent sinking into lethargy:

> *Africa [. . .] considers that it has been marginalized by historical evolution [. . .]. Its impoverishment stems from the cumulative effects of three hundred years of slavery, of one hundred years of colonization, and since independence, from the economic domination that has taken the form of the exploitation of its resources and the labor of its population via the perpetual historical tendency of prices to fall.[1]*

In other words, all of the problems described above are due to the nations that supported slavery, then colonization, before becoming "economic imperialists." This is a discourse whose arguments, repeated for at least the last 60 years, have led to a system fueled mainly by guilt. This guilt in turn forces Europe and the United States to intervene in order to "repair their wrong doings" under pressure from pro-Third World or Afro-American groups clinging to the famous "right of interference" so dear to media-glamorized French doctor Bernard Kouchner.[2] It is a guilt which, at the same time, permits African leaders to take shelter behind the childish excuse of "It's not me, it's them," and has proved to be an excellent lever to raise mountains of "international aid" in areas that are nonetheless strictly Africa's own responsibility.

This is what we designate as the "victimization paradigm" — a terrible hindrance to any legitimate, cool-headed appraisal of the African situation and an ideological limit buttressed by arguments so worn out they have become dogmatic. We intend to prove in this book, for Africa and for its sake alone, that these arguments are not only false, but suicidal.

---

[1] It is worth noting that, although agriculture supports 800 million Africans and represents more than 30 percent of the continent's economy, it is strangely absent from this formula.

[2] Translator's Note: Bernard Kouchner was one of the famous "French doctors" who helped found the non-governmental organization (NGO), Médecins sans Frontières, which began its operations in Biafra during the civil war in Nigeria (1967-1970) before intervening in many other of the world's "trouble spots." Kouchner later became the French Minister of Health, and more recently, the UN Administrator for Kosovo after the NATO occupation.

Part One

The Victimization Paradigm

According to the assertions of many African leaders, Africa is underdeveloped because the slave-owning states emptied it of its "best and brightest" by means of the slave trade and then funded their industrial revolutions with the profits, before plundering the continent through colonial exploitation. Propagated first by a certain number of ideologically motivated historians in the 1960s and taken up later by sloppy researchers or lazy plagiarists, such ideas ended up turning these debilitating myths into dogma for intellectuals on the African, American, and European continents.

The most serious consequence is that these myths prevent a lucid and clear-headed examination of the relationship between the Dark Continent and the white world. Furthermore, they deprive Africans of the means of finding the strength to overcome their present difficulties in their real historical substrata. Unfortunately, this is occurring exactly when Africa requires that examination most.

The introductory chapters of this book will show why all such claims are historical distortions.

Chapter 1

Slavery: When Africa Sold Its Children

The prosecution's case rests initially on the painful question of slavery. The weight of past sufferings, the traumas within the collective memory, and the combativeness of African-American pressure groups have all combined to make slavery a highly emotional and explosive question. The exposition of this case generally consists of a collection of clichés whose historical basis, if not questionable, is, for the most part, obsolete. Errors exist concerning the extent and consequences of, as well as the responsibility for, the slave trade.

The Real Nature of the European Slave Trade

Europeans had two methods of procuring slaves. The first was fixed geographically, and known as the "factory." It consisted of coastal settlements in which the prisoners were assembled by African enslavers. These forts were held by a few employees of the European companies, charged with ensuring the quality of the "product" and paying the suppliers. The ships stopped by regularly to pick up their human cargo, destined for the Americas.

The second was mobile. It involved a kind of coastal navigation along the African shores, during which the ships filled their holds little by little with the unfortunate people purchased on the coast.

However, it is important to note that:

[. . .] *In the one case as in the other, the system was, in the final analysis, under African control.*[1]

---

[1] On the subject of contemporary or ancient slavery and behavioral influences in Africa, one can read the excellent article by Roger Botte, "Le spectre de l'esclavage" [The Specter of Slavery], in *Les Temps Modernes*, Nos. 620-621, August-November 2002, pp 144-164.

Whites numbered only in the handfuls and lived entrenched in 40 or so forts that dotted the coasts from Senegal to Angola. Thus, with the exception of the *pombeiros,*[1] Europeans never penetrated the continent's interior and were hardly in a position to play an active role in the two most crucial phases of the "ebony trade:" the capture and the delivery of slaves to the coast. These two tasks were carried out entirely by Africans.

Indeed, the African slave states, who were not ignorant of the laws of capitalism, initiated the slave trade. They knew how to rarefy and regulate "supply" according to demand. From the depths of the continent to its shores, they set up veritable distribution networks with tolls and tax payments, hubs and slave markets in the hinterland, far from the coastal ports that sheltered the white Europeans. And this traffic was a considerable source of profit and power for those Africans who were the associates, partners, and suppliers of the Europeans. In fact, a strong interest bound "the black and white partners together involved in a profit-making economic operation,"[2] and part of Africa became rich by selling the other part.

Not all contemporary Africans have been duped into thinking otherwise. They know these facts and have condemned those responsible. *Andagaman,* the film by Ivorian director Gnoan M'Balla, released in June 2001, deals with this subject explicitly. According to this director, the film presents:

> *[. . .] the complicity of the African people who sold their brothers to the slave traffickers. African tribes rushed off to conquer other tribes, the vanquished were taken prisoner and exchanged for guns and rum.*

The weekly *Jeune Afrique* [Young Africa], dated July 28, 1998, also mentions that certain descendants of slaves in the French West Indies have begun to recognize this fact, proclaiming in a shocking headline:

> *We Have Nothing to Do with the People Who Sold Us.*

And the magazine goes on to say:

> *At a time when Africans are demanding reparations from Europeans for their role in the sale of slaves, the West Indians want to call Africans*

---

[1] People of mixed black African and Portuguese race operating in Angola.

[2] F. Renault & S. Daget, *Les Traites négrières en Afrique [The Slave Trade in Africa]*, 1985, p.87. One should also read S. Daget, *La Traite des Noirs [The Slave Trade in Black Africa]*, 1990.

to account: "Africa sold its children," they accuse. [. . .] It does indeed seem, in fact, that Martinicans need, for the first time, to ask questions about Mother Africa and to openly express their anger with her, in order to clear the air.

Let's clear the air, then. The slave trade was only possible because black Africans captured other black Africans to sell them to slave traders.[1] Indeed, the sale of men and women who were treated as livestock and turned into the economic system commonly called slavery was not introduced on the African continent by Europeans. The reality of the slave trade is that it was black Africans who sold their "brothers" to the European slave traders. What Europeans did was to redirect a traditional practice to their own benefit and thus contribute for a time to its perpetuation.

In studying the quotas within the slave populations, David Ellis highlights the preponderant role of the African slave traders.[2] He shows how European buyers, even though they preferred young men, were forced to pay for women and children, as they were entirely dependent on the supply from the Africans, over whom they had little influence. Once their human "merchandise" was purchased, the ships departed as rapidly as possible for the Americas by the "Middle Passage," a direct route with favorable winds allowing an Atlantic crossing in record time.

The liberties taken with history can be judged by Patricia Rozema's film adaptation of Jane Austen's famous novel, *Mansfield Park*.[3] Contradicting historical facts, the filmmaker imagines a scene (that does not appear in the novel) in which the heroine is traveling along the English coast in a horse-drawn carriage. She hears groans coming from the sea and questions her driver. The latter informs her, without batting an eye that it is a slave ship and that these agonizing cries are coming from the unhappy slaves packed in its holds. This is, of course, impossible since no slave trader would have taken the risk of "spoiling his ebony" by dawdling in the English Channel. The ports of Liverpool or Nantes never saw any black captives, other than in an anecdotal fashion. The boats left the European ports loaded with goods to exchange with the suppliers

---

[1] Illife, J. *Africans: The History of a Continent*, 1995.
[2] D. Ellis, "Fluctuations in the Age and Sex Ratio of Slaves in the Nineteenth Century Transatlantic Slave Traffic," *Slavery and Abolition*, No. VII (1986).
[3] Paperback edition from Oxford University Press.

Map III: The Atlantic Slave Trade
(15th – Early 19th Centuries)

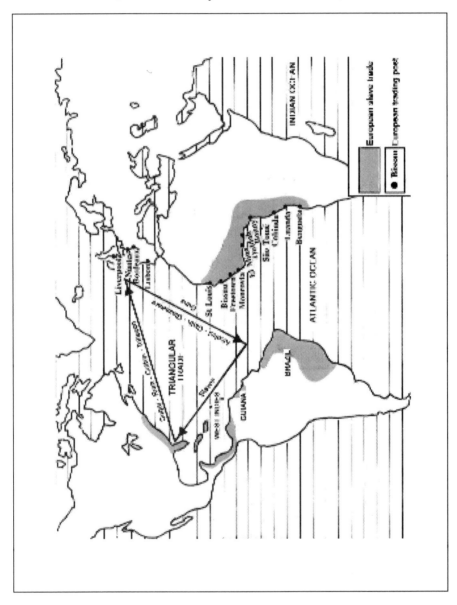

in payment for their captives and came straight back loaded with produce from the Americas. This gave rise to the term "triangular trade."

Who were these black African slavers, these partners of the white traders? There existed both on the coast and inland, African slave states that collaborated in the slave trade and built their wealth on it. (Map IV) Hugh Thomas has described how some of them enjoyed remarkable prosperity derived from the sale of their "brothers" to the Europeans.[1] The "terms of trade" were always favorable to the African slavers.

One of the great contributions of David Richardson[2] has been to show that the phenomenon only grew in scale as it persisted. The value of the goods and merchandise given in payment for each "head" by the European slave traders to their African suppliers continued to increase in the latter's favor, with a considerable rise from 1750 onwards.

It is known, for example, that Tegbessou, the king of Abomey who reigned around 1750, sold over 9,000 slaves to white traders every year.[3] The monarch enjoyed revenues well in excess of those of ship owners in Nantes and five times greater than rich landowners in England.

Most West African states during this period were slave-owning. Four of the biggest coastal states owed their fortunes and their development to commerce in slaves: Abomey (or Dahomey), Benin, Ashanti, and Oyo.

The history of Oyo, the least known among them, reveals the real nature of the slave trade. It is once again quite different from the image complacently transmitted by the media or works of fiction. Situated to the northeast of the West African forest, the kingdom of Oyo developed a remarkable military imperialism at the end of the 17th century. Historically, its warrior force, and above all, its cavalry, had permitted an abundant harvest of captives who were taken in raids from the Yoruba to the southwest, and from the Bariba and the Nupe to the north. These prisoners of war originally had become slaves within the victors' own society. With the appearance of the European slave trade, however, some of them were diverted to the coast. Then, as the Oyo began to realize that the slaves it supplied to the coastal kingdoms would permit it to make con-

---

[1] H. Thomas, *The Slave Trade, London*, 1997.
[2] D. Richardson, "The British Empire and the Atlantic Slave Trade," 1660-1807. In Vol. II of *The Oxford History of the British Empire*, 1998, pp. 440-464.
[3] R. Law, "Slave-Raiders and Middlemen, Monopolists and Free-Traders: The Supply of Slaves for the Atlantic Trade in Dahomey c. 1715-1850," *Journal of African History*, No. 30 (1989) pp. 45-68.

Map IV: The Slave Gulf

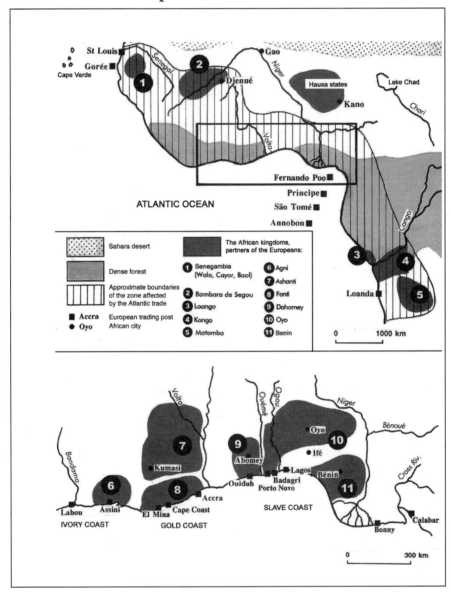

siderable profits if it sold them directly to the Europeans, they decided to reach the ocean in order to establish direct contact with the Whites. In other words, they wanted to cut out the middlemen.

And so, the kingdom of Oyo sought to control the southern routes leading to the European ships gradually and methodically. Between 1650 and 1670, Allada, Jaquin, and Porto Novo[1] became commercial dependencies of Oyo, and thereafter it was the latter kingdom that supplied these ports with captives sold at full profit for Oyo to the white slave traders.

All was "for the best" for several decades, until the kingdom of Abomey appeared as an emergent power close to these three principalities. Abomey quickly tried to deprive Oyo of its maritime outlet and cut the commercial routes leading inland. Allada, Jaquin, and Porto Novo were no longer able to guarantee the security of the free zones between kingdoms through which these routes passed[2]. The principalities were conquered one after the other by Abomey's armies.

The kingdom of Oyo, for which the revenues from the slave trade were vital, quickly understood that it was essential to eliminate this rival. Around 1725, it entered into a war against Abomey. Despite the violence of the clashes, neither of the belligerents managed to obtain a decisive military advantage. Peace was based on a compromise: Abomey would keep the outlets on the ocean and the slavery windfall, but would pay a handsome tribute to Oyo. But this "reasonable" arrangement was never really applied. The kingdom of Abomey continued to increase its deliveries of slaves and to develop its power. Oyo, rather than launch any new and uncertain military campaigns, preferred to strengthen its links with one of the principalities, Porto Novo, as the route leading to this port was easier for it to control directly.

However, in the second half of the 18th century, the kingdom of Oyo slowly fell apart, giving ground to blows from its peripheral provinces, who also wished to profit more from the economic benefits of the slave trade. In the 19th century, the importance of Porto Novo faded, as its supplies were less reliable than the two great slave-trading ports in the region, which were thereafter Badagry and Lagos.

The history of the kingdom of Abomey, studied notably by B. I. Obichere,[3] is no less rich in lessons:

---

[1] Three small principalities on the coast of the present state of Benin.
[2] Zones known as "hinterland."
[3] B. I. Obichere, "Women and Slavery in the Kingdom of Dahomey," *Revue Française d'Histoire d'Outremer,* Vol. LXV (1978) No. 238, pp. 5-20.

Since its origins, the kingdom of Dahomey was a predatory state. It conquered and annexed several small states. In its expansionary wars, Dahomey clashed with the peoples living on its northern and eastern frontiers, respectively the Yoruba and the Mahi. The inhabitants of these regions were captured as prisoners-of-war and brought to Abomey, the capital.

These captives were sold at numerous traditional markets located at the center or at the periphery of the kingdom. With each of these markets, a place was reserved for the slave trade. In all, again according to Obichere, there were 20 such markets throughout the kingdom. This was a considerable figure compared to Dahomey's relatively small area at the time. All of these markets functioned on a daily basis. They were already in existence when the Europeans made their first explorations, and they were still there when the Whites penetrated further into the country in the 19th century.

The Muslim Slave Trade

Another weakness in the effort to pin the blame for slavery on Europe is that it accounts only insufficiently for the fact that two types of slave trade coexisted: the European trade that arrived from the ocean, and the Muslim trade that came from the north and northeast of the continent.[1]

The more familiar of these, the European trade, began in the 16th century and came to an end at the beginning of the nineteenth century. We will return to its abolition later.

The other, the Arab trade, began 700 years earlier and never really stopped until the end of the 19th century with the colonization of Africa. This colonization rendered abolition effective because it controlled territories hitherto dominated by Muslim slave traders.

In the eyes of the media, however, commerce in slaves is almost always regarded as an iniquity imposed by the peoples of Europe or America; even if, amid the chaos that reigns in Africa today, this Arabic Muslim slavery still persists in certain regions.[2] It has become marginal, fortunately, but in Africa still there are black slaves belonging to Arab, or Muslim, masters.

---

[1] M. Gordon, *L'Esclavage dans le Monde Arabe du VIIe au XXe Siécle [Slavery in the Arab World from the 7th to the 20th Century]*, 1987.

[2] On Mauritania and also on Sudan, see the Report of Amnesty International: *Mauritania: A Future Face of Slavery* 2002 (on *http://web.amnesty.org*).

One of the reasons for this ignorance regarding the Muslim slave trade is that it is impossible to obtain reliable figures. Figures from Arab sources showing the effects on African demography and others were produced late in the day and largely exaggerated by Christian missionaries who saw, in this continuing Muslim slave trade a major argument justifying their installation in the continent's interior. Only the slave trade in East Africa – which became quite important in the 19th century – took place in a zone providing any reliable historical data.

It is known, however, that the Muslim slave trade hindered the conversion of sub-Saharan Africa to Islam. The law of Mohammed would have required the slavers to give up their human "merchandise" since only non-Muslims can be enslaved. By converting newly discovered African tribes, the Arabs would have deprived themselves of a "raw materials deposit."

The idea that filters down through from Arab sources is that there is a contempt for black Africans which has been present since the beginnings of the Muslim expansion. Thus, Iyad al-Sabti (1083-1149) writes the following:

[They] are all the most corrupt of men and the most given to procreation. [. . .] Their life is like that of the beasts. They pay no attention at all to the affairs of this world, if they do not concern food or women. Outside of that, nothing is worthy of their notice.

For the famous historian and man of letters, Ibn Khaldun (1332-1406), also cited by Murray Gordon:[1]

The only peoples to accept slavery are the Negroes due to their inferior degree of humanity, their place being closer to the animal state.

And this as well, also penned by Ibn Khaldun:

The behavior of those in the Sudan (the Muslim term for Africa) is generally characterized by levity, inconsistency, and exuberance. They are given to dance from the moment they hear music, and to eccentricities, in all their countries [. . .] Further south, there is no civilization worthy of interest. One only finds men closer to beasts than to intelligent beings [. . .] Sometimes, they eat one another. One cannot count them among the numbers of humans.

---

[1] M. Gordon, op cit., 1987.

Map V: The Muslim Slave Trades
(9th - 19th Centuries)

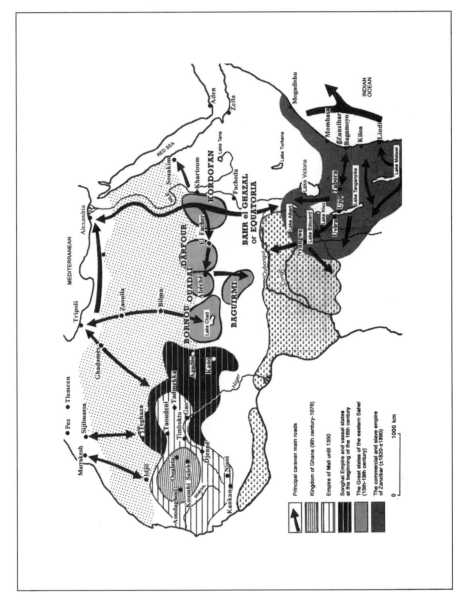

It would be fallacious to insinuate here that only Arabs have written such racist slurs. But we should at least recognize that colonialist literature is quoted much more often than Andalusian letters.

As to the form of slavery practiced by the north of the continent, it presented at least two important differences from the European trade:

—Firstly, while the Europeans participated neither in slave-hunting operations nor in the delivery of "catches" to the point of sale, Arab Muslims were directly involved in both these activities in the Sahel zone of Africa, which is sparsely populated regions at the southern border of the Sahara.

—Secondly, while the Europeans traded primarily in men, the Muslim trade was directed first at women, next at children, and lastly at the men.

This Muslim trade affected three vast regions of black Africa that were separate centers of commercial expansion. We will start with the Saharan trade,[1] which affected Sahelian West Africa. Here, the commerce in slaves was a component in trans-Saharan exchanges that linked the two fringes of the "Sea of Sands." This trade, the oldest, started with the opening of trans-Saharan trails by Muslims, and Arab sources dating back to the 9th century mention this form of commerce. The practice would continue until the 20th century, and in a clandestine form, even up to the start of this century.[2]

From the north, the Arabs carried goods, which shared three advantages: they were non-perishable, they were not very cumbersome, and they had a high market value. These included jewels, cloth, and arms as well as slabs of salt loaded during the journey. On their return, the traders brought back from the south ivory, gold, feline skins, feathers, and. slaves, who were even more "practical" to transport since they followed the caravan on foot. But in the case of slaves, the traders did not generally capture their victims themselves. Local tribes, sometimes given arms for their pains, did the job. Little by little, the organized states in the north coordinated these raids, relying on ethnic groups that became specialized in manhunts.

Numerous European accounts from the 19th century contain reports of this Saharan trade. Examples include those written by the Scotsmen, Mungo

---

[1] On this subject, see François Renault, "La Traite des Esclaves Noirs en Libye au XVIIIe Siècle" [The Black Slave Trade in Eighteenth. Century Libya], *Journal of African History*, no. 23 (1982), pp. 163-181.

[2] Amnesty International, op cit.

Park (1771-1806) and Hugh Clapperton (1799-1839), as well as by the German, Gustav Nachtigal (1834-1885). They describe the ravages caused by the slavers. The men were decapitated, and their remains were abandoned on the spot, while the women and children were dragged along the Saharan trails, where the ordeal of a long forced march awaited them. And the mortality rate was enormous. In 1822, Clapperton followed some slavers bringing their human loot back to the north for five days, and the caravan trail was strewn with dozens of bodies still shackled.

In 1895, the Fulbe (Peuhl converted to Islam) devastated the whole of what is now eastern Chad and seized thousands of captives. In this part of the Sahel, peace would only return with the death of the slaver chief, Snoussou, killed in a battle with French troops in 1911. The colonial military presence probably prevented the depopulation of this region, and, once the European troops were installed there, the inhabitants learned to live again without constant fear of raids by horsemen from the north. This was no doubt a fear of the same order as that once provoked by the raids of Drakkar Vikings in Europe.

The Saharan slave trade would thus last over 1,000 years. It is impossible to give a precise scale however, because the Muslim traders, as opposed to the Westerners' slave ports and colonial companies, left no archives.

Next, there was the slave trade in the northeastern corner of Africa, which was primarily Egyptian, but also Arab, in origin. Reports of this trade began in the 12th century. It was mostly due to the search for women, who were primarily affected by it. Indeed, the women of the Nilotic settlements of the southern Sudan gained such a reputation for their beauty that they were much sought after. When they evoked the subject, the Arabs waxed lyrical, as in the case of the famous geographer al-Idrisi (1100-1166), speaking about the Nubian women, one of the principal ethnic groups in this region:

> [They] are of a very great beauty. They have been excised. They are of a noble origin that has nothing to do with that of the other peoples of the Sudan. Throughout the territory of the Nubia, women are distinguished by the beauty and perfection of their features: fine lips, small mouths,

white teeth, smooth hair. Nowhere, among the peoples of the Sudan, whether they be the Makzara, Ghana, Kanem, Bedja, Habasha, or Zandji [does there exist] this sort of smooth, floating hair possessed by the Nubian women. For marriage, there are none more beautiful. A [Nubian] slave costs about three hundred dinars. Also, as all these qualities are prized by the kings of Egypt, the latter tend to overbid the sale prices.

During the first half of the 19th century, Egypt adopted an imperialistic policy towards Nubia, in the present-day Sudan. The fruit of this expansion into Nubia, was the city of Khartoum. It was founded in 1830, and trading posts were created further south. Ivory and slaves constituted the bases of commerce along the axis of the Nile, and fairs were held in all the major Egyptian cities. Specialist traders offered black captives to buyers from all over the Middle East there. As late as 1890, 78 slave merchants officially plied their trade in Cairo, and 73 were well-established in Alexandria.

The principal "hunting grounds" of the Egyptian slave traders, as well as their Arab counterparts, were Bahr-el-Ghazal, the Fashoda region, and Equatoria.[1] These regions, to the north of Lake Albert, were populated by Nilotic tribes who spoke languages of the Nilo-Saharan group and who are still today at the heart of the conflict between the Arab-Muslim and black African worlds that has plagued southern Sudan for nearly half a century.

The accounts left by European travelers of the 19th century are terrifying. Georg Schweinfurth (1836-1925), a German who explored these regions from 1868 to 1871, described the burnt villages and the decomposing corpses of men. Only the young, both boys and girls, were taken captive.

This Muslim penetration southwards met with resistance. That of the Shilluk, for example, was particularly fierce. Also a Nilotic tribe, they rebelled in 1860, then in 1868, and once again in 1874-1875. Each time, the Egyptian reprisals were merciless. During the last of these revolts, the regional capital, Fashoda, was transformed into an enormous slave market where numerous Shilluk were sold. These raids, which decimated entire regions, moved ever further to the south into the region of Equatoria.

---

[1] See Map V: Muslim Slave Trades.

There they came up against European philanthropists. One of them, Samuel Baker (1821-1893) had, beginning in 1869, won over the populations of this region. His accounts "turned the stomachs" of respectable London society.

It was once again abolitionist Europe which mobilized against such practices, and Egypt gave way in the face of international pressure. To demonstrate his good faith, the Khedive of Egypt, Ismail (1830-1895) named European governors in the Sudan. In 1877, another Englishman, Gordon, was appointed Governor-General of the Sudan. In 1878, Eduard Schnitzer[1] became governor of Equatoria. From 1880 onwards, the situation in this immense region was thus, in theory, under the control of these European governors appointed by the Egyptian Khedive.

In 1881, however, they had to face a Muslim "fundamentalist" uprising led by a warlord who called himself al-Mahdi, "the envoy of God." Mahdi managed to gather around him all those who were opposed to Egyptian hegemony, from Muslim leaders who did not accept the domination of Cairo to the slave traders who could not tolerate the obstacles to their lucrative commerce being set up by the European administrators. In the space of a few months, the Egyptian presence was swept from the region.

At the same time, in the Red Sea region, commerce in slaves was also flourishing. Some of these captives came from the peripheral regions of Ethiopia, notably the south of the empire, where the slave trade was still important even on the eve of the First World War. It was only the installation of Great Britain at Aden in 1839, followed by that of France at Obock in 1862 and at Djibouti in 1884, that helped to reduce this traffic.

However, the best-known, if not the most important, form of slave trade originating in the Arabian peninsula, was undoubtedly the Eastern trade. More recent than the Saharan trade, it has been studied by numerous historians, to whose publications we refer.[2]

In 1840, the Sultan of Muscat[3] decided to take up residence on Zanzibar, making this now legendary island, offshore from what is today called Tanzania, the capital of his sultanate. This was no mere whimsy on his part but a logical

---

[1] A German who became famous under the name of Emin Pasha.
[2] F. Renault, *Lavigerie, L'Esclavage africain et l'Europe [Lavigerie, African Slavery and Europe]*, Toulouse, 1971, 2 Vols. See also Marissal, J., *L'Islam et les royaumes interlacustres de l'Afrique de l'Est au XIXe siècle [Islam and the Nineteenth Century Great Lake Kingdoms of East Africa]*, doctoral thesis in History, University of Paris I, Centre de Recherches Africaines, 1976, 2 Vols., and J. Marissal, "Le Commerce Zanzibarite dans l'Afrique des Grands Lacs au XIXe Siècle" [Zanzibar Trade in the Great Lakes Area of Nineteenth Century Africa], *Revue Française d'Histoire d'Outremer*, Vol. LXV (1978) No. 239, pp. 212-235.
[3] Ruler of the country now called the Sultanate of Oman.

consequence of his commercial plans. Until that time, the Arabs had not taken the initiative in making contacts and exercised no control whatsoever over the lines of communication in the interior of the African continent. It was the Yao in northern Mozambique, the Kamba in what is now Kenya, and above all, the Nyamwezi, living to the south of Lake Victoria, who held the monopoly and made "coastal deliveries" in the same way that occurred with the European trade on the other side of the continent.

During the first half of the 19th century, however the new resolve of the Arabs to work their way "upstream" along the three trails, which all led deep into the heart of the interior and were used respectively by the Yao, the Kamba, and the Nyamwezi, represented a considerable change. These routes became the axes of penetration for their imperialism in this region. Here again, the search for ivory and slaves was at the root of these Arab initiatives. In 1830, the trading post at Tabora was created; in 1840, the port of Ujiji was founded on Lake Tanganyika; and Buganda, a black kingdom in the south of present-day Uganda, was reached in 1844. From that point on, mixed race Afro-Arabs proceeded to carve themselves vast empires within the Congo river basin.

Among them was a certain Hamed ben Mohammed el-Murjebi, known as "Tippo Tip." Born around 1840 on Zanzibar, and probably dying June 13, 1905, on the same island, he belonged to a trading family from Muscat that had settled in eastern Africa. He became the master of an immense commercial empire in the Congo basin where he exploited the potential riches of raw ivory (tusks) and black slaves. In 1887, the Sultan of Zanzibar, Seyyid Bargash, appointed him governor (vali) of the whole Stanley Falls region. Tippo Tip resided at Nyangwe,[1] a trading post founded in 1860 on the right bank of the Lualaba river, where Dr. Livingstone would be the first European to stay, from March to July 1871. On July 4, 1893, Belgian soldiers took control of Nyangwe, which had become the sumptuous enclave of a nabob living in grand style and systematically draining the region's wealth. The troops of King Léopold II thus put an end to the slave trade in the Congo basin.

Having returned to Zanzibar to finish out his days, Tippo Tip wrote his

---

[1] See Map V: Muslim Slave Trades.

memoirs on the advice of his friend, Dr. Heinrich Broch. They were published in 1901, in German, and then were republished with commentary by F. Bontinck under the title, *Autobiographie de Hamed ben Mohammed el-Murjebi, Tippo-Tip* (1840-1905).[1] They constitute an important resource on the question of slavery and have made Tippo Tip famous among experts in African history.

Rumaliza was another Muslim slaver chief who wielded his power to the north of Lake Tanganyika. Each of these chiefs demanded that the brokering or "protected" tribes under their command supply them with slaves and ivory in the greatest possible quantities.

Three slave trades, in addition to the familiar European one, thus ravaged Sahelian Africa and all of eastern Africa in a vast zone bordered on the north by the Sudan, on the south by Mozambique, on the east by the Indian Ocean, and on the west by the Congo river. The geographical boundaries of these trades, as well as an empirical idea of the losses they inflicted upon Africa, are only known thanks to the accounts left by European travelers.

The most detailed are those of the explorer Richard Burton (1821-1890), who traveled all over the Lake Tanganyika region from 1857 to 1859. And those of Dr. Livingstone (1813-1873), who made two journeys to central Africa: the first from 1858 to 1864, and the second from 1866 to 1873. We also have the accounts of John R. Stanley (1841-1904), who went in search of Livingstone for the *New York Herald* and found him in the Great Lakes region in 1871, before going off again to Zanzibar in 1874, then to the Congo at the behest of Léopold II. Less known is that of Verney Cameron (1844-1894), who, traveled up and down these lands from 1873 to 1876. And lastly, those of numerous other travelers, who have fallen back into anonymity.

One suspects, and these accounts confirm, that wars were the great suppliers of many slave markets in the Arab or North African Muslim world. Every important city had its own market. The captives were exhibited and sold there, the most sought after of which were women (60 percent of "catches") and young boys. The latter were often emasculated to provide harems with eunuchs.

---

[1] Académie Royale des Sciences d'Outremer, Brussels, 1974.

The survivor of castration thus became the guardian of the sexual well-being of a rich lord, who may have bought his mother or sister as part of the same lot. The estimates of the number of small boys dying from the aftermath of this form of mutilation, provided by Charles Gordon when he was governor of Khartoum, were dreadful; he speculated that only one child in 200 (0.5 percent) who was mutilated in this way survived the virulent infections that followed this operation, if a hemorrhage did not empty the victim's blood on the sandy ground of the market.

Once caught and sold to the Arabs, these unfortunate souls were divided into two lots: some remained in the African interior as slaves of the Arab trading posts, while the great majority took the direction of the Indian Ocean, or the Red Sea. In the caravans, the captives were bound to one another. Women and children were simply tied with ropes, while the men were chained together in groups of 10 to 20. The journey lasted two or three months, and, on each interminable march, losses were enormous. The descriptions of the captives' sufferings are hardly believable. In 1869, over the course of several weeks, Livingstone came across caravans from central Africa.[1] These originated at Maniema.[2] Hundreds of the chained captives carried elephants' tusks. The women and children followed behind. During the march to the ocean, those that could not keep up were killed.

Burton was also witness to a terrible scene:

> *The leader of our caravan remains behind because a young girl, one of last purchases, cannot continue the route due to a wound in her leg. Seeing that there is no remedy, he cuts off the poor child's head.*[3]

The Africans were exported from numerous ports along the East African coast, most destined for Zanzibar. The dhows, or Arab ships, that made these crossings could hold between 150 and 200 people, who were forced to squat throughout a voyage lasting one to three days. For each slave disembarked, the dhow's captain had to pay customs duty. Burton observed in 1859 that this entry fee varied from one to three dollars per individual, depending on the ethnic group. The immediate consequence of this tax was that the ill and dying,

---

[1] *The Last Journals of David Livingstone in Central Africa from 1865 to his Death,* London, 1874.
[2] In the eastern savanna of the present-day Democratic Republic of Congo.
[3] R. Burton, *The Lake Regions of Central Africa: A Picture of Exploration,* London, 1860, 2 Vols.

having become unprofitable, were thrown into the water.

Before their obligatory passage through the market, the slaves had a period during which to recuperate the strength they had lost after their capture. They were fattened up and washed, and when they were judged "presentable," they were led to the market, held daily from 4 p.m. The sale was made in a procession. It was led by the seller, while his criers boasted of the quality of the men, women, and children being presented. When a spectator was attracted by one of them, the procession halted and the "product" that had aroused the interest of the prospective buyer was examined from head to toe. In 1866, Livingstone described this market:

> *Three hundred individuals, approximately, were being put on sale. Except for the children, all of them seemed ashamed of their position. The teeth were looked at, the skirt lifted up to examine the legs, then a stick was thrown so that, in retrieving it, the slave showed his quickness. Some were dragged into the middle of the crowd, and their prices were constantly being shouted out loud. Most of the buyers were Arabs from the north and Persians.[1]*

If we do not know the prices paid at the source of the slave trade because the Europeans did not venture into the interior of the continent, we do, however possess information concerning the Eastern slave trades. The profits were considerable. Between the zone of capture and sale on Zanzibar, the value of a slave was multiplied five or six times. According to Burton,[2] a slave bought for two to six dollars at Tabora in 1859, was sold for between 13 and 20 dollars on Zanzibar.

Marissal's work,[3] based on records of Zanzibar customs receipts, shows that, from 1830 to 1875, 743,000 slaves were sold at this market alone, giving an average of 16,500 sales per year. These figures only concern Zanzibar's official trade and do not take into account either contraband, deaths during the journey or the activities of numerous ports on the mainland coast that traded directly with the Arabian peninsula. Regarding "transport losses," Marissal estimated that, for each slave sold at the market on Zanzibar, four or five perished en route or at the time of their capture. Once again, even if these estimates

---

[1] Op cit., 1876.
[2] Op cit., 1862.
[3] J. Marissal, "Le Commerce Zanzibarite dans l'Afrique des Grands Lacs au XIXe siècle," [Zanzibar's Trade around the Great Lakes of Africa in the 19th Century] in *Revue Française d'Histoire d'Outremer*, Vol. LXV (1978) No. 239, pp. 221-235.

allow extrapolation as to the scale of the massacres, it is impossible to give a global evaluation of the Eastern trade, due to the lack of reliable sources. The same cannot be said about the European trade, and yet it is the latter, and only the latter, that is blamed for demographic thinning out and African underdevelopment due to the "triangular trade."

The Myths of Slavery

To begin with, these myths are based on a quarrel over some very problematic numbers. What has happened is that prosecutors of the case against Europe have advanced reprehensibly imprecise estimates that are then broadcast by public figures who are, at best, ill-informed.

Here is just one of many examples that is representative in many ways. Koffi Yamgnane, the brilliant engineer of Togolese origin, who was elected mayor of the town of Saint-Coulitz in France in 1989 and then became the French Secretary of State for Integration under the presidency of François Mitterand, had no hesitation in 1992 in affirming:

The figures I know are that 150 million Africans were taken as slaves.
I believe it is important that apologies be presented to us.

We will demonstrate that, between this declaration, made by a top-ranking official of the French state, and historical reality, lies a gap that separates received ideas – propaganda – from scientific truth.

Let's finish once and for all with wildly fanciful evaluations of this type. There are "maximalist" ones, such as that by Koffi Yamgnane we have just cited. We do not, in fact, even know to which slave trade(s) he was referring, but no doubt everyone assumed he meant the "European" form, but also those which minimize the impact of slavery and, which are just as dangerous because they contribute equally to distorting public perceptions of the issue.

The first serious attempt to estimate the volume of the European slave trade dates back to 1966. D. Fage's[1] estimate that it only removed about 15 million black Africans from the continent caused considerable controversy.

In 1969, Curtin[2] did a new study based on a verifiable reality (the only one which is unquestionable) of the number of slaves who disembarked in the New

---

[1] D. Fage, *An Introduction to the History of West Africa,* London, 1966.
[2] P. Curtin, *The Atlantic Slave Trade: A Census,* Madison, 1969.

Fage's Estimate of the Volume of the Slave Trade

16th century	900,000
17th century	2,750,000
18th century	7,000,000
19th century	4,000,000
TOTAL	14,650,000

Curtin's Estimate of the Volume of the Slave Trade

From 1450 to 1600	200,000
From 1601 to 1700	2,000,000
From 1701 to 1810	7,000,000
From 1811 to 1870	2,000,000
TOTAL	11,200,000

World. The figures he put forward in a refined estimate, divided not by centuries but by historical periods, show less than 12 million slaves.

As the result of a considerable amount of research, in particular monographs about the slave ports, the global estimates by Curtin were later revised upwards, notably by Lovejoy and Richardson,[1] in order to take account of losses at sea.

Up until the beginning of the 18th century, the deaths caused by transport in the slave shifts are assessed at about 20 percent of the slaves initially shipped. That figure is thought to have fallen to about 10 percent by the end of the century, and then to 5 percent in the 19th century. As far as the British trade is concerned, Richardson writes that mortality at sea was high until about 1680 before reaching an average of 10 percent in the second half of the 18th century. It dropped again after 1788, when the Dolben Act came into effect. This imposed rules of hygiene aboard slave vessels and a reduction in the number of slaves transported in relation to the size of the holds. In all, about 450,000, or a little over 13 percent, of the 3,400,000 Africans embarked on British ships between 1662 and 1807, died during the voyage.

---

[1] P.E. Lovejoy, *Transformations in Slavery: A History of Slavery in Africa*, Cambridge, 1983.
D. Richardson, "Slave Exports from West and West-Central Africa. 1700-1810: New Estimates of Volume and Distribution," *Journal of African History*, No. 30 (1989), pp.1-22.

Since they concern the fates of men, women, and children, these terse figures, even considered as relatively "low," send a chill down one's spine. To understand them correctly, however, one needs to recall the living conditions aboard sailing ships in the 16th and 17th centuries for whoever was embarked upon them. Set side by side, the figures for slave losses compared with those of losses of crew members, embarked at Liverpool, Plymouth, or Nantes, are about the same, and slave mortality was sometimes even lower:

The slave trade demands and consumes sailors and captains. And here the verb takes its full force; many die in the trade. On average, 20 percent of a crew, statistically more than the black cargo.[1]

In short, it was not healthy living onboard one of His Majesty's vessels (or French ships) and slaves were no worse off than their jailors.

Today, there is a consensus on the parts of historians regarding the global volume of the Atlantic slave trade. Research has generally confirmed the figures given by Curtin in 1969.

In a study that summarized the existing state of knowledge in this field, H. Thomas wrote:

The attempts to establish the exact measure of the number of persons transported between the 15th and 19th centuries are futile. [I consider] that the approximate figure must be 11 million, give or take 500,000.[2]

In any case, do these 11 or 12 million victims, to which must be added the unknown numbers who died in the raids by the black African suppliers of the "ebony trade," explain the state of contemporary Africa? Does the abduction by Europeans of African men and women between the 16th and 19th centuries, alone suffice to explain the slow development of Nigeria or the Congo in the 20th and 21st centuries? Any such assertion runs into a major problem: to evaluate the impact of the tragedy on the population, one must be able to estimate the total numbers and life expectancy of that population. Since we do not know anything at all about the continent's demography before the start of the slave trade, we must base our assumptions on theoretical estimates.

Somewhat arbitrarily, Catherine Coquery-Vidrovitch, one of the most

[1] F. Renault & S. Daget, *Les Traites Négrières en Afrique [The African Slave Trades]*, Paris, 1985, p. 87.
[2] H. Thomas, *The Slave Trade*, London, 1997.

ardent critics of Europe's role in creating Africa's ills, sets the population of black Africa at 100 million in 1650.[1] Is this figure well-founded? Whatever claims she makes, we simply do not know the answer. In an equally peremptory fashion, she reduces this figure by five percent over a century because there were only 95 million in 1750. Thus, Coquery-Vidrovitch can speak of "stagnation." Now, according to her, this stagnation could only have been due to the slave trade, which disrupted and broke natural growth. The evidence is that the Chinese population doubled and that of the Indian subcontinent both rose by 1/3 in this same period.

Her postulate suffers from two fatal inconsistencies. The first is of a demographic nature. Let us suppose that Coquery-Vidrovitch's figures are right, and that the black African population was indeed 100 million in 1650. How does this relate to the most reliable estimate of the slave trade over four centuries or 20 million (the 12 million attested to by Curtin and Thomas to which are added eight million who died in the course of being captured). Dividing 20 million by 400 years gives an average figure of 50,000 victims per year, or 0.5 percent of the total population of black Africa. While that is too many, it is lower than any conceivable birth rate.

Therefore, in absolute terms and over four centuries, there would have been a total loss of 20 percent (0.5 percent multiplied by 400 years) of the initial population. That may appear to be enormous, but it seems obvious to everyone that this reasoning is fallacious, since it assumes that this population had not evolved in 400 years.

Let's suppose that the black population had stagnated, meaning that each African woman had only given birth, on average, to slightly over two surviving children. If we estimate that the life expectancy of an African was 50 years,[2] in this period, the African population would thus have been renewed seven or eight times during these 400 years. At that rate, the abductions by the slave trade would not have been borne by a population of 100 million but by 700 to 800 million. With a loss of 20 million, a high "maximalist" estimate, the European slave trade would have cost Africa 2.5 percent of its population in the period under consideration.

---

[1] C. Coquery-Vidrovitch, "The Pillage of Equatorial Africa in History," No. 83, July-August, 1978 and *Black Africa: Permanent Sand Breaks*, Paris, 1985.

[2] A highly "optimistic" assumption, because the reality was closer to 35 years than to 50.

While this represents a considerable cost on the personal level, it ends up being very little in terms of the demographic flux of a population. The question then becomes whether such a toll would have compromised significantly, and definitively, the future of a continent.

A comparison with human catastrophes experienced by other countries, and notably, by Europe, may help to answer this question. It is estimated that the great plagues decimated between 30 percent and 60 percent of the European population, depending on the region. To match the European losses due to the Black Death in 1348-1349, which killed, on average, 40 percent of the population, the loss of 20 million would have meant that the total population never exceeded 48 million. Assuming this loss occurred over seven or eight generations and with a life expectancy of 50 years, the population of Africa would have to have been at most six million inhabitants to start. But an estimated population of only six million Africans on the Dark Continent in the 16th century is obviously completely farfetched.

Similarly, the Thirty Years War depopulated a great portion of Central Europe, and, in general, the wars of religion involved massacres that one can scarcely imagine today. Moreover, these catastrophes eliminated large percentages of the population in very short periods of time, sometimes in only a few years, not over four centuries as was the case with the Atlantic slave trade. Even so, these terrible bloodlettings did not block the development of Europe.

The second inconsistency in Coquery-Vidrovitch's argument is the assumption that the slave trade was practiced in a uniform fashion. In fact, these human levies were not always taken at the same times, or in the same places, or under the same conditions.

Thus, the abductions in Senegambia and in the Upper Guinea regions were proportionately heavy in the 16th and 17th centuries, but these were the least important centuries as far as the slave trade was concerned. The numbers declined in those areas at the end of the 17th century.

In the 18th century, when the non-Portuguese slave trade was at its height, the levies were mostly carried out along the Gold Coast and the Slave Coast in the zone occupied by the present-day states of Ghana, Benin, Togo, Nigeria, and Cameroon – encompassing the entire Niger delta. But today, these Ibo, Yoruba, Akan, and Ewe lands are among the most densely populated in coastal Africa. If the arguments of those who attack Europe were correct, we should, instead, find human deserts there.

In 1980, Yves Person, holder of the Chair in African History at the Sorbonne, wrote that locally, instead of emptying the regions of their peoples, the slave trade tended to "sponge off" the surplus of a growing population.[1] Why is such an assertion so politically incorrect? Quite simply because the introduction of American plants by the Portuguese explains this growth. Plants such as manioc, corn, and beans revolutionized the diets of Africans and significantly increased the life expectancy, bringing about an important spurt in population.

Hugh Thomas, for his part, shows that the slave trade ultimately had little effect on the overall demographic balance sheet in Africa. The greater part of the continent escaped the consequences of the slave trade, while the agricultural revolution of American imports more than compensated for slavery's negative demographic impact, even stimulating a growth in population during the 16th and 17th centuries. He writes:

> *The population of West Africa was probably of the order of 25 million at the start of the 17th century, with a rate of growth of 1.7 percent. The slave trade which took 0.2 percent of the population could at most have only slowed its increase.*[2]

In short, whatever angle you look at the argument of the historians who attack Europe, the conclusion is the same: they are obviously distorting history, for purposes which are, in the author's opinion, ideological.

In the final analysis, the slave trade did not bring about the depopulation of Africa, even if it sometimes modified the demographic distribution. John Illife sums up this reality in a catchy phrase when he writes that the demographic levy taken by the slave trade was for Africa "a disaster, but not a catastrophe."[3]

It was a human disaster, for each man and each woman uprooted against their will, put in chains, and condemned to hard labor. That much is painfully

---

[1] Person, Y., "The Population of North Africa during the 18th and 19th Centuries" in *Culture and Society*, Vol. III, 1980, pp 26-49.
[2] H. Thomas, *The Slave Trade*, op cit.
[3] J. Illife, Africans: *The History of a Continent*, op cit.

obvious. But a demographic catastrophe from which an entire continent could not recover? Certainly not.

In any event, Europeans do not deserve the catastrophic evaluations which are regularly hurled at them. The vision of an Africa depopulated by the merchants of Nantes or Liverpool is a mental construct which is seriously damaging to present-day relations among Africans, Europeans, and Americans.

Historically, the practice of commerce in men and women was not the result of European intervention; it pre-existed, traditionally, the "triangular trade." But it remains the case that the "factories" on the coast profited from this practice and lent it an almost industrial character, so that this commerce constituted the economic basis not only of numerous African kingdoms, but also of all the European and American plantations of coffee, indigo, cotton, and sugar.

From this observation, a second historical postulate has emerged and developed. It states definitively that it was thanks to the profits stemming from the slave trade that the European industrial revolution came about. Thus, the human substance stolen from Africa was the origin of Europe's wealth.

This postulate does not stand up to factual analysis either. The European slave trade was largely the work of the Portuguese. During the century when it was at its peak, between 1701 and 1810, Curtin has shown that 40 percent of the Atlantic slave trade drew its "raw material" from a vast region between Cameroon in the north and Angola in the south. About 70 percent of the slave trade in these areas was then controlled by Portugal alone. That amounts to saying that, out of every 100 slaves torn from their land, a little less than 1/3 were taken for the sole benefit of slave traders in Lisbon or Brazil. If industrial development was proportional to the profits derived from the commerce of slaves, Portugal should therefore have been one of the nations best provided for in this respect.

This idea is obviously absurd since it is common knowledge that Portugal was, as recently as two decades ago, still practically an enclave of the Third World in Europe. In fact, Portugal never had its industrial revolution. Nor is this theory supported by the industrialization of Germany, Sweden, or the former Czechoslovakia, since these three countries never participated, or only participated in a marginal way, in trading slaves.

The common rebuttal to this line of reasoning states that the the lack of correlation between European industrialization and the slave trade is because: "One hundred percent of the slaves were disembarked in the Americas and look what the United States of America has become." However, if the two phenomena were linked, then the industrial revolution should have taken place in the South of the United States, the slave region, and not in the abolitionist North. Yet the South remained essentially agricultural. Indeed, one could argue that the slave trade and the whole system stemming from it immobilized the South and that that is precisely why it had not experienced the industrial revolution by the time of the Civil War which ultimately turned in favor of the North, which was lucky not to depend on a slave economy and had therefore become industrialized.

Another argument is that perhaps Portugal and the southern states in the U.S. did not know how to manage their "windfall," and that it was this incompetence which was responsible for their lagging behind. In contrast to other countries, they simply did not know how to use the massive profits.

There again, the counter-argument crumbles once it is examined carefully. The idea that the European countries practicing the slave trade built their standard of living upon the gains derived from industrialization that was itself rendered possible by profits generated by that trade is based on the works of Eric Williams. Williams was an historian born in Trinidad, the southernmost island in the Lesser Antilles, where he later became Prime Minister. Proclaiming himself a proponent of "dialectical materialism," he defended a thesis at Oxford in 1938, titled *Capitalism and Slavery*, which he later developed in a book published in 1944. Williams put forward the idea that the Caribbean sugar cane plantations, needing an abundant, servile labor force, generated such great profits that they enabled the propertied classes in England to enrich themselves. That is true, at least in the case of some individuals.

Several contributions to the *Oxford History of the British Empire* refute this position, even if the thesis upon which it rests was for a long time dominant.

In Volume II of *The Oxford History of the British Empire*,[1] David Richardson deals with the question of the profits which the British derived from the slave trade.[2] He writes that fortunes were made based upon this odious commerce, but he strongly minimizes the real benefits obtained from this activity. He calculates a return on investment of eight to ten percent at the end of the 18th century. Thus, an Englishman who invested £100 in the Caribbean in 1791 would have received £10 per annum for this investment. That was more than could usually be earned in the stock market in our times but was not enough to build a financial empire.

He goes on to show that the idea of these profits having permitted the financing of the British industrial revolution is false. Around 1790, the total sums invested annually in the slave trade were slightly in excess of £1,500,000, in the currency of those times. At the annual return rate of 10 percent, these investments generated, at most, profits of £150,000 per annum. Supposing that a third of these profits, or £50,000, had been invested in the new industrial activities, this would have represented less than 1 percent of all domestic investment linked to the industrial revolution. It is safe to conclude, therefore, that the wealth of England does not rest on the suffering of black slaves.

Richardson even writes that:

[. . .] the slave trade was in no way crucial to the finance of the first British industrial revolution.

Only one point might weaken the force of Richardson's demonstration: the possibility that the dynamism of the London stock market, which permitted the British industrial revolution, was due, at least in part, to the profits made in the Caribbean with the sweat of slaves. That issue remains unresolved to this day, and the article "The Caribbean" in the *Oxford History of the British Empire,* along with other works, is inconclusive on the subject.

Clearly sensing that their arguments on these points have been demolished, the prosecutors of the case against Europe have pushed forward other pawns. Thus, the slave trading activities introduced by the Europeans are said to have had another harmful effect on African societies. Specifically they argue

---

[1] *The Oxford History of the British Empire,* five volumes published between 1998 and 1999 under the direction of W.M. Roger Louis.
[2] *The British Empire and the Atlantic Slave Trade, 1660-1807,* op cit.

that, by devoting themselves to capturing slaves, those societies abandoned their traditional economic activities. This secondary impact was an aggravating factor of African underdevelopment.

The evidence tends to contradict this claim. For example, in a study of the kingdom of Loango and the Vili tribe, Renault and Daget[1] state:

> [. . .] sale for exportation did not cause the deterioration of the internal institutions because the captives sold to the Westerners were never captured within the kingdom; they came from outside after a long search, perhaps even as far as the large kingdoms of Luba and Lunda that touched the Great Lakes. Thus the Vili population that was not implicated in the slave trade continued its traditional agricultural and fishing activities.

Abolition: Humanitarian vs. Economic Causes

Abolition came at last. What were the real causes behind it? During the first half of the 20th century, historians admitted that the abolition of the slave trade by the British Parliament in 1807, then of slavery itself in 1833, resulted from the action of a powerful, philanthropic abolitionist movement, whose roots were religious in nature and were notably incarnated by William Wilberforce's Society for the Mitigation and Gradual Abolition of Slavery.[2]

Although historically well-founded, this explanation was strongly disputed by Eric Williams, the Marxist historian and future Prime Minister of Trinidad and Tobago, already cited. Williams' argument was inspired by the work of Lowell Ragatz[3] and opposed previous theories. It rested on the idea that abolition did not result from a new moral awareness but was due to a fall in profits; the sugar economy was dying, and cynical investors decided to place their capital in other regions that would generate greater profits, notably Asia. According to Williams, the monoculture of sugarcane had exhausted a poor and fragile soil. The Caribbean plantations were no longer profitable, and neither was the importation of slaves to maintain them. In Williams' view, Parliament voted in favor of abolition because the profits generated by the slave trade were no longer sufficient to satisfy its backers.

---

[1] Op cit., 1985.

[2] For the historiography on this question, see G. Heuman, "Slavery, the Slave Trade, and Abolition," in Vol. V of *The Oxford History of the British Empire*, 1999, pp. 315-326.

[3] L. Ragatz, *The Fall of the Planter Class in the British Caribbean, 1763-1833: A Study in Social Economic History*, New York, 1928.

Written at a time when Marxism exercised its intellectual domination over university studies, Williams' thesis won the favor of historians. It largely served to support the anti-colonial struggle, and it is still very widely accepted in ill-informed circles.

It was not until the 1970s that these arguments were solidly opposed.[1] And, as a resounding closing note, when *Volume II* of the *Oxford History of the British Empire* in 1998 was published, two chapters, one written by J. R. Ward[2] and the other by D. Richardson,[3] reduced the arguments of Williams and his successors to tatters. Ward showed that exports from the British Caribbean had never been greater than during the period when slavery was suppressed. Far from being on the decline, the plantations were at the height of their production and profitability.

This was due essentially to agronomical causes. A new variety of sugarcane with a much higher yield had been introduced. This variety was combined with improved techniques, notably for crushing the stems and refining the molasses, which permitted very significant gains in productivity.

In addition, the raising of livestock was developed in these regions, where it had hitherto not existed on any significant scale, allowing for the production of fertilizing manure that also increased yields per acre for the sugarcane crop. Together, these improvements had reached the point that commerce in sugarcane required no less than half the British merchant fleet and represented 1/8th of Crown receipts.

If it has previously been established that the slave trade was not the origin of England's wealth, it is no less evident that a good number of English fortunes were made in plantations whose economy rested on the servile labor. Fortunes served the owners but not the industrial revolution of the United Kingdom.

Thus, contrary to what historians who blame Europe contend, the most up-to-date studies absolve the slave trade from any significant impact on black African demography or the underdevelopment of African societies. Nor do they credit it for the development of European societies. Lastly, they stress the role of pressure from public opinion and the European anti-slavery associations as the reason of abolition.[4]

---

[1] They were notably opposed by Roger Anstey, in his article, "Capitalism and Slavery: A Critique," *Economic History Review,* second series, XXI (1968), pp. 307-321. Anstey directly attacks Williams' thesis, as did Seymour Drescher in his work, *Econocide: British Slavery in the Era of Abolition,* Pittsburgh, 1977.

[2] J. R. Ward, "The British West Indies in the Age of Abolition, 1748-1815" in *The Oxford History of the British Empire,* Vol. II, 1998, pp. 415-439.

[3] D. Richardson, op cit.

[4] S. Drescher, "Whose Abolition? Popular Pressure and the Ending of the British Slave Trade," *Past and Present,* CXLIII (1993), pp. 136-166.

The scandal of slavery was stopped because Europe finally took notice of its iniquity and its savagery. The European slave traders who persisted in their commerce were severely repressed, their "cargoes" were seized and repatriated to African lands,[1] and the European "ebony trade" was finally halted in a relatively short time, due to improved means of spreading information during this period. In less than 30 years, four centuries of the slave trade had become shameful; offenders were hung from the yardarms of ships.

This abolition was unilateral. No one asked the opinions of the African kingdoms that had built their wealth by selling their black brothers, nor was any attempt made to consult with the Arab traders in this matter, and the latter would continue to prey on the eastern coasts of the continent.

Yet it was Europe that would finally shut down the Arab slave trade. In 1822, the British imposed a restriction of this commerce to the coast of East Africa, the Persian Gulf, and Arabia upon the Sultan of Zanzibar, Seyyid Said. Realists, the British knew full well that they lacked the means to put a complete stop to the slave trade without effective territorial occupation, and for over 60 years they hesitated to take this step, trying to control and then to contain the traffic without ever really having the ability to interrupt it.

They proceeded by degrees. Thus, on October 2, 1845, the Hamerton Treaty, signed by Seyyid Said, forbade the exportation of slaves outside the Sultan's African possessions. An exemption was granted for the labor force in the clove-tree plantations.

The Royal Navy scarcely had the means to control the application of this treaty. Renault[2] explains that, from 1867 to 1869, only 2,600 of the 37,000 slaves exported in defiance of the Hamerton Treaty, were intercepted and freed by the British. This gives some indication of the real volume of the Arab slave trade. In 1871, the government in London ordered its navy to set up a temporary blockade around Zanzibar. In 1873, Sir Bartle Frere and the British consul John Kirk, forced Seyyid Bargash, the new Sultan, to accept closure of the market on Zanzibar, the end of the slave trade, and the confiscation of all slave ships. In under 24 hours, the market was shut.

---

[1] With consequences we shall discuss below.
[2] Op cit., 1972.

But the trade continued in the interior of the continent. It only retreated in the face of unrelenting assaults led by religious missionaries. This was the work of the Protestants in the Church Missionary Society who founded their first mission in 1844 at Mombasa. In 1862 and in 1873, the French Pères du Saint-Esprit installed themselves on Zanzibar itself and at Bagamoyo. But the missionary movement reached its highest level with the Missionnaires d'Afrique or Pères Blancs under Cardinal Lavigerie, who discovered the African field for their proselytizing in 1878.

The slave traders were also being hunted by private organizations, such as the International Association for the Exploration and Civilization of Central Africa, which put together expeditions with the aim of building outposts at the crossroads of the trails used by the caravans. It was in this way that Karema and Mpala were founded on Lake Tanganyika. It was also this association which sent Stanley to create stations along the Congo river. The struggle against the slave trade was therefore largely the result of a philanthropic mobilization, a mobilization that would eventually lead, in part, to the colonization of Africa.

The colonial powers had to mount their own military expeditions before the slave traders were finally defeated. On Lake Victoria, the Germans were forced to engage in veritable naval battles. In the Congo, the Belgians were obliged to organize campaigns against the slave traders. Without the colonial conquest, millions of black Africans would have continued to take the direction of the slave markets on Zanzibar, then those of Cairo, Alexandria, Muscat, or elsewhere.

The Island of Gorée: A Small Example of a Big Distortion

The "Gorée legend" is typical of the misinformation spread by those who would portray Europe as guilty of all of Africa's problems. Located off the shore of Dakar, the Island of Gorée is an obligatory stop for all tourists visiting the Senegalese capital. It is presented to them as one of the bases for the slave trade, through which millions of unhappy souls transited before being sent to the New World. The travel agents in the United States offer African Americans a "pilgrimage" visit to the island through which their ancestors may have passed.

Gorée has thus become, for black Americans, a kind of macabre equivalent of what Ellis Island represents for the descendents of immigrants from Ireland and Central Europe. The idea has been accepted to such a point, that in February 1992, during a trip to Senegal, Pope John Paul II was deeply moved at the sight of Gorée, the "slave island."

The culmination of visits to Gorée is naturally the sadly famous "Slaves' House," where the presentation is particularly well staged. Here, the tourist guides narrate in full detail the edifying history of this house. Built by the Dutch in the 17th century, it was originally an "esclaverie" (a holding prison for captive slaves), an element at the heart of the regional slave trading system that revolved around Gorée. Its walls have seen hundreds of thousands, if not millions, of black Africans torn from their land to be sold to the American plantation owners. A visit gives one an idea of the living conditions endured by these unfortunate people. The décor is tragic. Still in place are chains that held the captives, alcoves where the victims in transit were packed, the door to the sea through which the ill or recalcitrant were thrown out, cells for the men and women, and even those for the children.

And here is the dungeon, ladies and gentlemen, where hotheads were beaten into submission. See the drainage channel dug in the floor where the blood of these unfortunates ran.

UNESCO has registered both Gorée and the "Slaves' House" on its official list of places belonging to the Heritage of Humanity, and the Slaves' House looks quite impressive since its restoration. A plaque also informs the visitor that its sponsors include a prestigious association, the Fondation France Liberté, presided over by Madame Danielle Mitterrand, the widow of a former President of the French Republic.

The only problem is that "Slaves' House" is not one, and the Island of Gorée was never a slave-trading center. But the economic virtues of tourism have reasons that historical reason knows not.

The real history of this house, which is, in fact, familiar to Senegalese historians and others has nothing to do with the official legend of Gorée. It was not the Dutch who built it in the 17th century, but the French, in 1783, to be exact. This was a period when the slave trade had practically ceased in the region of Senegambia. The construction was commissioned by a rich signare,[1] Anna Colas. Like all colonial residences of this period, it housed numerous domestic servants, and it is probable that these included some slaves to carry out the most onerous tasks. But the housing presented during visits and in the guidebooks as "cells" were never used in the slave trade; they were warehouses for merchandise.

As for Gorée being a "slave trading post," even in the period when the slave trade was flourishing in Senegambia, the island was never a major center for this activity. At the peak of this commerce, that is to say, the 17th and perhaps the beginning of the 18th century, it is estimated in fact that only 200-500 slaves transited there annually. This is very few in relation to Curtin's overall figures for this period.

After abolition, the island even served as a "transit camp" as one would call it today, for the unfortunate slaves "rescued from the sea." We know, for example that it sheltered the 272 prisoners who escaped from the holds of the Illizia, a Brazilian slave ship caught red-handed with "contraband ebony" and boarded offshore in 1846 by the L'Australie,[2] a French military steamship. Fifty-six of those rescued (27 men, 27 women, and two children born on Gorée), would later become the first black "colonists" who founded Libreville, the present-day capital of Gabon.

It is understandable that African-American visitors who come to the site want to find their roots and learn a little about the tragedy of their ancestors' deportation. But the historical distortion represented by the choice of Gorée as an "emblem of the black slave trade" deceives them. It is time they knew the truth in order to reconstitute their identity on a real historical basis.

Two other African sites along the former colonial Gold Coast (present-day Ghana) are still visible today: the Dutch fort of Elmina and the old English settlement of Cape Coast. Visits there are much more instructive than to the Gorée fraud.

* * *

[1] Translator's Note: An African or half-caste woman that Europeans would marry "according to the custom of the country" (that is to say for the time spent in the colony).
[2] J. L. Donnadieu, in *Historia Thématique* No. 80, Nov.-Dec. 2002, p. 77.

The reason for exposing these facts is to highlight the gap between historical knowledge and its representation to the public. In the case of the slave trade, the distortions and lies are voluntary, deliberate ones. They are made by all African-American groups who depend on this faked history for veritable "secure dividends" that they derive from the political and emotional exploitation of this shameful period of Afro-European history.

As for Africa's political leaders, Roger Botte correctly points out that:

[. . .] *some will go as far as to deny the existence of any slavery internal to Africa [. . .]. In all frankness, how could the African states have justified their demand for expiatory and compensatory indemnities, during the United Nations World Conference Against Racism at Durban in September 2001, if they had recognized that in their own countries [. . .]; their ancient oligarchies had participated in the crime against humanity constituted by the slave trade?*[1]

---

[1] R. Botte, "Le Spectre de l'Esclavage," [The Ghost of Slavery] in *Les Temps Modernes*, Nos. 620-621, Aug.-Nov. 2002, pp. 144-164.

Chapter II

Colonialism: Good Deeds, Not Good Business

The issue of colonization constitutes another essential element in the case made against Europe's role in Africa by its critics. Colonization is presented as nothing more than a gigantic pillage operation. Let's look at the facts.

By 1880, the European presence in Africa was limited. After the slave trade ended earlier in the century, West Africa no longer interested the Europeans. The Danes had completed their retreat from the area around 1850. In 1865, the British Parliament began studying the possibility of an evacuation of all Crown possessions in the region, with the exception of Sierra Leone, and the Dutch abandoned their last outposts between 1870 and 1872. France was in Algeria and Senegal and possessed some isolated outposts along the coast. Portugal had some settlements in the region of Luanda and in Mozambique. Great Britain had a colony at the Cape of Good Hope, and the Boer Republics of Orange and Transvaal were partially under its control. Spain was present on some islands and in two enclaves on the Moroccan shore.

Ten years later, in 1890, the situation had completely changed. The European powers (i.e., France, Great Britain, Germany, Portugal, and Italy), had launched themselves into a veritable race to acquire colonies. In those 10 years a vast movement was initiated that would end less than two decades later by dividing up Africa.

The impression that dominates today, fueled by interested parties, is that

Map VI: The Europeans in Africa Around 1820

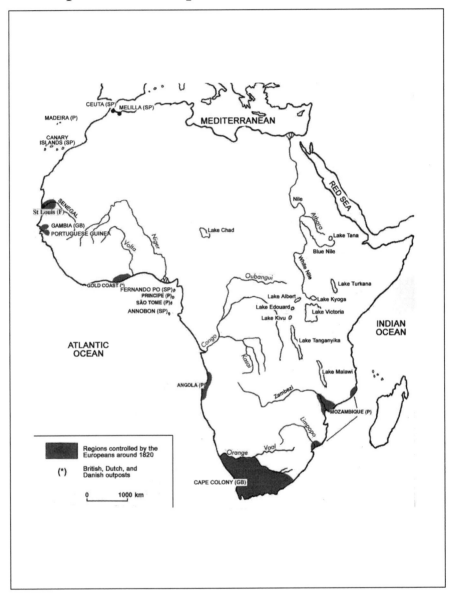

ATLANTIC
OCEAN

INDIAN
OCEAN

MEDITERRANEAN

RED SEA

CEUTA (SP) MELILLA (SP)
MADEIRA (P)
CANARY
ISLANDS (SP)

SENEGAL
St Louis (F)
GAMBIA (GB)
PORTUGUESE GUINEA

GOLD COAST (*)
FERNANDO PO (SP)
PRINCIPE (P)
SÃO TOME (P)
ANNOBON (SP)

Nile
Albara
Lake Tana
Blue Nile
White Nile
Lake Chad
Volta
Niger
Oubangui
Lake Turkana
Lake Albert
Lake Edouard
Lake Kivu
Lake Kyoga
Lake Victoria
Lake Tanganyika
Congo
Kasai
Lake Malawi
ANGOLA (P)
Zambezi
MOZAMBIQUE (P)
Limpopo
Orange Vaal
CAPE COLONY (GB)

| | Regions controlled by the Europeans around 1820 |
| (*) | British, Dutch, and Danish outposts |

0   1000 km

Map VII: The Europeans in Africa Around 1880

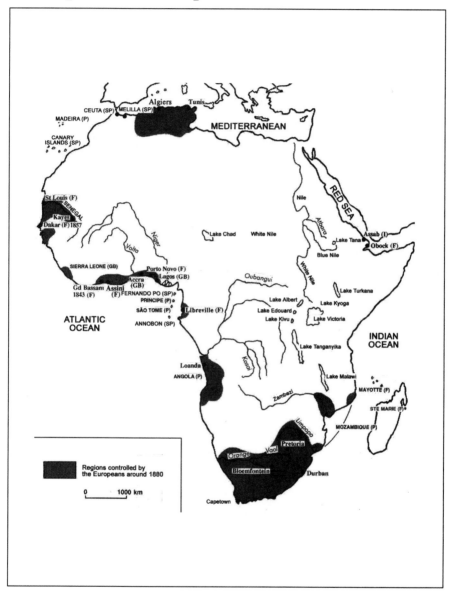

Europe was waiting in ambush for an opportunity to carve up Africa. But the impulse to colonize was nothing so self-evident or foreseeable. The European powers even tried to slow the movement that took off between 1890 and 1895 with a "Scramble for Africa."[1]

It was Britain that initiated the movement in South and East Africa, followed shortly by France in West Africa, and it was triggered by philanthropic, ideological, and/or strategic concerns, as opposed to economic ones. This sudden movement of geographical occupation ended in 1898-1900 with the victories of Horatio H. Kitchener over the Mahdists and those of the missions by Foreau, Lamy, Joalland, and Gentil over the slaver chief Rabeh.

It was an extremely limited episode in African history. Since the independence movements began in the 1950s, colonialism was, in the end, only a 60-year parenthesis in the "long march" of Africa (except for the special cases constituted by the possessions claimed at the beginning of the 19th century that we mentioned above).

The Role of Left Wing Ideas in French Colonialism

In 1870, France only possessed some islands and outposts scattered around Africa, Asia, and the Americas. Its only important colony was Algeria, which was clearly seen as a colony destined for settlement since 10 percent of its two and a half million inhabitants were Europeans. However, in less than 20 years, between 1880 and 1900, France would build its own colonial empire.

In retrospect, this movement may seem to have been consensual. But in actual fact, the subject was argued bitterly at the time and a large segment of the population was opposed to colonization. Until the eve of the First World War, the debate was lively between those who put forward France's continental vocation and those who militated in favor of overseas expansion.

It is astonishing to observe, for those who are only familiar with contemporary debates on African questions, that it was the French Right which was anti-colonialist, while the Left defended the idea of the creation of this colonial empire. Indeed, a large part of the Left and the liberal current believed that it was through an active colonial policy that France could recover the interna-

---

[1] "The Drive for Colonies".

tional influence and role that had been badly dented by the defeat to the Germans in 1870 and the loss of Alsace and Lorraine.

It was under Léon Gambetta and Jules Ferry, both men of the Left, republicans, and humanists, that the French Third Republic set forth on the road to colonial expansion. Gambetta, who exerted considerable influence over Jules Ferry, was not far from thinking that France might some day exchange colonial territories with Germany in return for Alsace and Lorraine.

Jules Ferry clearly defined his colonial program during a famous speech made before the French National Assembly on July 28, 1885. For him, French colonial expansion met three essential needs: first, France's political concerns, by restoring her influence as a great power; next, her economic needs, since a colonial empire would doubtless furnish markets for French industry; and lastly, a philosophical need, since France, the "Homeland of the Enlightenment," should spread its universal message to the peoples of the world who still lived in ignorance. In the thinking of the French Left, this ideological, moral, and universal dimension was of major importance. For example, it was Jean Jaurès, the French Socialist leader, who shouted out at a public meeting in 1884:

When we take possession of a country, we should bring with us the glory of France, and you should be sure that it will be warmly welcomed, because it is as pure as it is great, totally imbued with justice and goodness.[1]

French colonization was to a very large extent the "Daughter of the Enlightenment" and that of the revolutionary humanists of 1789. The Société des Amis des Noirs [Society of Friends of the Black People], created in 1788 to fight against slavery, thus changed its name at the beginning of the 19th century to the Sociéte des Amis des Noirs et des Colonies. Colonization was understood here as a "liberation" of Africans through the influence of the Enlightenment and civilization. A filial relationship was seen between the colonial movement and the abolitionist movement. Since civilization had fought slavery, it should continue to carry out its civilizing mission to completion. That is why Victor Schoelcher, the emblematic figure of the cause of abolition,

---

[1] Quoted by A. Ruscio, in *Le Credo de l'homme blanc [The White Man's Creed]*, 1996.

revered by the Left today, was the logical choice to become the French Secretary of State for the Colonies. In 1889, he did not hesitate to co-preside over the International Colonial Congress, alongside General Louis Faidherbe, the man who conquered Senegal.

In 1870, the principal spokesman of progressive thinking, the "Conscience of France," Victor Hugo himself, made a speech in Victor Schoelcher's presence following a banquet:[1]

> [. . .] Already, two colonizing people have seized Africa, France holds the West and the North, England the East and the South. Here is Italy which accepts its share of this colossal work. Mountain passes, trails, and straits are now practicable; this universe that once frightened the Romans, now attracts the French. In the 19th century, the White has made the Black into a man; in the 20th century, Europe will make Africa into a world. [Applause]. The problem is, how remake a new Africa, and render the old Africa amenable to civilization. Europe will resolve it. Go forth, Peoples. Take control of this land. Take it. From who? From no one. Take this land from God. God has given the land to men. God has given Africa to Europe. Take it. Where the kings brought war, bring concord. Take it, not for the cannon but for the plow; not for the sword but for commerce; not for the battle but for industry; not for conquest but for fraternity. [Prolonged applause] Pour your excess into this Africa, and at the same time, resolve for your social questions, and turn your proletarians into property owners. Go forth, and do it. Build roads, build ports, build cities. Grow, cultivate, colonize, multiply, and on this land, more and more freed from the priests and the princes, the divine spirit will affirm itself by peace, and the human spirit by freedom.

There was enthusiastic applause, and the diners exclaimed:

Vive Victor Hugo, Vive la République.

Not all of the Left, however, was won over to colonial expansionism. Its opponents included Georges Clemenceau. In a famous discourse, known as the

---

[1] *Discours sur l'Afrique, [Discourse on Africa]*, pronounced by Victor Hugo on May 18, 1870 at the banquet commemorating the abolition of slavery.

"stewpot speech," made before the French National Assembly on July 31, 1885, he addressed Jules Ferry:

> [. . .] Supposing that Monsieur Jules Ferry's theory about the profits from colonial expeditions will ever be justified, expenditures of this order can never be more than a luxury. Before giving in to luxury, let us therefore give an hour to the politics of the stewpot, let us provide stew, schools, and tools. While you are lost in your colonial dreams, there are, at your very feet, men, Frenchmen, who demand spending of a useful, fruitful nature [. . .]

Clemenceau's criticism was in many ways prophetic:

> It by constantly increasing the charges on the budget that you propose to open markets, whereas there are neighboring countries who, not having paid for colonial expenditure, fight with us on the very same terrain. Since their budgets are not burdened by the cost of these expeditions, they present a formidable competition and take trade from us even in our own markets. [. . .] New markets cannot be opened by firing cannon.[1]

The nationalist Right, for its part, completely opposed this colonial adventure. According to this element of the political spectrum, France would have to choose between "revenge," which would permit the re-conquest of Alsace and Lorraine, and colonial expansion, which they considered to be a chimera offering only a future that would distract the French from the "Blue Line of the Vosges."[2] In the aftermath of the defeat of 1870, all of France's energies, according to these nationalists, should be turned towards the lost provinces. They considered the colonial adventures almost a form of treason.

This right-wing anti-colonialism was embodied perfectly by the French writer and politician, Paul Déroulède. For him, the issue was obvious: the colonies would never compensate for the losses of 1870. And it was in this frame of mind that he declared to Jules Ferry:

> I've lost two sisters, and you're offering me twenty servants.[3]

In his eyes, the colonial mirage was a dangerous trap laid by the enemies of France. In a striking turn of phrase, he opposed the fantasy of a "Greater

---

[1] Quoted by J. P. Biondi, Les anticolonialistes en France (1881-1962), [The Anticolonialists in France] 1996.
[2] Translator's Note: i.e., the eastern frontier at that time with occupied Alsace and Lorraine.
[3] Quoted by R. Girardet, L'idée coloniale en France de 1871 à 1962, [The Colonial Idea in France], 1996.

France," that is to say, this hypothetical empire that threatened to make Frenchmen forget about "setting true France back on her feet." And Déroulède maintained this stance even after this empire was actually constituted. In 1905, when France was almost unanimously won over to the cause of colonial expansion, he still wrote the following about her colonial successes:

> [They] created a diversion [and] also a dispersion. They made the Germans much too happy not to give the French cause to worry.[1]

In fact, by this time, part of the Right had become colonialist, and, for this group, it was not the Germans who were France's rivals, but the English. Their error in perspective was total, since French diplomacy was patiently spinning a web to isolate Germany through the Franco-Russian alliance and through a step-by-step rapprochement with London, which meant giving way to the colonial appetites of the British. In opposition, the colonialist Right and the Colonial party pressed for war against Britain over border disputes in Africa, notably at Fashoda.

This much talked about Colonial party was not a political party properly speaking, but a constellation of pressure groups, geographical associations, regimental clubs, etc. that all militated in favor of the country launching itself with force into overseas expansion. The most important of these groups was the Comité de l'Afrique Française (CAF), founded in 1890, whose position was original insofar as its members saw the French colonial vocation as being first of all Mediterranean, and then more generally African, with Algeria as the pivot of the future French colonial empire.

After having hesitated a long while, and without any hurry, France embarked on a policy of colonial expansion. It followed the Congress of Berlin, convoked by the German Chancellor, Bismarck, which took place between June 13 and July 13, 1878.

The goal of this Congress was to settle what was then called the "Oriental Question," that is, the issue of the Balkans and the problems caused by the inexorable corrosion of the Ottoman Empire, the former dominant power in the region. Russia was extending itself towards the Balkans, and Britain

---

[1] Quoted by R. Girardet, op cit., p.423.

ardently wished to maintain a status quo. They wanted the straits leading to the Mediterranean, the Bosphorus and the Dardanelles to be held by a future Turkey to prevent the Russian fleet from leaving the Black Sea. As for Austria-Hungary, it feared seeing its Slavic subjects escape from its rule by demanding protection from the Russians.

Thus, the division of the Ottoman remains gave rise to hard bargaining. In the end, Russia inherited Bessarabia, and Austria-Hungary obtained Bosnia, thus preventing the latter from joining Serbia, with all the subsequent problems that we know. Britain, having obtained the island of Cyprus without protest from France, felt obliged to offer the French a reward. Such "compensation" could only be taken from territories belonging to the Ottoman Empire. On the diplomatic front, Bismarck was hoping to distract France from Alsace and Lorraine, place Paris in competition with London on the terrain of their respective colonial ambitions, and annoy a jealous Italy, with whom France was seeking to constitute an alliance against Germany. The upshot was that Tunisia, although much coveted by Rome, was given to Paris.

Tunisia was in theory a Turkish province administered by a "Pasha," but power had passed in actual fact to the military commander, the "Dey," who was eventually supplanted by a civil administrator, the "Bey." In the 1860s, the Tunisian authorities, wishing to modernize the country, had gone deeply into debt, notably with French banks. In 1867, incapable of repaying its loans and prevented from contracting new ones, Tunisia was in a state of bankruptcy and passed into the control of its European creditors.

The "gift" was a poisoned one. It was a destitute state that the participants at the Congress in Berlin offered France. France, however, had no interest in carrying the burden of the Tunisian bankruptcy and did not rush to take possession.

For a time, France ignored Tunisia in favor of reviving Faidherbe's old West African project, in Senegambia. Under the Second Empire, Louis Faidherbe had been governor of the outpost France possessed there since the 17th century, first from 1854 to 1861, then from 1863 to 1865. He had grand development projects for this region, but the war of 1870 against Prussia placed them on hold.

From 1879 to 1880, within the government of Charles de Freycinet, Admiral Jauréguiberry became the French Minister of the Navy and the Colonies. In September 1880, he made Lieutenant-Colonel Gustave Borgnis-Desbordes director of operations in all Upper Senegal and placed the western Sudan under military authority.

It wasn't until three years after the Congress of Berlin, in 1881, that the French finally reversed their appraisal of the Tunisian question. This would turn out to be France's first real step into the whole trap of colonialism.

By then, Britain was the mistress of most of the key points in the Mediterranean, including Gibraltar, Malta and Cyprus. Egypt would soon follow. Bismarck was meanwhile pressing Paris to intervene in Tunisia, threatening to support Italy's claim instead. At the same time, the idea took hold that Algeria's security depended on controlling the totality of the Maghreb. In these conditions and, while waiting for an opportunity to do the same with Morocco, occupying Tunisia became useful.

The nomadic tribe of the Kroumirs, which regularly violated the frontier between Tunisia and Algeria, offered a pretext for intervention. On April 7, 1881, the French army penetrated Tunisia, officially to help the "Bey" of Tunis to restore his authority over the rebel tribesmen. On May 12, 35,000 soldiers presented themselves before the Bardo Palace, the residence of the Bey. He was given two hours to study and sign the Bardo Treaty, which turned his country into a French dependency, and then in 1883, a protectorate.

A second step towards French colonization occurred in sub-Saharan Africa. Here, France found itself engaged in Madagascar, again owing to an international agreement.

This agreement involved putting an end to a dispute over eastern Africa among Germany, Britain, and Portugal. Since both Berlin and London wanted their territorial arrangements made official by a consensus of the great powers, they involved France, which already possessed the neighboring island of Reunion and was beginning to become interested in Madagascar. The French parliamentary members of the Catholic Right were certainly still opposed at this point to any policy of colonial expansion, but they were also concerned about the Catholic missions which were facing hostile competition from their Protestant counterparts. They therefore supported the idea of a military intervention on the island. In 1883, Paris officially claimed a protectorate in Madagascar, and it was eventually recognized by London and Berlin in 1890.

In December 1894, France occupied Tamatave (now called Toamasina), Diego Suarez (Antsiranana), and Majunga (Mahajanga). An expeditionary corps then marched to the central plateau, the heart of the Imerina kingdom, which was reached on September 26, 1895. The protectorate treaty was signed the following day by Queen Ranavalona III, who kept her throne. But a revolt soon took hold of the country. The immediate consequence was that Madagascar was purely and simply annexed in 1896, the monarchy was abolished, and the island was absorbed into the French colonial domain.

The result was that France, which had long been hesitant, had become an imperialist nation. And it plunged, this time with ardor, into the race to acquire colonies.

Its ardor arose partly when uncertainties as to the nature of the French political regime were lifted with the failure of General Boulanger in 1889.[1] Thereafter, the French Republic would no longer be seriously challenged.

Secondly, the country was no longer isolated diplomatically, and a Franco-Russian alliance was taking shape. This rapprochement occurred during the crisis between France and Germany, when the Russian Czar declared that he "would not let France be crushed." The alliance was solidified in three stages between 1892 and 1894, and it permitted France to dispose of an ally in Germany's rear. Thereafter, the great policy of expansion advocated by the Colonial party could be put into place.

Senegal in the west, and Porto Novo and Cotonou in the south, were the starting points of the penetration destined to place all of western Africa under French sovereignty. The goal was to establish a new pivot around Lake Chad which would soon effectively become the junction of French military columns, thus covering the hinterlands of Algeria, Senegal, and the outposts in the Gulf of Guinea.

In February 1883, Bamako was occupied, then in February 1891, Louis

---

[1] Translator's Note: Georges Boulanger (1837-1891) was a French general who founded a League of Patriots that attracted the support of nationalists, Bonapartists, and other right-wing elements, and threatened in January 1889 to seize power in Paris.

Map VIII: The Conquest of West Africa (1890-1900)

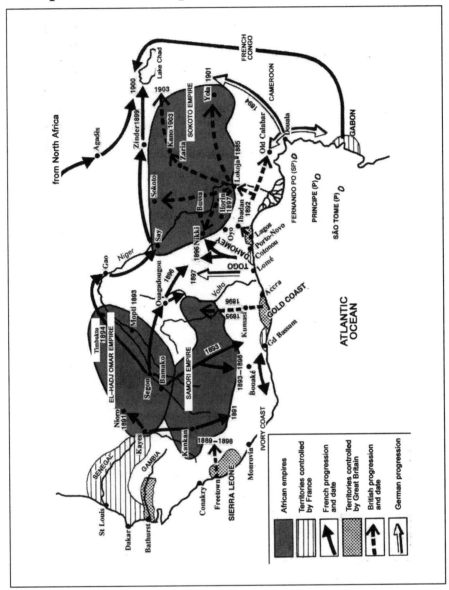

Archinard took Segu, the capital of the Toucouleurs kingdom.

This expansion was so rapid that, in just five years, from 1893 to 1898, France achieved all its goals. The French expansion in West Africa spread essentially from west to east and followed the axis of the Upper Niger river, thus bypassing to the north the coastal kingdoms that might have presented obstacles to its progression. In the case of the British "competitor," its push was from south to north, and the Lower Niger was its main pivot.

It was at the crossroads of these axes that the two imperialist powers met. The question of access to the Niger would create strong tensions between the French and British powers. Finally, reason prevailed, and they negotiated a convention signed on June, 1898 that settled their dispute in the region and permitted the British to create the immense colony of Nigeria.

Having been given a free hand on the Niger, France then had Lake Chad as its objective. Several expeditions were launched in 1899. In February 1900, the connection was made between the columns led by Gentil, which departed from southern Congo, and those of Foureau and Lamy, which came from Algeria across the Sahara. Paris had succeeded in linking up its three colonial zones, and all that remained was to "pacify" the Sahara.

British Colonization: A Reluctant Enterprise

The question of when British imperialist policy towards Africa really began has been the subject of extensive debates.[1] London, which wanted to control the strategic points along the route to India, had established a foothold very early on at the Cape of Good Hope. During the winter of 1794-1795, the revolutionary contagion that had spread from France to Holland led to the proclamation in March 1795 of a Batavian Republic, sister of the French Republic. The king of Holland, who had taken refuge in England, was no longer in a position to exercise his sovereignty, and the Dutch East India Company (VOC in its Dutch initials) at that point asked London to temporarily take charge of its overseas interests, notably the important staging post at the Cape. This was carried out on June 11, 1795 when Admiral Elphinstone and General Craig

---

[1] On the British colonial question, see: C. Newbury, "Great Britain and the Partition of Africa, 1870-1914," *The Oxford History of the British Empire*, Vol. III, 1999, pp. 624-650. Also J.E. Flint, "Britain and the Scramble for Africa," *The Oxford History of the British Empire*, Vol. V, 1999, pp. 450-462.

Map IX: British Ambitions in Southern Africa

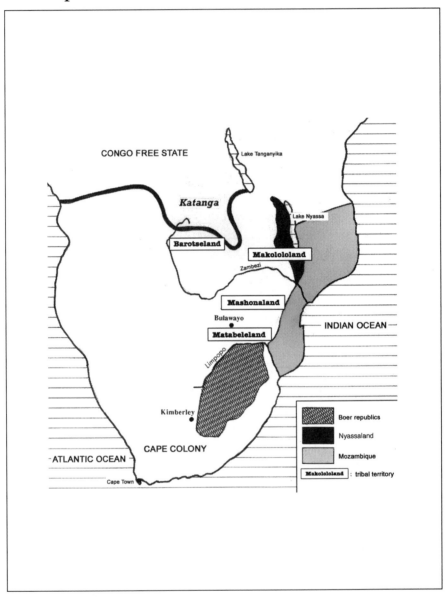

disembarked there with their Royal Marines.

In 1802, France and Britain signed the Treaty of Amiens. London, which recognized the existence and the legitimacy of the Batavian Republic, consequently had to return the Dutch outpost at the Cape of Good Hope. But war between Britain and the Napoleonic Empire resumed the following year, and London decided to reoccupy the Cape on January 7, 1806. In 1814, Holland sold its former possession to London for the sum of £6 million. A few months later, the Congress of Vienna ratified the transfer of sovereignty that had taken place in southern Africa.

During the first years of British rule, Cape Colony was only considered to be a stronghold, a "Gibraltar of the Indian Ocean," destined to protect the access to India. But little by little, and most often unwillingly, London found itself attracted by the lands in the interior.

Everything changed in 1879, when this "attraction" ended in the annexation of the Kimberley region, a desert territory situated to the north of the Cape Colony, where the first diamond fields were discovered in 1867.

Starting around 1880, the push by the Boer Republics towards the Limpopo River became a pressing issue. The Portuguese, who occupied Mozambique, opposite Madagascar, were increasing their presence in the area of Lake Nyassa at the time. In 1886, the Portuguese explorer Serpa Pinto proposed a Portuguese protectorate to the Makololo people living to the south of this lake, in Makalololand. For London, the danger became clear. Next, Mashonaland might also come under Portuguese control.

In order to contain this expansion, the British became interested in Mashonaland (the territory of the Shona tribe, which constitutes most of present-day Zimbabwe) and Matabeleland (territory of the Matabele), both of them to the north of the Limpopo. However, it did not engage in any real attempt to conquer them.

The driving force of British conquest in this region was Cecil Rhodes, who acquired an enormous fortune in Kimberley through exploitation of the diamond mines. A member of the Cape Colony's parliament, he founded the

British South Africa Country (BSAC), which became a chartered company with considerable privileges recognized by London. There included rights to police, mine, trade, and create railways in an immense territory situated north of the Limpopo river, between Angola and Mozambique.

In March 1889, Rhodes arrived in London bearing a treaty signed by Lobenguela, the King of the Matabeles whose territory covered the south of what is today Zimbabwe. His influence even extended to a part of the Shona country. This treaty, which Lobenguela had signed without realizing its true import, accorded possession of the mineral rights in his kingdom to the BSAC. It was the BSAC that would open up this part of southern Africa to British colonization but without any direct intervention by London.

In January 1890, Great Britain demanded that Lisbon recall the meddlesome Serpa Pinto and abandon all its claims on Mashonaland and Makalololand. In 1893, Nyassaland (present-day Malawi) became a British protectorate. The same year, Sir Leander Starr Jameson, Rhodes' deputy, took Bulawayo, the capital of Lobenguela, king of the Matabeles. In May 1895, in honor of Cecil Rhodes, the territory was baptized Rhodesia.

However, Rhodesia was only one stage of the northward progression, and the BSAC's agents soon signed a new agreement with the Barotse (of Barotseland). The "savannas of the south" were thus reached, and the partition of what would become Africa's "Copperbelt" was agreed between the BSAC and the Congo Free State. This accord recognized the former's possession of future Northern Rhodesia (present-day Zambia) and the latter's claim to Katanga (southeast of what is now the Democratic Republic of Congo).

Besides the region of the Cape of Good Hope, the other area of interest to Britain was Egypt. "Stuck" at the southeastern extremity of the Mediterranean, Egypt had been a dead end until 1869, when the Suez Canal was inaugurated. Then it became almost overnight a crucial crossroads of maritime communications, an event which constituted a real geopolitical revolution.[1] But Egypt launched costly public works programs and rapidly outstripped its debt capacity, and Great Britain and France, its principal creditors, became more and more

---

[1] See Lugan, B. *Histoire de l'Egypte des Origines à Nos Jours [A History of Egypt from Its Origins to the Present]*, Paris, 2002.

mixed up in its affairs in order to ensure repayment of the debt. By the end of 1875, Egypt was no longer able to meet its financial obligations. Under Prime Minister Disraeli, London bought up the totality of Egyptian shares in the Suez Canal Company. That allowed a few months' breathing space to the country's finances but above all permitted London to become the majority shareholder of one of the essential points of passage for international trade.

In 1876, Egypt's creditors imposed upon the Khedive Ismail the appointment of two financial controller-generals, one French and the other British. In August 1878, Paris and London demanded that Ismail constitute a government composed of European experts who would take effective command of the country. Finally, in 1879, Ismail was forced to abdicate in favor of his son, who reigned until 1892 under the name of Tewfik Bey.

In 1881, Tewfik Bey was violently accused by opponents of being the "Europeans' lackey," and a popular revolt broke out. The movement, which took on a vast scale, was led by an officer named Ahmed Urabi (or Orabi) better known as Arabi Pasha (1839-1911). London obviously feared for the security of the Suez Canal but still hesitated to become engaged on the ground. Not desiring to take direct action, Britain asked Turkey to do so in its place. Then, a Franco-British intervention was contemplated, but, as was mentioned earlier, France was agitated at this time by the controversy—which found a large echo in its Parliament—for or against colonial expansion and "revenge" against Germany. In these conditions, the eventuality of French participation in an Egyptian operation was bitterly challenged. The debate dragged on, and, since Great Britain estimated that its vital interests were threatened, it decided to act alone.

On July 11, 1892, a body of Royal Marines was disembarked, and Arabi Pasha was defeated. In theory, this British presence was only temporary, but everything changed when Robert Arthur Talbot Gascoyne Cecil, third Marquis of Salisbury, became prime minister in 1887. When he came into power, the new and complex international situation can be summed up, from the British point of view, in the following way:

At a time when Russia was seeking access to the Mediterranean for its

Black Sea fleet, Britain's priority was to guarantee freedom of navigation to India via the Suez Canal. London therefore had every interest in maintaining the status quo in the Balkans reached at the Congress of Berlin in order not to weaken Turkey, the guardian of the Bosphorus and Dardenelles straits, any further. But visibly, the Turkish position would not hold so for very much longer; the wars in the Balkans continued one after another, and the Turkish retreat in the face of the Slavic push was plain for all to see. London was thus forced to remain in Egypt to ensure freedom of movement towards the Indian Ocean via the Suez Canal in the event the Russian fleet finally managed to open a passage to the Mediterranean.

This geopolitical situation naturally resulted in a growing involvement by Britain in the region. And the necessity of making Egypt secure led London to launch a campaign in the Sudan, an Egyptian colony since 1821.

Like Arabi Pasha's movement in Egypt itself, the Sudan had witnessed a nationalist revolt of a peculiar type. Beginning in 1881, a religious leader named Muhammad Ahmed Ibn Abdallah (1844-1885), who called himself al-Mahdi,[1] had started a powerful movement (Mahdism) that created turmoil throughout the region, with repercussions extending as far as Ethiopia.

On January 26, 1885, after a siege lasting several months, the Mahdists took Khartoum from the troops of Charles Gordon, the British governor of the besieged city. Four thousand British and Egyptian soldiers were massacred. Gordon suffered the same fate. His corpse was decapitated, then profaned. Now master of Khartoum, al-Mahdi founded a Mahdist state and gave himself the title of caliph.

In Great Britain, indignation was at its peak, and public opinion pressed for a war to "avenge Gordon." The government, which was aware of the difficulties entailed by such a venture, tried to calm the vengeful wrath of the public. After several years of hesitation, however, it resolved to intervene.

The reasons went well beyond popular recriminations. The British feared that Sudanese example risked becoming contagious and could have had grave consequences in the area of the Suez Canal. But, above all, the British needed

---

[1] See above, chapter I, "The Muslim Slave Trades".

to respond to recent French and the Italian successes in the scramble for new colonies. The French would soon reach Lake Chad, thus compromising the possibility of the "corridor" between Cairo and the Cape of Good Hope that some British imperialists wanted to establish. The Italians had installed themselves on the African coast of the Red Sea, threatening to ruin the efforts of the British to secure the area surrounding the Suez Canal.

In Khartoum, the Mahdi died a few months after his bloody victory, in June 1885. A successor was named, Caliph Abdallah, who tried to pursue the policies of the movement's founder. But in the course of a few years, he was challenged, criticized, and weakened. Once British spies had reported that his power was failing, the conquest of the Sudan was decided. In March 1896, an expedition placed under the orders of Horatio Kitchener slowly advanced south, at the same speed as the construction of the Cairo-Khartoum railway by which the prudent strategist was moving his troops and equipment. He was prudent but also solid, and the Mahdist armies were vanquished. On January 19, 1899, the Sudan became an Anglo-Egyptian co-dominion.

As far as the British Empire was concerned, it was timely. The French expedition led by Captain Marchand had reached the Nile at Fashoda, which set off a new crisis between London and Paris. But the will to create an anti-German front settled the matter. It occurred in two separate stages: first, in March 1899, a "gentlemen's agreement" between France and Britain granted the latter possession of a western tributary of the Nile, the Bahr el Ghazal; then, in 1904, Paris abandoned its last claims over Egypt. In "exchange," London left Paris a totally free hand in Morocco.

In West Africa, Britain's progression towards the Niger and Lake Chad was blocked for a long period, on the one hand by the Ashanti of the Kumasi kingdom, against whom the British fought four wars before succeeding in proclaiming a protectorate in 1896, and on the other hand, by the Sultanate of Sokoto. France thus had the advantage in western Africa.

"We Germans Don't Need Colonies"

This quotation from Bismarck sums up his position well and would define

Map X: Africa in 1914

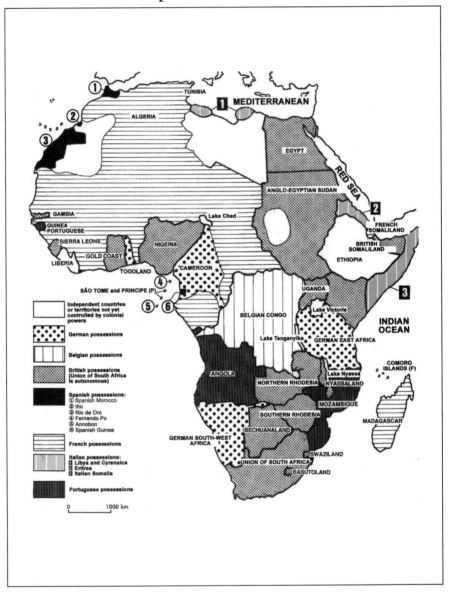

for over 20 years the German doctrine on the subject of colonies.[1] When war was declared in August 1914, however, the flag of the Second Reich, floated over Togo, Cameroon, South West Africa, and in East Africa, in a zone circumscribed by Lakes Victoria to the north, Nyassa to the south, and Tanganyika to the west. Germany had thus created an empire, and largely against the wishes of its own government.

Up until 1884, German priorities were European. Before 1870, there was a focus on achieving unification of the German states, and then, after the victory over France and proclamation of the Reich, there was a need to consolidate the latter.

In 1868, prior to the end of German unification, North German merchants proposed the acquisition of free territories in eastern Africa and present-day Mozambique to the King of Prussia. Bismarck, then Prussian Chancellor, responded clearly:

> *I think that the German Confederation should not become engaged in colonial enterprises, as these should be exclusively the work of private initiatives.*[2]

Bismarck did, in fact, believe that the German state should keep itself apart from the colonial movement, but nothing prohibited German commercial firms from entering overseas ventures at their own risk. After his victory in 1870, Bismarck followed the same political line. In his eyes, the constitution of a colonial empire could only weaken Germany by diverting part of its national energies, at the very moment when the Reich required all the state's resources and even those of its private citizens in Europe. Moreover, plunging into this enterprise with such dubious prospects risked creating diplomatic crises with France and Great Britain who regarded the Dark Continent as their "private hunting grounds." The objective of planting one's flag on a scattering of dispersed possessions, which would be indefensible in case of conflict, seemed illusory to the Chancellor, who officially declared that Germany harbored no colonial territorial ambitions. Under these conditions, the powers concerned should not perceive German traders as the representatives of any sort of

---

[1] See Lugan, B. "L'Allemagne et l'Afrique (1870-1918)" [Germany and Africa (1870-1918)], *L'Information historique,* special issue: *Concours Agrégation et Capes* (1993), Vol. LV, cahiers 4 & 5, pp. 169-176. And B. Lugan, *Cette Afrique qui était allemande [The Africa That Was German],* in Rocher, 1990.

[2] Letter of January 9 to Count von Roon, Minister of the Navy.

German imperialism. Berlin affirmed, on the contrary, that its only goal was of a commercial order, and thus of an entirely different nature than those of Paris or of London, who sought to acquire political control in as many colonial territories as possible. This went further than a simple refusal of overseas commitments, and Bismarck defined here a doctrine that Germany would maintain for a dozen more years.

Bismarck's position was justified as long as the "Scramble for Africa" had not yet begun. It later became untenable because France and Great Britain were subject to constraints on their sovereignty within their respective empires and thus could not accept the methodical and aggressive German commercial policies pursued at their expense in their colonial territories without responding. It was in effect thanks to the French and British infrastructures, administrators, and soldiers that the traders from Bremen or Hamburg were able to create and develop their businesses.

To this "grumbling" from the neighboring great powers, there was soon added that of German economic circles. As early as 1878, a journalist wrote:

[. . .] it's a matter of knowing whether Germany will decide to do something else in Africa besides sending scientific missions or planting the bones of its explorers [. . .].

Bismarck was thus progressively forced to define a new policy. It was elaborated under the pressure of events in the period between 1884 and 1890. Three arguments had "tempered" the Chancellor's certainties: the problem of German immigration, that of the German navy, and lastly, the question of the Reich's prestige.

A country of emigration throughout the 19th century, Germany had witnessed the departure (without any hope of return) of three and a half million of its people between 1819 and 1885, a veritable human hemorrhage. The colonial pressure groups, such as the Colonial League, founded in 1883, actively militated in favor of diverting this flow to settlement colonies belonging to Germany, which never happened.

Germany, having launched an ambitious maritime program committed to guaranteeing its commercial freedom on all of the planet's seas, did not have secure footholds, ports, or outposts. It thus needed to possess colonies.

And finally, private commercial initiatives allowed the German state to avoid becoming engaged in colonial entanglements, except in those regions where no other European authority prevailed. There, it simply could not allow German traders to be threatened without intervening.

Bismarck had not, however, become a committed colonialist. While he could no longer oppose the movement to join the race for colonies, he tried, nevertheless, to control it and slow it down. While he accepted the establishment of the first elements of colonization in Togo, Cameroon, and eastern Africa, he declared these were not the constitution of a colonial empire, but only a means of supporting German trade. There was no question of territorial conquest.

On April 24, 1884, after long delay, Bismarck telegraphed the German consul at the Cape informing him that the 1,500 kilometers between the Orange and Cunene rivers, south of present-day Angola, were thereafter under the protection of the Reich. On July 6, 1884, the German flag was raised at Lomé, in Togo, on July 12, a German protectorate was declared in Cameroon. Germany thus took its place among the nations interested in Africa.

In order to prevent colonial rivalries from becoming armed conflicts between the great powers and also to ensure that Germany had a "fair share" of Africa, in line with its strength in Europe, Bismarck gathered together an international conference in Berlin, from November 15, 1884 to February 26, 1885. Fourteen European nations took part, focusing on three objectives: ensuring freedom of trade in the Congo basin; ensuring freedom of navigation on the two major African rivers, the Niger and the Congo; and deciding on procedures to observe when new possessions were taken along the African coast.

The Berlin conference was a success, and if there ever was a meeting to "carve up" the continent,[1] it was really this one, rather than the Congress of Berlin in 1878. The division was effectively organized and codified, even though this would not prevent severe crises between the colonial powers which emerged in later years.

---

[1] Léopold II, King of the Belgians, notably asked for and obtained personal sovereignty over the Congo.

In 1890, Bismarck was removed from power by Kaiser Wilhelm II, but his replacement, Chancellor Caprivi, had the same global views on the matter of colonization: "It was urgent to wait." In 1894, Hohenlohe-Schillingfürst took over from Caprivi, and it was he who committed Germany to a real colonial policy, allowing a significant increase in credits for the colonies, which rose from (DM) 2 million in the budgetary year 1890-1891 to nearly (DM) 10 million in 1896-1897.

Beginning in 1898, Berlin launched itself vigorously into a program of colonial acquisitions. Led by the Kaiser himself, Germany sought to establish positions everywhere, although Wilhelm II favored the Far East. A convention signed by China and Germany on March 6, 1898 gave Germany a 99-year lease on the bay of Kiaochow and the port of Tsingtao. On February 12, 1899, Germany bought the Caroline, Marianas, and Palaos islands from Spain and then acquired the islands of Bougainville and Buka.

Effects on the Colonizers

As we have seen, after much hesitation, prevarication, and backtracking, a variety of pressures had turned Europe into an imperialist power in Africa. These were predominantly strategic and philanthropic concerns rather than commercial or financial, contrary to what certain ideologically-driven historians continue to affirm.

The idea that the African colonies were "good deals" for the colonial powers is a heresy. Yet this heresy provides justification for numerous African countries to call on the former colonial nations to repent. They demand international aid and try to condemn them to the payment of indemnities, as was the case at the Durban summit in fall 2001, thus enabling them to flee from their own responsibilities. Because, in fact, the colonizers did not plunder Africa. Quite the contrary.

In 1956, journalist Raymond Cartier was the first to challenge the pious taboo against questioning France's colonial policies. At this time, he wrote in the French weekly, *Paris Match:*

Holland has lost its East Indies under the worst conditions and yet a few years have sufficed for it to enjoy more business and well-being than ever before. Perhaps it would not be in the same situation if, instead of drying out its Zuiderzee and modernizing its factories, it had been obliged to construct railroads in Java, cover Sumatra with dams, subsidize cloves in the Moluccas and pay for family allowances to the polygamous inhabitants of Borneo.

Cartier was saying publicly what experts had been writing for several decades: the colonies were a worthless burden. France had exhausted itself building 50,000 kilometers of paved roads in Africa, as well as 215,000 kilometers of trails passable by motor traffic, 18,000 kilometers of railroad, 63 equipped ports, 196 airports, 2,000 modern medical dispensaries, 600 maternity wards, and 220 hospitals where treatment and medicine were free.

In 1960, 3.8 million children in the African colonies were receiving an education, and in black Africa alone, 16,000 primary schools and 350 secondary high schools were operating. Also in 1960, 28,000 teachers from France, 1/8 of its entire teaching corps, were working on the African continent. For the single decade between 1946-1956, France spent the colossal sum of $1.4 billion on the infrastructure of its colonial empire.

The example of Madagascar provides a good illustration. It is an island, a closed territory which, with its 587,999 square kilometers, is bigger than France, the country which annexed it in 1896.

As a result, the great epidemics (bubonic plague, cholera, smallpox, typhoid fever) were vanquished. In 1935, in Tananarive (present-day Antananarivo), the French doctors Girard and Robic created the vaccine against bubonic plague.

By 1960, the effects of French health policy were clear. Madagascar's population had grown from around 2.5 million in 1900 to over six million in 1960. By the same year, 50 percent of children were in school, and France had endowed Madagascar with 28,000 kilometers of track, 3,000 kilometers of paved roads, hundreds of construction works, and railroads linking Antsirabe,

Tananarive (Antananarivo), Tamatave (Toamasina), Lake Alaotra, Fianarantsoa, and Manakara. It also bequeathed her four equipped ports: Diego Suarez (Antsiranana), Tamatave (Toamasina), Majunga (Mahajanga), and Tuléar (Toliary), along with several airports. In the agricultural domain, which was the French priority on the island, agronomists established profitable plantations of coffee, vanilla, cloves, sugarcane, and tobacco. Black pepper was introduced, along with cotton, sisal, fruit trees, grapes, and potatoes. Traditional rice-growing had been developed, and, starting in 1920, Madagascar exported 33,000 tons a year. The French civil engineers battled against erosion by actively reforesting the high plateaus. Dams were built and constituted reserves for irrigation. Industries for transforming agricultural produce were created, such as oil works, sugar refineries, and canning factories for meat and fish.

In 1960, the Malagasy Republic obtained its independence. When independence came, Madagascar was perhaps the only country of all those formerly controlled by France in sub-Saharan Africa truly on the path to development. At the time, agricultural self-sufficiency was assured, and rice exports were frequent and regular.

What remains today of those 64 years of "pillage?" Certainly, there are important legacies from the French, of which the country's territorial and political unification, carried out from the start by Gallieni, is not the least valuable. However, the roads no longer exist, and the population is threatened by famine. Civil war has nearly ruined a country already ravaged by corruption.

In 1984, Jacques Marseille published a book of paramount importance for understanding France's colonial problem. It was titled *Empire Colonial et Capitalisme Français, Histoire d'un Divorce [Colonial Empire and French Capitalism, History of a Divorce].*[1] It could have been titled, instead, "The Real Price of Empire."

What Marseille showed is that the African adventure was ruinous for France. The French government was constantly forced to compensate for private, capitalist enterprises, which turned away from the whole affair, quite simply because Africa was not profitable "business." France ended up

---

[1] See, also by Jacques Marseille, "L'héritage Colonial Français: au-delà des Légendes" [The French Colonial Heritage: Beyond Legends], in Rony Braumann (ed.), *Le Tiers-mondisme en question,* Paris, 1986.

exhausting itself building infrastructure, not even counting all the purely local expenses that were also funded by the mother country.

The Fonds d'Investissement pour le Développement Economique et Social (FIDES: Social & Economic Development Investment Fund) was in theory financed 90 percent by France and 10 percent by the overseas territories. Increasingly, however, there was a decline in the share these overseas territories were charged, and even when they did manage to pay their share, it was by means of French Treasury loans through the Caisse centrale de la France d'Outremer (CCFOM), whose funding came directly from the French budget in the form of long-term loans at reduced interest rates. These loans were never repaid. Finally, following a government decree of October 6, 1956, the mother country financed 100 percent of all public works projects in the social, agricultural, and industrial fields laid down in official development plans. And the same applied to investments in health, education, urban development, housing, town streets, rural improvements, agricultural production, hydraulic works, forestry, cattle raising, fishing, tourism, industrialization, electrification. The colonies were a bottomless pit.

Between 1948 and 1955, on capital investments alone, the French treasury spent FFR1,340 billion overseas, which is the equivalent of $4 billion or three percent of French national income.[1] This did not even include ongoing expenses, such as the salaries of civil servants and military spending. The global amount was enormous. In 1952, for example, total spending by France in its colonies, including those linked with the war in Indochina, represented 1/5 of its national budget.[2] A burden of this size was economically intolerable for a country that had to reconstruct all the infrastructure on its own territory that had been destroyed in the Second World War.

All of this spending was a pure loss for France, as well, since it never managed to supply itself cheaply from its African empire. As Jacques Marseille explains, France not only subsidized the farming of produce in its colonies but subsequently bought it up at prices artificially raised above the levels of the world market. So it was that, in 1958, 22 percent of all French colonial imports were constituted by Algerian wine, at a cost of $35 per liter, when Spanish or

---

[1] F. Walter, "Le Paradoxe Économique de l'Union Française," [The Economic Paradox of the French Union], *Le Monde*, October 9, 1955.

[2] M. de Bieville, "Contribution Métropolitaine aux Dépenses de l'Union Française," [Metropolitan Contribution Spent on the French Union] *Revue Politique et Parlementaire* (March 1953).

Portuguese wine of the same quality cost only $19.

From 1954 to 1956, colonial imports cost France FFR360 billion. At world market levels, these should only have cost FFR310 billion; hence, it lost FFR50 billion. Moreover, apart from Moroccan phosphates, coal from Tonkin, and a few products in other sectors, the French empire produced nothing valuable.

These extravagant expenses severely reduced the national investment capacity, hindering industrial modernization and the conversion of the French economy at the very moment when its world competitors were gaining a decisive lead with respect to France. The empire thus constituted a "ball-and-chain" that weighed down the country and threatened to lead it to asphyxiation and decline. It was urgent, even crucial, for France to decolonize.

What about Britain? Contrary to the predominant idea, British imperialism was not the result of colonial exploitation. The British industrial revolution came about as the result of a process, an evolution which was internal, prior to colonial expansion.

We know from the work of P.J. Cain and A.G. Hopkins,[1] that England was the first country with a modern banking system. It was in place by the end of the 17th century, before the period when the plantation economy and the slave trade developed. Because of it, the City of London to become the principal financial center in the world, providing both commercial credit, with short- or medium-term loans, and long-term investment credit. By this time also the industrial revolution had started there. It was a process that lasted a century, enriching the country and permitting it to become the world's foremost naval power.

From a chronological point of view, there was thus no direct link between the British economy and its colonial expansion in Africa. At the end of the 18th century, having completed its first industrial revolution, Britain found itself at the head of an immense American and Asiatic empire. A century would go by, until the 1890s to be precise, before Great Britain became interested in Africa, and for strategic rather than economic reasons. It occurred at a time when surplus goods at low prices resulting from the British industrial revolution began to appear causing Britain to start looking for external outlets. As a result,

---

[3] Notably since the publication of *British Imperialism,* London, 1993.

London embarked on a policy of opening up international markets. British imperialism was not the cause of the industrial revolution but instead was a result of that revolution.

The cost of Britain's African empire is not as easy to calculate as that of the French. The studies available to us are generally devoted to the British Empire as a whole, and only estimates of Africa's percentage are given. The British Empire did indeed spread to all of the continents, and it was composed of territories that were very different from one another. The dominions (Canada, Australia, New Zealand, and South Africa) had a greater economic importance than the colonies. Moreover, among the latter, some, like India or Ceylon, had a much greater weight than the African territories.

That being said, we have known for a decade now, thanks to numerous academic publications,[1] that British power in the 19th and 20th centuries was not the result of exploitation of the Empire. The figures even indicate, on the contrary, that the share of the colonies in its Gross National Product (GNP) was negligible.[2]

The most recent studies concerning the share of foreign trade in the British GNP indicate that, during the period 1871-1913, Great Britain obtained 31.5 percent of its revenues from abroad, whether from the dominions or the colonies or from outside the Empire altogether. What then, was the Empire's share, and above all, that of Africa in this percentage?

British historians have compared the rates of return on investment made overseas and those made at home, those made within the Empire, and those beyond its frontiers. In this way they have discovered that investments within the Empire earned more, to be sure, than those within the territory of Great Britain itself, but also that investments in the rest of the world were even more profitable than those within the Empire.

Let us take the example of railways. Between the years 1870 and 1913, the projects carried out in Great Britain earned 3.8 percent, those carried out in the Empire 4.5 percent, and those in the rest of the world 5.7 percent. During these same years, a study taking into account 566 securities, including variations in

---

[1] For example: M. Edelstein, "Imperialism: Cost and Benefit," in R. Floud & D. McCloskey (eds.), *The Economic History of Britain since 1700*, Cambridge, 1994, Vol. II, pp. 173-216.

[2] For a detailed bibliography on this question, see A. Offer, "Costs and Benefits, Prosperity, 1870-1914," *The Oxford History of the British Empire*, Vol. III, pp. 690-711.

capital, indicate a return of 4.6 percent for investments at home and 5.7 percent for those in the Empire and the rest of the world, an increase of only 1.1 percent. Taken over the entire period, which was a time of great national prosperity, these figures permit A. Offer[1] to affirm that the difference between these different types of investment represented only 1.6 percent of the British national income. In other words, that the investments outside the British Isles were in the end not particularly attractive and those in the Imperial domain even less so.

Offer even writes that, for a long time, the rates of return on investments within the Empire, which only represented a small fraction of the total volume of overseas investments, were overestimated. He estimates that profits on investments from the Empire amounted at most to only 0.4 percent of national income in 1913, at the Empire's height.

As for trade, the profits from the Empire as a whole were at most between five and six percent of British national income. This permitted Offer to conclude that, in the end, if the contribution of the Empire was not totally negligible, it was not the basis for Britain's wealth. Even if the colonial empire of His Majesty had not existed, the country's economy would have surpassed those of France and Germany.[2] In short, the wealth and prosperity of Great Britain did not rest on the exploitation of its colonies.

Moreover, the share of Africa in this percentage—between five and six percent of national income —was negligible. It is estimated to have been at most between one and two percent. For the City of London's financiers, Africa did not count.

Given these conditions, was Britain's African empire a good deal? During the 60 years of its colonial presence, did it enrich itself at the expense of its African possessions?

The answer is complex, because imperial policy constantly wavered between two tendencies: the one rested on international free trade, and the other on the priorities to be given to economic relations with the Empire. In any case, Africa was only a secondary component of the imperial order. In the end, the Empire as a whole only played a relatively important role during

---

[1] Op cit.
[2] Op cit, p. 708.

periods of crisis and particularly during the two World Wars.

As D.K. Fieldhouse has shown,[1] total British capital (in the mother country and in the rest of the world) amounted to £5,783 million in 1914. It was distributed as follows[2]:

Distribution of British Capital in 1914

	£ Billions	Share
Mother Country	1,828	31.62 %
Empire	1,488	25.73%
All Others	2,467	42.65%
Total	5,783	100%

The figure that interests us directly is that of the Empire, that is, £1,488 billion, which represented 25.73 percent of British capital. Of this sum, 70.22 percent was located in the dominions (Canada, Australia, New Zealand, and South Africa), 19.21 percent in India, and 10.48 percent in the rest of the Empire. The latter's share, amounting to £156 millions, represented barely 2.7 percent of all British capital in 1914 and less than 4 percent of the capital exported outside the British Isles that same year. Knowing that, this "rest of the Empire" category encompassed Ceylon and numerous island possessions off the American and Asian coasts as well as Africa, one realizes that Africa was practically nonexistent within British capital markets in 1914, at the height of the Empire.

Still referring to Fieldhouse's figures, we find the same tendencies concerning trade:

British Imports in 1913 and 1934 (in £ millions)

Imports	1913	Share	1934	Share
Dominions	103	13.3%	157	21.7%
India	49	6.4%	42	5.7%
Colonies	39	5.1%	58	7.9%
All Others	577	75.2%	470	64.7%
Total	708	100%	727	100%

[1] D.K. Fieldhouse, "The Metropolitan Economics of Empire," *The Oxford History of the British Empire,* Vol. IV, 1999, pp. 88-113.
[2] In the monetary values of the period.

British Exports in 1913 and 1934 (in £ millions)

Imports	1913	Share	1934	Share
Dominions	92	17.5%	88	23.3%
India	70	13.4%	37	9.8%
Colonies	33	6.3%	41	10.8%
All Others	330	62.8%	212	56.1%
Total	525	100%	378	100%

In 1913 and 1934, the colonies, including Africa, only represented between 5.1 percent and 7.9 percent of all British imports and between 6.3 percent and 10.8 percent of all exports. Africa represented at most a third of these figures, and probably even less, giving us a figure of barely one to two percent of British imports and two to three percent of exports.

Moreover, the permanence of these historical facts is striking; the figures are practically identical to those of present-day flows of British trade with the independent African states, which are 2.1 percent of imports and 3.2 percent of exports.

The Empire in Africa thus was of no real economic interest to Great Britain, and it certainly did not enhance the economic independence of the mother country. All the less so, in fact, since London, like the other colonial powers, was subject to constraints of sovereignty (the provision of infrastructure, protection of property and persons, etc.) that it had to support financially. Thus, from 1946 to 1954, the Colonial Development and Welfare Fund, the British equivalent to the French FIDES, was financed by the Crown's budget to the sum of £123 million, of which £121 million took the form of grants, an amount which was on average three times greater than British imports from Africa and two times its exports to the continent.

As in the French case, it was the British Treasury which intervened constantly to assist the development of the Empire in Africa, The only major exception was in the Rhodesian colonies which were capable of balancing their budgets from 1935 to1940 onwards. Great Britain's Empire in Africa was thus as unprofitable as that of France. The vast spaces of Africa were economically marginal.

The Belgian Paradox

Only Belgium, which became imperialist against its will had a colony that barely cost it anything at all.

When Léopold II was crowned king of Belgium in 1866, he wanted a colony. Knowing that Belgian public opinion, both on the Right and the Left, was opposed to such a project, he planned on financing it out of his personal fortune, which was considerable. On October 24, 1869, he wrote to Hubert Frère-Orban, the head of his cabinet:

I solemnly promise to ask for nothing from the Ministry of Finance.

On July 15, 1880, in another letter sent to the same official, he said:

Belgium will have its share in the African movement and the opening of this continent, without state expenditure.

In 1885, the Etat Indépendant du Congo (EIC – Congo Free State) was created. Léopold II became the colony's sovereign. This was authorized by the Belgian Chamber of Parliament after some hesitation due to worries over the cost of the undertaking. But the king reassured the representatives by affirming to them that it was only a "personal union," and that the administration and finances of the Congo would be separate from those of Belgium. Moreover, the Congo would not be a burden to the home country, since local resources would ensure its autonomy.

As considerable as it was, Leopold's fortune was nevertheless rapidly exhausted. The amounts spent on the Congo between 1878 and 1885 reached a total of 10 million gold francs. The "local resources" turned out to be nonexistent at the time, and, by 1890, the EIC was bankrupt. Contrary to his promises, the king then turned to the Belgian government, which, in 1890 accorded a first loan to the EIC of which 25 million gold francs of which five million were paid out immediately and the rest in 10 annuities of two million each. In return, the king bequeathed the Congo to Belgium.

In 1895, when the last annuity from the first loan was paid, bankruptcy threatened again. This time, six million was needed. This was only made avail-

able by the Belgian Chambers after a sharp debate over the wisdom of pos-
sessing the Congo. The parliamentary representatives did not want to let themselves be dragged into a budgetary spiral, as had occurred in Holland, where,
without a separate colonial budget, the state budget was constantly forced to
meet the deficit of its colonies.

In 1896, a reversal of past trends took place. Revenues from ivory, and
above all, from rubber, at last permitted the EIC to balance its budget.
Thereafter, it produced a surplus, and the territory no longer cost Belgium anything. On the contrary, starting in 1900, Léopold II drew on the resources of
the Congo to launch a public works program in Belgium. With this end in
mind, he created the Foundation de la Couronne (Crown Foundation), to
which he allocated about a tenth of the Belgian Congo's area.

It was this Foundation which received the estate revenues from the colonial concessions. A dark period in the history of Belgian colonialism ensued,
with a genuine policy of exploitation based on forced labor and the harsh treatment that accompanied it.[1] Congolese rubber undeniably enriched the building
heritage of Brussels, which found itself gifted with the Arcade du
Cinquantenaire (costing six million gold francs, the Tervuren Museum,
eight million, and an extension of the Laeken Royal Palace, 12.5 million. The
total of all these projects was 30 million gold francs.[2] This provoked the anger
of the "colonials," who protested against this policy of taking Congolese
resources for the benefit of the mother country on the one hand and, on the
other hand, an emotional outburst on the part of the public. Eventually, a campaign was launched in the United Kingdom aimed at denouncing the abuses of
the Leopoldian regime. Finally, in 1908, the Belgian state took control of the
Congo and abolished the Foundation.

As regrettable as it was, the "dark period" of Belgian colonialism only
lasted about 10 years. Starting in 1908, the Congo returned to lawful rule, with
its resources devoted to its own development as the Belgians launched an
impressive construction program of new roads, railroads, and ports in their
colony. But this brief parenthesis, with its exceptional misconduct, has been

---

[1] For a report on the issue, despite its polemical title and its largely ideological position, it is provided in Adam Hochschild's book, *The Ghosts of King Leopold II: A Forgotten Holocaust*, Editions
Belford, Paris, 2001.

[2] For more details, see J. Stengers, "Combien le Congo a-t-il coûté à la Belgique?", [How Much Did
the Congo Cost Belgium?], *Académie Royale des Sciences Coloniales*, Vol. XI, fascicule 1, 1957,
pp. 330-340.

utilized to describe colonial practices as a whole. Nothing could be further from the truth, or more dishonest.

On August 20, 1908, a year before the death of Léopold II, the Parliament in Brussels voted the annexation of the Congo by Belgium. By then, the Congo had cost the country nothing, and the finances of the distant territory were in the black. In all, during the first "Leopoldian" period, from the start of the adventure to 1908, Brussels had spent 50 million gold francs there, and had withdrawn 66 million, primarily to repay its loans. So, it had made a profit of 16 million, somewhat less than the cost of building the Palace of Justice in Brussels (43 million). This 16 million did not, in fact, represent much within the budget of a state such as Belgium.

The situation continued along these lines throughout the second "post-Leopoldian" period, until the crisis of the 1930s, when the Congo was ruined for a time. The price of copper collapsed, bringing with it a sharp rise in unemployment and forcing numerous European managers to return home. The Belgian state was then forced to intervene. It created the Colonial Lottery which raised 58 million francs while the Belgian Treasury intervened with contributions amounting to 104 million between 1933 and 1940. This colonial lottery was nothing other than a tax levied in Belgium on behalf of the Congo, a tax subtracted from the wealth of the mother country.

In the final analysis, and as Stengers sums up well:

In 1908 [. . .] at the moment when the Congo was taken over by Belgium, the Congo had yielded 26 million gold francs to the Belgian state. From 1908 to 1950, colonial expenditures by Belgium [. . .] reached a total of 259 million gold francs. During this period, the benefits derived by Belgium thanks to the Congo amounted to 24 million. Net spending by Belgium, from 1908 to 1950, thus totaled 235 million.

The Congo had yielded 26 million at the time of the takeover. It cost 235 million since then. In all, it thus cost Belgium, until 1950, 209 million gold francs.[1]

---

[1] J. Stengers, op cit., p. 350.

These 259 million gold francs was the equivalent of 7 billion francs in postwar Belgium, and in 1950 represented less than 1/10 of the annual spending by the Belgian government. By way of comparison, the annual Belgian budget for pensions was 12.5 billion in 1950, which is the same as saying that annually, spending on this item alone was nearly twice as much as 70 years' involvement in the Congo[1] cost.

The Congo thus barely had any impact at all on the Belgian economy. From the beginning, the Belgian government did not intervene in the Congolese budget, except in the case of grave crises, and vice versa. Their finances were separate, From 1918 to 1939, the budget for the colonies averaged 1,300,000 gold francs per year. From 1945 to 1956 it rose to 1,500,000 gold francs.[2]

The budget of the Belgian Ministry for the Colonies can be analyzed as follows:

Share of the Ministry for the Colonies in the Belgian and Congolese Budgets

Year	Share of the total Belgian state budget	Share of the Congo's budget
In 1910	0.15%	3%
In 1930	0.13%	1.8%
In 1950	0.10%	1.6%
In 1956	0.08%	0.6%

In short, Belgium's Congolese adventure was a paradox. The Congo was the only colony which cost the mother country nothing, or very little in terms of the total budget, and it was the only one which yielded profits, albeit practically none to Belgium, but a great deal to private investors.

How did this come about? Luckily for Belgium, the Congo did not require major military spending for its conquest and the few revolts that had to be put down by Belgian troops were mere skirmishes compared to those the French troops had to contain in Tunisia[3] and in Madagascar,[4] for example, or again the "Herero rebellion" in South West Africa, which, between 1904 and 1905, cost the Germans 400 million gold francs.[5]

---

[1] J. Stengers, op cit., p. 351.
[2] A. van Bilsen, "Pour une politique congolaise nouvelle" [For a New Congolese Policy], *Revue Générale Belge* April 15, 1956, p. 911.
[3] Costing 142 million gold francs between 1881 and 1886.
[4] Costing 80 million gold francs between 1895 and 1896.
[5] M.E. Townsend, *The Rise and Fall of Germany's Colonial Empire (1884-1918)*, New York, 1930, p. 340.

As was noted earlier, the initial infrastructure was financed out of Léopold II's private purse, and the investments necessary for exploiting the potential mineral and forest resources, which were considerable, were taken charge of by private consortia. Infrastructure such as education and health were subcontracted to the Catholic missions, who were only too happy to proselytize.

Another heavy budgetary burden borne by the other colonial powers was the cost of market support to stimulate colonial production and the purchase of goods at a loss. Here again, the Congo proved an exception. Belgium chose to respect the terms of the Congo Act of Neutrality, refusing to accord any privileges in commercial exchanges between the colony and the mother country.

To sum up, the Congo was a "profitable enterprise" and was managed as such, to the advantage of investors who placed their capital in the colony. The "Congo enterprise" had sufficient self-financing capacity to satisfy its needs, carry out its ten-year development plans, and meet its "operating expenses." Of course, loans were necessary, but what enterprise of this size could have operated without relying on external capital to some extent? The Congo's economy was prosperous and still generating wealth, when, in 1960, at the moment of independence, Belgium bequeathed it to the République Démocratique du Congo (RDC).

In the case of Ruanda-Urundi (the present-day states of Rwanda and Burundi), another Belgian possession, the situation was different, and much more comparable to the French and British colonial territories which incurred loss-making expenses. In just six years, from 1950 to 1956, these two territories cost Belgium more than two billion — a third of what the Congo had cost in 75 years.

In hindsight, did the Congo enrich Belgium? Yes, briefly, before 1908. And while Belgium later provided support as necessary, there was seldom any call for this because the colony was economically healthy and possessed efficient infrastructures. One should not lose sight of this history when one observes the catastrophes that independent Congo has caused for its unhappy populations.

* * *

In conclusion, it is fair to assert that, as a general rule, the colonial empires in Africa, which were founded on the basis of strategic and philanthropic interests, became economic burdens for their respective mother countries, due, as Jacques Marseille put it, to ruinous "constraints of sovereignty." For the European powers, condemned to feed, educate and provide medical treatment for ever-growing populations and their infrastructures, the vast spaces of Africa became a bottomless pit. In economic terms, decolonization became an urgent necessity.

Chapter III

The Balance Sheets of Colonialism and Decolonization

Colonialism was a brief parenthesis that only spanned 60 years of the whole of Africa's long history. The myth of "colonial pillage" rests on the same kind of assumptions as those that make the slave trade the basis of the Industrial Revolution. According to this myth, the wealth of the countries in the north was ultimately due to their pillage and exploitation of the south.

Beyond the fact that there are no grounds for such assertions, these same partisan arguments provoke the same logical responses. If present wealth could be attributed to the immense colonial possessions of yesteryear, then today Portugal ought to be the foremost European industrial power because it only decolonized in 1975; and Germany, which lost its colonies after its defeat in 1918, should, on the contrary, be a sort of Romania.

The Real Colonial Balance Sheet

In the field of health, the work accomplished by the colonizers was considerable. They rid Africans of leprosy, measles, trypanosomiasis ("sleeping sickness"), cholera, smallpox, typhoid fever, and widely introduced quinine, the only means of combating malaria. These achievements by the colonial doctors appear to have been forgotten today. Yet the list of those, who from Indochina to Madagascar and from Djibouti to Dakar, risked everything to save the populations living in the tropics, is long.

Let us recall Georges Girard and Jean Robic, for example, already mentioned in connection with their work in Madagascar. Trained at the French School of Naval Health in Bordeaux, then at the Pharo Institute of Tropical Medicine in Marseille, and finally at the Pasteur Institute in Paris, they were posted to Madagascar at a time when bubonic plague was ravaging the island. With great tenacity, they succeeded in creating a vaccine against this disease which had once decimated Europe. As the race against death became more pressing, they even injected one another with the vaccine, thus serving as human guinea pigs. Thanks to them, the epidemic was stopped, and the disease eradicated.

There were other Girards and Robics who, in less dramatic circumstances, were no less generous. They were doctors and agronomists, hydraulic engineers and geologists.

Between 1900 and 2000, thanks to such people, the population of the continent multiplied sevenfold. Should colonization be blamed for that?

Indeed, while colonization was partly responsible for the disaster that has befallen contemporary Africa, its responsibilities do not lie where they are most commonly assigned. They are instead partly philosophical and partly geographical.

Colonization was, at its core, very largely philanthropic in nature, imposing upon Africa and its "noble savages" a doctrine which was foreign to the continent and unleashing a profound trauma on populations that could not understand the way this doctrine favored the individual over the collective. Furthermore, colonization tended to benefit the weak at the expense of the strong. The colonizers were welcomed by those who wanted to escape from other, "predatory" peoples.

In this respect, colonial responsibility was effectively enormous. In the name of the oppressed, white Europeans interfered in local power relations that extended beyond their immediate comprehension and in social networks that resisted their mode of understanding the world. They destroyed empires that resisted them, often to the benefit of former subordinate peoples. It was a major shock for a continent whose values were neither charity, nor compassion, nor tolerance, but prestige and force. The long history of Africa had, in effect, been written around dominant peoples who commanded other dominated peoples, in the name of their own peculiar values borne by collective definitions. Never the reverse. The reality of "dominant versus dominated," although it clashed with democratic sensibilities and a philosophy based on the "Rights of Man," was nevertheless at the root of all ancestral inter-African relations.

Colonization also traced new "frontiers" on the ruins of the vanquished African empires. This was an unfamiliar and even bizarre notion in Africa. In doing so, it disturbed the internal equilibrium of great zones of cattle-raising, where age-old patterns of seasonal migration were territorially amputated. Ethnic groups were often cut into two or more segments by these artificial lines of partition. Without the slightest historical basis, they soon formed impassable legal barriers between close cousins, while these same lines made yesterday's implacable enemy into an artificial "compatriot." Elsewhere, colonization assembled fragmented worlds, divided into tens, hundreds, and even thousands of ethnic, tribal, or village entities and made groupings that seemed administratively coherent to the eyes of the colonizers. But they were purely artificial and not viable.

With hindsight and thanks to the proliferation of academic studies, colonization can be described as an African "Golden Age," compared to the continent's present-day disasters. Under colonial rule, with honest and efficient administrations, devoted and passionate agents, health facilities, infrastructures, and schools, African populations lived in peace, were well fed, and received medical attention. More generally, colonization brought order and respected the principles of law.

This globally positive balance sheet is not in any way a blissfully naive apologia of colonization. Three of the chapters in this book provide an in-depth critique. Darker and more shocking aspects did indeed exist: the actions of the Congolese concessionaires already mentioned above, certain forms of forced labor, or the bloody Voulet-Chanoine mission. All the same, from a historical point of view, these were exceptions, reprehensible, to be sure, but not in any way general practices, as some would argue.

Only blind prejudice prevents the intellectuals of the "white" world and those of the "black" world from recognizing that, for millions of Africans, life was better in colonial times, before the botched independence processes delivered these same millions of Africans to the quarrels between the Eastern bloc, eager to spread its proletarian revolution, and the Western bloc, with its foolish egalitarian pieties, supported by capitalist greed.

Decolonization was accelerated by the Second World War, which sounded the death knell of the colonial empires. The two principal victors of the war, the United States and the USSR were, for different reasons, opposed to them. The new world order, defined in the United Nations Charter, proclaimed the right of self-determination for the colonized peoples. Already, in 1941, France had been forced to recognize the independence of Syria and Lebanon, while Great Britain had set in motion the process that would lead to the independence of India. The colonial period would thus soon come to a close.

As opposed to Asia and North Africa, where wars took place, the process of decolonization in black Africa was carried out, with some rare exceptions, in a peaceful fashion. Among the French, British, Belgian, and Portuguese empires, however, the evolution of the situation differed.

French Decolonization

France possessed two great territorial groupings in black Africa: Afrique Occidentale Française (AOF – French West Africa), and Afrique Equatoriale Française (AEF). The AOF was composed of eight colonies and a UN mandate territory: Senegal, Mauritania, Guinea, Côte d'Ivoire, Soudan Français,[1] Niger, Dahomey,[2] Upper Volta,[3] and Togo. The AEF was formed by four colonies: Gabon, Moyen Congo,[4] Oubangui Chari,[5] Chad, and another mandate territory, Cameroon. In addition to these two groups, there was Madagascar with its dependency, the Comoro Islands, and French Somaliland.

When the Second World War ended, it was necessary to explore the future

---

[1] Present-day Mali.
[2] Present-day Benin.
[3] Present-day Burkina Faso.
[4] Present-day Congo, known as Brazzaville, as opposed to the Democratic Republic of Congo.
[5] Present-day Central African Republic.

of the French empire. That is why, in the final phase of the war, a conference of top French colonial officials was held at Brazzaville from January 30 to February 8, 1944. The paradox is that this conference is referred to today as if it had been the catalyst for the emancipation of French Africa, when the conference's preamble in actual fact rejected any notion of independence, or even of autonomy:

> [. . .] the goals of the civilizing work accomplished by the French rules out any idea of autonomy, any possibility of an evolution beyond the French bloc of the Empire; the eventual constitution, even in the future of self-governments; [in English in the text]; in the colonies must be dismissed.

At the very moment when the United States and the USSR were affirming the right to freedom of the colonized peoples, France maintained its traditional imperial line. It was, moreover, all the more justified in doing so because, independence was not the Africans' principal demand at the time. They wanted more liberty, more equality, and, as the final recommendations of the Brazzaville Conference made clear, a closer association with the management of their territories, in order to temper the French system of centralized administration that was generally applied.

The impact of the Brazzaville Conference was mainly symbolic. Except in the economic field, it only issued recommendations. A plan for industrialization and development was foreseen, which would later lead to the creation of the Fonds d'Investissement du Développement Economique et Social (FIDES).

A real evolution began in 1946 when, by referendum, the French voted for a new constitution providing for the creation of the Union Française [French Union], a sort of "social contract" passed between the mother country and its colonies. In the French National Assembly, the debates surrounding the creation of this Union were lively and passionate. The newly elected parliamentarians had all emerged from the French Resistance, and it was this assembly, with its left-wing majority, which would nevertheless refuse to give equal political rights to populations of the colonial empire. In this, they followed Edouard Herriot, the great leader of the French Left, a humanist radical, Mayor of Lyon,

Map XI: French Africa at Its Height

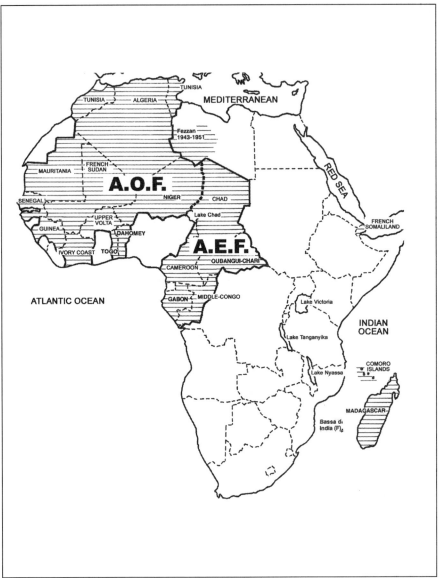

Prime Minister of France in 1924 after the victory of the left-wing "Cartel des gauches," president of the National Assembly on the eve of the Second World War, and who, in an address on August 27, 1946, declared from the rostrum of the Assembly:

If we give equality of rights to the colonial peoples, we would be the colony of our colonies.

This declaration provoked the indignation of three "colonial" representatives; the Algerian Ferhat Abbas, the Senegalese Lamine Guèye, and Léopold Sedar Senghor, who described the statement as "racist." However, this criticism did not prevent the National Assembly from wholeheartedly approving Edouard Herriot's position.

Under the terms of Title VIII in the French Constitution of 1946, largely inspired by Léopold Sedar Senghor himself, France was declared an "indivisible Republic forming with the overseas states and territories a freely consented union." The Constitution recognized the existence of territorial entities freely administering themselves, on the one hand, and groups of territories placed under the authority of a resident minister, on the other. The French Union was guided by a Haut-conseil de l'Union, made up of representatives of the French government and of the associated states, and by an Assemblée de l'Union Française, half of which was composed of parliamentarians of metropolitan France, designated by the National Assembly and Senate, and the other half of overseas representatives, elected by the territorial assemblies.

If, both in spirit and in letter, the differences with the prewar situation seemed minor, the change they represented in actual practice was to the contrary quite considerable, because of internal, and above all, very important external pressures. The events in Indochina, then later in Algeria, and the priority given to decolonization in the polarization around the two superpowers, profoundly affected the international situation. And all this would very quickly render the principles of the French Union obsolete and lead inevitably to independence.

It was in this context that the "Loi cadre" [Framing Law], or the Defferre Law, was passed on June 20, 1956. This was the last serious attempt by France to preserve its empire. It established universal suffrage and a single electoral college for the election of the territorial assemblies, but, since it arrived late with respect to events, it was almost immediately outdated since as the internal autonomy it announced could only lead to independence.

In May 1958, upon his return to power, Charles de Gaulle drew lessons from this evolution. At this point, he proposed replacing the French Union, which he judged to be too constraining and too directive, with a more flexible federal structure that would permit each territory "by an act of free determination" to join the Franco-African Community. It was a veritable constitutional revolution; it sought to set up a genuine federation in which each colony would have an autonomous government but would accept to entrust France with its foreign policy, its defense, its currency, its economic policy, and even its justice system.

In August 1958, General de Gaulle made a trip to black Africa in order to present France's new policy. Everywhere on his journey he offered the choice between association and secession. The tour was triumphal, except in Guinea, where Sekou Touré declared, with an emphatic dignity, that his country preferred "poverty in freedom to wealth in slavery."

The African referendum that followed was a plebiscite for de Gaulle. To the question posed concerning joining the Community, the Africans voted 7,470,000 (87 percent) in favor and 1,120,000 (13 percent) against. Even then, among the "no's," more than half (636,000) were those of Sekou Touré's Guinea, which separated itself from France on October 2, 1958, six days before the vote on the new French Constitution held on October 8, that election established the Franco-African Community and replaced the French Union.

But this new juridical construction did not survive for long in the face of nationalist demands, and De Gaulle understood that his policy of a Franco-African federal association had failed. Being a realist, he did not oppose its breakup. And an independence explosion followed. Between January 1 and November 28, 1960, 14 member countries of the Franco-African Community became independent. France's African empire had expired.[1]

As we have seen, colonization and decolonization were both predominantly

---

[1] The question of the decolonization of North Africa is another subject, which we will not deal with in the book since it is devoted to sub-Saharan Africa.

two left-wing ideas. It was very much the Left in France which advocated the great "humanist" idea of philanthropic colonization. By its constant refusal to recognize that there exist differences between people, French colonization was carried out in the name of a utopian will to assimilate, a sort of secular and republican messianism which claimed to deliver the "revelation of the Enlightenment" everywhere from Dunkirk to Fort Dauphin in Madagascar and to administer Middle Congo in exactly the same way as the French département of Corrèze. But ideological fashions change, and, when the French Left adopted another moral imperative, it then mounted the chimera of independence, provoking a new catastrophe for which it was, once again, fully responsible.

British Decolonization

In 1945, besides the Anglo-Egyptian Sudan, Great Britain's possessions in West Africa included the Gold Coast,[1] Sierra Leone, Nigeria, and Gambia, plus part of the former Togo and Cameroon. In East Africa, its empire included Kenya, Uganda, Zanzibar, and the formerly German Tanganyika[2] over which it exercised tutelage. In southern Africa, Britain was present in Nyassaland,[3] Northern Rhodesia,[4] and Southern Rhodesia.[5] It also exercised a protectorate over Bechuanaland,[6] Basutoland,[7] and Swaziland.

In contrast to France, there was a consensus in Great Britain among the entire political establishment about decolonization, and London admitted very soon that the movement toward independence was inevitable. Under the circumstances, Britain was concerned, on the one hand, about not letting itself be pushed into conflict, and at the same time, about organizing the transition in the best interests of both the mother country and its former colonies.

In contrast also to French imperial practices, the British colonial system was largely decentralized. Once decolonization had been decided, it sufficed to reinforce the legislative and executive councils that existed in each colony, then to increase little by little the number of elected members in relation to those who had been appointed, and finally to widen the electoral base of those charged with electing them. With the exception of Kenya where, in 1952, the

---

[1] Present-day Ghana.
[2] Present-day Tanzania, born of the union between Tanganyika and Zanzibar.
[3] Present-day Malawi.
[4] Present-day Zambia.
[5] Present-day Zimbabwe.
[6] Present-day Botswana.
[7] Present-day Lesotho.

Map XII: British Africa at Its Height

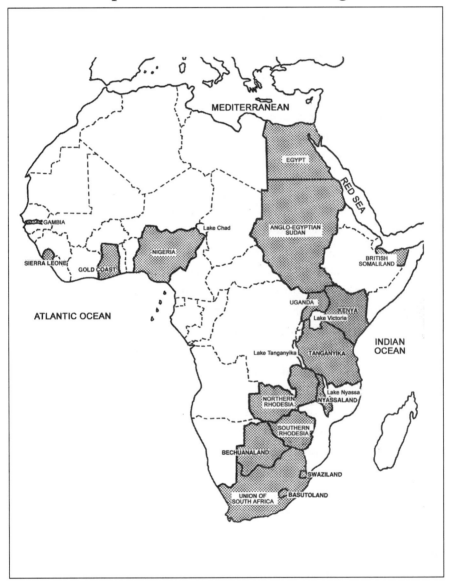

"Mau-Mau" revolt erupted within the Kikuyu ethnic group, and of Southern Rhodesia, where the white minority unilaterally declared its independence in November 1965, the decolonization of British black Africa went smoothly and peacefully. At the end of the process, the British governors were replaced by African presidents and independence was acquired without clashes, major disruptions, and at the conclusion of a constitutional evolution that was perfectly controlled from start to finish.

The first independent country was the Sudan, which obtained a statute of internal autonomy in 1953 before proclaiming its independence in 1956. It was followed by Ghana in 1957, Sierra Leone in 1961, then all the other territories in a rush.

For the record, we should not forget two particular examples: the Union of South Africa[1] and Southern Rhodesia. The first had been a dominion since 1910, and then became an independent republic in 1961. The second was a rebellious colony from 1965 to 1979 under a white regime, then temporarily became a colony again until its definitive independence in 1980 under the name of Zimbabwe.

Decolonization and the Other European Powers

If Belgian decolonization appeared chaotic, it was because it was rushed. Brussels, which had prepared a movement in the longer term, found itself propelled by outside events.

On June 30, 1960, independence was granted to the former Belgian Congo, and a kind of state was set up to preside over the destiny of this huge ethnic conglomerate. As far as its economic health was concerned, this did not present any problems; the Congo, as we have seen, had healthy finances, a balanced budget, and was able to fund its own investments. However, it was in no way prepared politically. This unique example in Africa honestly allows us to take measure of the full scale of the disaster and the waste that took place following independence.

Independent Congo immediately sank into anarchic chaos, beginning

---

[1] The present-day Republic of South Africa (RSA).

with the secession of Katanga in 1960. This provoked a long and bloody civil war, a mess that was aggravated still further by the "help" of troops sent by the United Nations in 1963. As for Rwanda and Burundi, which became independent in 1962, they had never in fact really been colonized, and Belgium left behind a potentially explosive situation there, as later events, alas, would show.

Portuguese decolonization was the latest since it only took place in 1975. It was provoked by the military coup d'état of April 25, 1974 which overthrew the Estado Novo regime established in the mother country in 1926.

Present in Africa since the 15th century, Portugal was the only European power to attempt to swim against the current of the international evolution. It considered its colonies of Angola, Mozambique, and Guinea-Bissau, along with the islands of Cape Verde, and of Sao Tome and Principe, integral parts of the Portuguese nation according to the constitutional principle, which laid down that Portugal was one and only one "before and beyond the sea." In application of this principle, Portugal squandered colossal sums on its African empire, far beyond its means.

Young, "progressive" (meaning Marxist) officers belonging to the Movimento das Forças Armadas (AFM – Armed Forces Movement), led by Captain Otelo Saraiva de Carvalho, took power in Lisbon. It was the "Revolution of the Carnations." Their position was clear: Portugal had to decolonize as quickly as possible, and they granted independence to the colonies, transferring power to the movements in Africa to whom they felt closest in ideological terms. Decolonization would thus occur in a manner that profited local African Marxist revolutionary parties. Angola and Mozambique, after a hurried process lasting barely two years, were abandoned to themselves after a bondage that had started five centuries earlier.

It was thus not colonization, but decolonization, which was catastrophic for Africa. It delivered, in the 1960s, new "ready to occupy" artificial states to predatory "nomenklatura" who, with regularity of a metronome, diverted both national resources and international aid to their personal profit.

Then, in the 1990s, when the Western bloc won the East-West duel, these artificial African "states" were impelled by Western ideology along the road to a democratic system. The trauma resulting today from this attempt to introduce "Western democracy" is considerable. Whether it is a good system for Western civilizations is debatable. That it is in no way beneficial to African civilizations is a fact. We'll come back to that point shortly.

* * *

In the final analysis, the only reproach that one could make against the former colonizers is that they put an end to what they considered to be the "law of the jungle," interfering in things that were none of their business. Yet that is what they have been asked to do yet again in Sierra Leone, in Somalia, in former Zaire, in Rwanda, in Burundi, etc. Under pressure from the "humanitarians," heirs of the philanthropists who had pressed in favor of "colonizing to free the blacks," in the 19th century, the Western world is repeating the same mistakes. Clearly, the white man is incorrigible and lacks enough memory even to recall his own history.

The reality is that contemporary Africa has bridged the colonial parenthesis and returned to its original patterns. In the 19th century, before colonization, the continent had been consumed by wars in the east, the south, the center, and the west. In the view of the European philosophy of that time, colonization was morally justified. Europeans brought peace and put an end to the massacres and the turpitudes of those who were then characterized as "black tyrants." Today, the same argument is made, modernized under the term of the "right of interference," with the same humanitarian pretext and without any greater understanding of the problems.

Chapter IV

Scientific Analysis of Afrocentrism

"Afrocentrism" was born in the United States, alongside the development of the Civil Rights movement. It is a form of cultural nationalism with a racist basis that affirms the creative primacy of negritude. Inspired by the work of the Senegalese Cheikh Anta Diop, Afrocentrism postulates that humanity originated with the "Negroes,"[1] as did Egyptian civilization, and even of the founding of America. In short, it is the true source of practically everything. Rather than Afrocentrism, it would be more accurate to speak of a "negrocentrism," since it claims that all of mankind's primordial inventions were made by Egyptians, who were in actual fact black Africans and that Egyptian civilization was the source of all the intellectual developments that subsequently took place in the Mediterranean basin, notably in Greece. It also contends Whites have disguised these truths because of racism and in order to impose the image of a white civilization. According to Afrocentrism, the very first falsifiers were the Greeks, who shamelessly appropriated Egyptian science, philosophy, and mythology.

Fiction vs. Fact

In an effort to evaluate these claims, let's begin with the comical story of the discovery of America. It is an interesting example of the kind of logic that prevails in the Afrocentrists' theses.

---

[1] The word being employed here and throughout this chapter, in the noble sense given to it by Léopold Sedar Senghor, Aimé Césaire, and the Negritude movement that Césaire created with Léon-Gontran Damas, from 1934 onwards.

Map XIII: The Afrocentrist Legend
of the Discovery of America

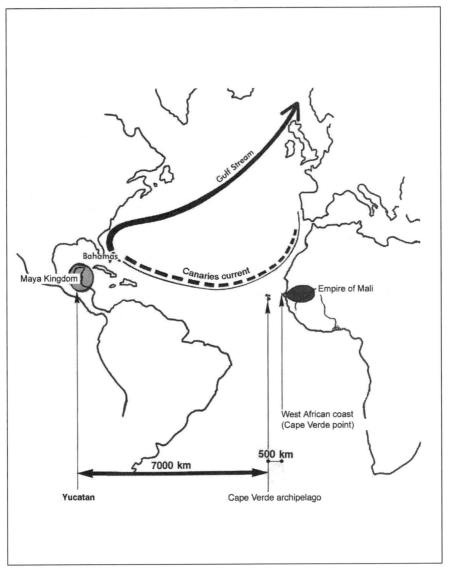

On what historical basis has this farfetched hypothesis been constructed? It rests almost solely on the text of an Arab author, Al-Omari, which appears to date from around 1337.[1] He recounts that Abu Bakr, the emperor of Mali, wanting to know the limits of the ocean, was said to have sent 200 pirogues (dugout canoes), westwards. This was a total failure because only one of these boats returned. It was then that the emperor constituted a second grand expedition, which he commanded in person, leaving power at home in the hands of his son, Kango Moussa. In Al-Omari's text, the fleet was lost with all hands, and none of the explorers ever reappeared on the coasts of Africa. But it is nevertheless on this text alone that Afrocentrists have built an entire thesis postulating that black Africans reached what is today Mexico, and produced a mixed race with the Mayas before returning to their land to introduce corn.

According to Afrocentrists, Abu Bakr II discovered America around 1310.[2] In their version, he embarked at the head of a fleet of 2,000 pirogues, crossed the Atlantic from east to west and reached the Americas, before returning in triumph to his empire, bringing back the gift of corn.

During the reign of their adventurous emperor, the Malians—and in general, the West Africans—utilized pirogues without keels, or outriggers, and propelled them by paddles. They did not know how to use either sails or oars. They would thus have had to paddle more than 2,000 kilometers (1,250 miles) across the ocean before encountering the Canaries current, the only one capable of permitting them to drift to the west over 6,000 kilometers (3,750 miles) from that point. Before that, they would still have had to first reach the Cape Verde archipelago which stood across their route to the open ocean. But these islands, situated "barely" 500 kilometers (310 miles) from the westernmost point (Cape Verde Point) of the West African coast controlled by the Empire of Mali, were unknown to the Africans. At the moment of its discovery on behalf of Portugal by the Genovese Antonio Noli, in 1450, the archipelago was uninhabited and never had been visited previously.

The brave pirogue paddlers of Abu Bakr II thus traversed the Cape Verde archipelago without seeing it, then navigated to the "arc of the Antilles," the

---

[1] Quoted by Bernard R. Ortiz de Montellano, from a translation by Gaudefroy-Demombynes, op cit. p. 252.

[2] For the critique of all that relates to the myth of the "discovery" of America by the Africans, see the excellent article by B.R. Ortiz de Montellano, "Black Warriors Dynasts, l'Afrocentrisme et le Nouveau monde" [Black Warrior Dynasts: Afrocentrism and the New World], *Afrocentrismes*, Paris, 2000, pp. 249-270.

Caribbean islands which they did not explore, either but, shrewder than Christopher Columbus himself, who mistook the land he set foot upon, they meandered through the hundreds of islands that blocked their way to the American continent and directly reached the Yucatan, where their race became mixed with the natives.

During their return voyage to Africa, still by means of paddle, they visited the Bahamas, then let themselves be carried by the Gulf Stream. Certainly that was the only obvious means of getting back home; how else could such small craft have managed the return journey solely by paddling against the Atlantic currents that brought them over on the outward leg? The only problem, but a big one, is that the Gulf Stream would have taken the 2,000 pirogues of Abu Bakr II, or at least those that survived such an expedition, not back to Africa, but to Ireland, Wales, or even Scandinavia. The arrival of such an exotic fleet in those waters would surely not have gone totally unnoticed.

Even if this was the only "attested" expedition, it is claimed in any case that regular crossings were made between Africa and America, even before Abu Bakr II, a reality "established" by the "Negroid features" of Maya statues and by the practice of mummification, taught to the inhabitants of the Andes by Egyptian travelers, and thus by black Africans.

As for the mummification of human bodies in the Andes, which would "prove" the existence of Egyptian expeditions to America, the techniques used have nothing to do with those practiced in Egypt. In addition, the most ancient "mummy" discovered in these high mountains has been dated as originating at the beginning of the sixth millennium B.C., 2,000 years before the historical beginnings of Egypt, a civilization moreover where mummification only started during the Old Kingdom, that is to say, 1,000 years later still (approximately 2,700 to 2,200 B.C.).

But there's another even more fantastic notion being tossed about. According to I. Van Sertima,[1] one of the leading lights of Afrocentrism, the Nubian sovereigns or "Black Pharaohs" of Dynasty XXV, who reigned in Egypt for less than a century (from around 715 to 663 B.C.) sent a maritime expedi-

---

[1] Ivan Sertima, *They Came Before Columbus,* Random House, New York, 1976, and *African Presence in Early America,* Transaction Publishers, New Brunswick, N.J., 1992.

tion to the west. It is said to have reached the Gulf of Mexico, where the Olmec people, still in a primitive state, then asked the Nubians to become their kings. It was thus black Africans who presided over the birth of the Olmec civilization. The civilizations of Monte Alban, of Teotihuacan, and that of the Mayas having been influenced by the Olmecs, Afrocentrists can thus maintain that it was black Egyptians who were at the origins of all the pre-Columbian civilizations.

If these stories of the discovery of America seem comical, there are other Afrocentrist claims concerning the true past of Africa that are more destructive in historical terms.

Claims to "Negro Nations and Culture"

To understand them, let us turn to the theories of the principal instigator of Afrocentrism, Cheikh Anta Diop. Diop was born in 1923 near Diourbel, in the Baol region of Senegal. Having come to Paris to pursue studies in physics and chemistry, he registered as a student at the Sorbonne and took courses in philosophy taught by Gaston Bachelard, while also undertaking personal research on the history of the Wolof and Serer languages.

Very politicized, like many intellectuals of this period, his first postulates were formulated in February 1952 in the first issue of *La Voix de l'Afrique [Voice of Africa]*, the mouthpiece of the student section of the Rassemblement Démocratique Africaine (RDA). This party of Marxist persuasion, founded by Félix Houphouët-Boigny, advocated the emancipation and later the independence of France's African colonies. Diop's first article was titled: "Vers une Idéologie Politique Africaine" [Towards an African Political Ideology]. But these first elements were later taken up and developed in 1954 with the publication of his most famous book, *Nations Nègres et Culture, de l'Antiquité Nègre Égyptienne aux Problèmes Actuels de l'Afrique Noire Aujourd'hui* [Negro Nations and Culture: From Negro Egyptian Antiquity to the Current Problems of Black Africans Today].[1] In 1960, upon his return to Senegal, Diop founded the archeological laboratory of the Institut Français d'Afrique Noire (IFAN or French

---

[1] Présence Africaine, Paris, 1954, for the first edition. [Translator's Note: large excerpts of this work have been translated into English, in C.A. Diop, *The African Origin of Civilization: Myth or Reality*, Lawrence Hill, 1983]. One can also cite *Les Fondements Culturels, Techniques et Industriels d'un Futur Etat Fédéral d'Afrique Noire [The Cultural, Technical, and Industrial Basis of a Future Federal African State]*, Présence Africaine, Paris, 1960 [A revised edition was published with the title, *Black Africa: The Cultural and Economic Basis for a Federated State*, Lawrence Hill, 1987]; "Antériorité des Civilisations Nègres: Mythe ou Véritéhistorique", Présence Africaine, Paris, 1960 [excerpts translated in *The African Origin of Civilisation*, op cit.]; and *Civilisation ou Barbarie*, Présence Africaine, Paris, 1967 [translated as *Civilization or Barbarism: An Authentic Anthropology*, Lawrence Hill, 1991].

Institute of Black Africa], directed by Théodore Monod, and created an opposition political party to President Léopold Sedar Senghor, the Bloc des masses sénégalaises (BMS). He died in 1986. The University of Dakar today bears his name.

Whatever other merits this intellectual had, in the field of history, he was nothing more than a selective compiler, retaining from his reading only those elements that confirmed his arguments.[1] These can be summarized in three principal theses:

—His primary thesis is that first man was Black. The Australopithecines, the Homo erectus and Homo sapiens sapiens (modern man) were all Blacks. Through interbreeding, the Whites and the Yellows appeared later.

This question can be disposed of quickly.

For, if anything is certain, it is that the Australopithecines, and other pre-hominoids, notably those discovered in 2001 and 2002 in Kenya and in Chad, who lived four or five million years ago, were neither Black nor White. As for the rest, did they even have descendants? Might their relationship with men today not be reduced to the sole existence of a hypothetical common ancestor? It's not known. All of this is the subject of ongoing debates among the specialists in the field.

What is known, on the other hand, is that the genus Homo appeared later, between two and three million years ago, with Homo habilis, who, to this day, has only been discovered in Africa. Then, a little more than two million years ago, a newcomer came on the scene. This was Homo erectus, also called "pithecanthropus," whose remains have been brought to light in Africa, Asia, and Europe. Was Homo erectus the descendant of Homo habilis? Are both of them our ancestors? These questions have not been settled. The only certainty is that it is absurd to want to attach them to a race, in this instance to the "black race" as Diop nevertheless insists on doing.

The last to arrive was "Modern Man," Homo sapiens sapiens (or Cro-Magnon). His most ancient representatives have been discovered in the Middle East and in Africa, and they would be 150,000 to 100,000 years old.

On the subject of this "Modern Man," two great theories oppose one

[1] For an in-depth critique of Cheikh Anta Diop's theses, see A. Froment, "Origine et Evolution de l'Homme dans la Pensée de Cheikh Anta Diop: Une Analyse Critique" [Man's Origins and Evolution in the Thought of C.A. Diop: A Critical Analysis], *Cahiers d'Etudes Africaines,* 121-122, XXXI, (1991), pp; 29-64; and F.-X. Fauvelle, *L'Afrique de Cheikh Anta Diop, [The Africa of Cheikh Anta Diop]*, Paris, 1996; or *Afrocentrismes: L'histoire des Africains entre Egypte et Amérique,* [Afrocentrism: The History of Africans between Egypt and America], Paris, 2000.

another. One of these supports the African origin of all humanity. It is the "unicentrist" model, the theory of the so-called "African Eve," to which the Afrocentrists naturally subscribe. The second defends the idea of the simultaneous emergence of "Modern Man" in several places across the globe. It is called the multicentric model. In this hypothesis, Homo sapiens would have descended from archaic local lineages resulting from in situ evolutions of Homo erectus.

But, in the one case as in the other, "racialization" is largely posterior to the stages postulated by Diop, who does not say with whom the interbreeding would have taken place which would have given birth, from the Negroid (black) race, to the Caucasian (white) and Mongoloid (yellow) races.

—Diop's second thesis is more serious in terms of its consequences. It holds that Egypt, which (according to Diop) was "Negro" in its origins, was the mother of civilizations. It was the starting-point from which the continent was populated. That is why the cultural unity of Africa is a reality and therefore makes it possible to speak of the "African nation," since all the continent's cultures were engendered by Egypt.

To support his major postulate, Diop claims there was a relationship between the Egyptians and the Serer, a population which one finds today in Senegal, in contact with the Wolof. If one follows Diop's line of reasoning, several pharaohs of the first Egyptian dynasties were Negroes since they were of the "Serer race." This theory rests on the etymology of some of the pharaoh's names. There was Djeser, who was the first or second pharaoh of the third dynasty, and Peribsen, Sar or Sar-Teta, other sovereigns of Dynasty III (approximately 2700-2620 B.C.).

In a highly eccentric fashion, Diop goes on to claim that the skin color of the Egyptians who remained in the original river valley gradually lightened over the centuries. However, it was the Egyptian Negroes who discovered everything — mathematics, astronomy, history, science, religion, arts, agriculture, medicine, writing, architecture, etc. They were thus the source of all civilization.

Next Diop puts forth a theory of migrations that took place from Egypt towards the interior of the continent, from north to south, from the Nile valley to that of the Niger and beyond, during which the brilliant culture of the "Egyptian Negroes," faded away and crumbled because:

> When the Negroes of the Nile, due to overpopulation of the valley and the social upheavals penetrated more and more deeply into the interior of the continent, they met with different physical and geographical conditions. A given practice, or instrument, or technique, or science, once indispensable on the banks of the Nile, was no longer vitally essential in the loop of the Niger [. . .] One thus understands that certain elements of the Negro civilization of the Nile valley disappeared in the interior of the continent.[1]

—Lastly, reaching a conclusion that is self-evident in his own eyes, Diop says that the Whites, who could not admit their immense "debt" with respect to the black world, invented modern Egyptology. This scientific discipline was in reality only a racist plot aimed at destroying the proofs of Egyptian negritude by, among other things, eliminating the black mummies and displaying only the white ones.[2]

The Story Behind Negro Egypt

The question of contact between the Egyptians and black Africans is very well documented. We can validate that it began with Dynasty XVIII (approximately between 1543 and 1292 B.C.) as the sovereigns of that dynasty led expeditions into Nubia because representations of black Africans became more frequent in Egyptian paintings.

For the Egyptians, Nubia was the "miserable country of Kush," a barbarous region, the southern frontier of Pharaonic civilization. The Nubians the Egyptians described lived between the first and the fourth cataracts on the Nile. They had coppery skin but were not "Negroes." The "real" Blacks lived further to the south, beyond the region of Napata.

The Egyptians sought to deny the Nubians access to the middle valley of the Nile. They even tried to reinforce the "racial barrier" that separated them by establishing a hermetic frontier at the level of the second cataract and by

---

[1] *Nations Nègres et Culture, [Negro Nations and Culture],* op cit., p. 351.
[2] Diop uses the term "leucoderms" [derived from the Greek for "white" and "skin"].

building forts there. But, whenever Egyptian power weakened, the Nubians resumed their push northwards. Events of this sort took place at the end of the Middle Kingdom, during the Second Intermediate Period,[1] and during the Third Intermediate Period.[2] This last period even witnessed the triumph of the Nubians who, in Dynasty XXV or the "Cushite" Dynasty, took power for a century in Egypt itself between 730 to 636 B.C. In other words, contacts certainly existed between Egypt and Nubia and Nubia's population was well portrayed in Egyptian art, but there was still no indication that the population pool of ancient Egypt was Negroid.

On the contrary, the survival of the Egyptian physiognomy through the millennia is striking. Particularly eloquent in this respect are the Fayum paintings. Discovered at Fayum and throughout the Nile valley beginning in the first century of the Christian era, these distempered portraits on acacia panels faithfully reproduce the features of the deceased. They provide extensive documentation that enables us to affirm that the inhabitants of Fayum and the Nile valley between the second cataract and the Mediterranean at this time were Whites.[3] Nothing gives rise to the idea that those Whites could have committed "ethnocide" against black predecessors whose place they took.

As to Diop's claim that the coloring of the ancient Egyptians of the Nile valley had lightened little by little over the centuries, his proposition is also unsupported. The ancient Egyptians are both well known and clearly identified, both from the physical and the linguistic points of view.

In their art, the ancient Egyptians followed fixed rules when they portrayed themselves. Men were colored red and women were a lighter shade, sometimes white. Each foreign population was distinguished by a particular feature and by its color. Thus, when the Egyptians depicted populations such as the "Syrians" or the "peoples of the sea," they gave them lighter shades than their own. In contrast, when they represented people with a darker color, they knew how to render the entire palette from copper to ebony.

That the ancient Egyptians were physically Whites of a "Mediterranean" type is clearly established by their art. The population of ancient Egypt, how-

---

[1] Roughly between 1800 and 1543 B.C.
[2] Roughly between 1078 and 664 B.C.
[3] On this subject, see Susan Walker, "Ancient Faces: An Exhibition of Mummy Portraiture at the British Museum," in *Egyptian Archeology*, No. 10, pp. 19-23. Also see *Euphrosyne Dioxadis, The Mysterious Fayum Portraits: Faces from Ancient Egypt*, The American University in Cairo Press, 2000.

ever, was not homogeneous from a racial perspective. That is why, moving from the north to south in the Nile valley, towards Nubia, the coloring of the Egyptians became more and more "coppery," as is still the case today.[1] The Egyptian expansion in the direction of Nubia extended over two millennia, so it was thus probable that interbreeding occurred as a result. But that is not the same thing as saying that Egypt was Negro.

If the artistic representation of the human races by the Egyptians is instructive, the study of mummies is even more helpful. Diop wrote that Egyptian women had frizzy hair, which, according to him, can be seen in all the representations and thus permits him to affirm that they belonged to the black "race."[2] However, the Egyption mummies have straight or curly hair. The melanoderms[3] were rare, as were people with frizzy hair.[4] What Diop saw as a "constant concern of the black woman to adapt her frizzy hair to feminine grace" is nothing but the generalized wearing of wigs. Egyptians of both sexes wore them, the women over their natural hair and the men over shaven heads.

As for the linguistic question and the resemblances between certain names of pharaohs and the word "Serer,"[5] Diop's argument is simply inadmissible. Let's note first that, with the exception of Djeser, the other pharaohs cited by Diop cannot be confirmed. Moreover, there is little documentation of Dynasty III, and we know very little about the first three successors of Djeser and nothing at all about the six sovereigns who followed. Their names are not even known with any certainty.

In addition, establishing links among their names constitutes a misrepresentation in linguistic terms. Serer and Egyptian belong to two different linguistic families.[6] The former is a language of the Niger-Congo group, while the latter belongs to the Afrasian or Afroasiatic group.[7] This does not prevent Diop

---

[1] J.H. Taylor, *Egypt and Nubia,* British Museum, London, 1991.
[2] *Nations Nègres et Culture,* op cit., pp. 40-41.
[3] Meaning with black skin and/or presenting Negroid characteristics.
[4] D.R. Hardy, "Analysis of Hair Samples of Mummies from Semna-South," in *American Journal of Physical Anthropology,* No. 49 (1978), pp; 277-283. See also E. Rabino-Massa & B. Chiarelli "The Histology of Naturally Dissected and Mummified Bodies," in *Journal of Human Evolution,* Vol. I (1972), pp. 259-262.
[5] On the Egyptian Language, see Pascal Vernus, "Situation de l'Égyptien dans les Langues du Monde" [The Place of Egyptian Among the World's Languages], in *Afrocentrismes,* op cit., 2000, pp. 169-208.
[6] For more details on linguistic definitions and origins, see Chapter V of the present work, "The Peoples of Africa".
[7] C. Ehret, "Who Were the Rock Painters? Linguistic Evidence for the Holocene Populations of the Sahara," in *News 95 – International Rock Art Congress,* Turin, 30 Aug. – 6 Sept. 1995. Or see the same C. Ehret, "Reconstructing the Proto-Afroasiatic (Proto-Afrasian): Vowels, Tone, Consonants, and Vocabulary," in *Linguistics,* Vol. 126, University of California, 1996.

from peremptorily presenting Egyptian as a sort of Sanskrit, the mother tongue of all the African languages. His error is total. With the exception of the so-called Chadic languages, none of the languages of black Africa belong to the same family as that of the ancient Egyptian. Thus, they cannot, by definition, have descended from it.

As for the linkage of consonances based on the syllables "ser," "sar," or "sen," it proves nothing in scientific terms except that we have no reliable idea of the way ancient Egyptian was pronounced. The duplication of place names or other artificial connections may impress lay people but not linguists. Such artificial resemblances can be found among all languages. That is indeed what made the great French African historian, Raymond Mauny,[1] wonder, in refuting Diop's theses:

Are Sun Yat-Sen, Henrik Ibsen, Konrad Eisenhower and Roald Amundsen all Serer, too?

Similarly, does the existence of a Lake Kasba[2] in the Canadian province of Quebec permit one to establish a link between Algonquin and Arabic? Or does the fact that when the kings of France were buried, the corpse bearers in the procession were known as "hanouars"[3] authorize one to say that the Capetians descended from the Arabs? Obviously not. And yet, it is upon such superficial links and reasoning that Diop's historical readings are founded.

Moreover, on the list of Pharaohs that he claims were of the "Serer race," he cites one of the 36 nonattested pharaohs of Dynasty XVI, Osorta-Sen. But this dynasty was Hyksos[4] in origin, not Egyptian. So, were the Hyksos also Serer? That would be difficult to accept.

Diop's theory concerning the migrations from north to south, in addition to his linguistic incoherencies, is based only on pre-suppositions and not on attested elements. Let us reason as he does and, in the quotation from his work cited above, replace "Nile" by "Rhine," and "Negro" by "European." It is then possible to perceive the utter absurdity of his proposition:

When the [Europeans], due to the imperialist movement, moved more and more deeply into the interior of the continent, they met with different

---

[1] R. Mauny, "Recension de Nations Nègres et Culture de Cheikh Anta Diop," in *Bulletin de l'IFAN*, XXII, série B (1960), pp. 544-551; English translation: "Nations Nègres et Culture: A Review," *Problems in African History*, London, 1968, pp. 16-23.

[2] Meaning "house" in Arabic.

[3] A common Arab pronoun – Anwar Sadat, for example.

[4] A Greek term attributed to Manethon, the first historian of the Egyptian civilization. It means "chiefs of a foreign country", and designates the invaders from the east who ruled Egypt from 1730 to 1580 B.C., founding Dynasties XV and XVI.

physical and geographical conditions from those of [the Rhine]. A given practice, or instrument, or technique, or science, once indispensable on the banks of the [Rhine], was no longer vitally essential in the loop [of the Seine] One thus understands that certain elements of the [European] civilization disappeared in the interior of the continent.

Diop committed another error, but it would be unjust to reproach him for it, since accepted knowledge in his time did not permit him to correct it.

It was not in Egypt where the great discoveries of the Neolithic era originated, but in the Sahara. This was a Sahara in which the northern and central parts were populated by white proto-Berbers (Afrasians), and the southern part by black Nilo-Saharans. As we now know, it is in the Sahara that the most ancient examples of utilitarian pottery were discovered. They have been dated roughly from between 8500 and 6700 B.C. The idea of a Saharan home to the invention of ceramics thus seems plausible. The antecedence of the Sahara also seems to be attested to in connection with the domestication of bovines, since it started there around 7500 B.C. It would thus have slightly preceded, or have been nearly contemporary to, domestication in the Middle East. In any case, it was far more ancient than in the Nile valley, where the domestication of animals does not go back further than roughly 5000 B.C. The men who lived in the Nile valley, from the delta in the north to the first cataract in the south, were still Paleolithic hunter-fisher nomads when the Saharans had become Neolithic potters and cattle raisers.

The "birth" of Egypt was thus in all likelihood due to the meeting between these Neolithic proto-Berber Saharans and the natives living in the lower valley of the Nile. All of them spoke Afrasian languages, and their skin was white. Those who spoke Nilo-Saharan language, and whose skin was black, lived to the south of the fifth cataract. Egypt was thus indeed the creation of "Whites" rather than "Blacks."

We now know with the utmost certainty, thanks to the analysis of Chromosome Y's haplotypes[1], that the ancient peoples of Egypt were Berbers, not Negroids. Three main Y-haplotypes can be found in the Nile Valley. They are, by order of importance: the V haplotype, which hails from Berber; this

---

[1] Haplotypes are what provide chromosomes with their distinct identity. See Lucotte, G. and G. Mercier, "Brief Communication: Y-Chromosome Haplotypes in Egypt," in *American Journal of Physical Anthropology*, No. 121, pp. 63-66, 2003.

haplotype can be found with 40 percent of the subjects studied in Egypt. In the Nile Delta, this haplotype is predominant. It can be found with 52 percent of subjects. In Lower Nubia, on the contrary, the V-haplotype is present with only 17 percent of the subjects.[1]

The second haplotype, Haplotype-XI, is Oriental and/or Ethiopian and can be found with 19 percent of subjects. The third haplotype found in Egypt, haplotype IV, also known as the Negroid Haplotype, hails from Sub-Saharan Africa. It is common to only 14 percent of Egyptians (1.2 percent in the Nile Delta, 39 percent in Nubia, between Abu Simbel and the Second Cataract).

Egypt was thus peopled by "white" Berbers, an evidence heretofore negated by the Afrocentrists. The science of genetics pulverizes Diop and Bernal's postulates and confirms my hypotheses on the Berber origins of ancient Egypt[2].

The Heritage of Cheikh Anta Diop

Placed at the confluence of resentment, magic, and sometimes even invective, Cheikh Anta Diop's theses are those of an African griot (traveling poet) telling a story to fulfill his listeners' dreams and not the result of any real scientific approach. As Marcel d'Hertefelt, professor of African anthropology at the Royal Museum of Tervuren in Belgium, wrote so justly over thirty years ago:

> *Diop's theses demand that one decides once and for all to ignore everything that pre-historical and proto-historical archeology, iconography, and historical critiques of the ancient texts have taught us about the populations of the Middle East and Egypt, concerning the development and spread of agriculture and metallurgy, as well as the respective contributions made by these two cradles of civilization to the sciences and writing. One must decide from the start whether generations of archeologists, Egyptologists, experts on Sumer, the Indo-Europeans, the Semitic peoples, and even Africans have all been ideologically mystified to the point of falsifying cultural history, up to the moment when Diop discovered the truth. It's indeed asking a lot.[3]*

In 1954, however, Diop's theses found a considerable following within the community of black intellectuals, even among the most lucid. Aimé Césaire, for example, wrote about them:

---

[1] Fifty-eight percent of Moroccans, 57 percent of Algerians, 53 percent of Tunians and 45 percent of Libians carry this haplotype.

[2] Lugan, B., *Histoire de l'Egypte des Origines à nos Jours*, Paris, 2002, pp. 15-42.

[2] M. d'Hertefelt, *Eléments pour une Histoire Culturelle de l'Afrique, [Elements for a Cultural History of Africa]*, University of Rwanda, 1972, p. 151 (mimeographed course).

The most audacious thing that a Negro has ever written up to now, and which will no doubt count in the waking of Africa.[1]

What remains today of Diop? Very little, except a philosophy of history born in the context of the struggles for independence. It is taught by certain black African, Caribbean, and American intellectuals who have sought to invent a glorious history that would better justify their national or identity-based claims. In short, it is, above all, a question of ideology. Except for that, everything in Diop's work is erroneous, even when his intuitions are correct.

Scientifically, Diop was mistaken. His writings should no longer be taken into consideration other than on the level of the historiography of Africa. They are essentially "testimonial mounds" left over from the anti-colonial ideology of the 1950s and not based on knowledge about the past.

And yet, Diop's theses are still regarded as official history and are being taught. A relevant example of this is the monumental *History of Africa* in eight volumes that is constantly being re-edited and published in the principal world languages by UNESCO. The second volume, *Ancient Africa,* reserves a generous portion of its pages to Cheikh Anta Diop, to the extent that it is his vision of the settlement of Egypt that is retained by UNESCO and not the scientific conclusions. For African readers and for others, Diop thus appears to be right, and that is how false history triumphs.

Martin Bernal and Black Athena

Martin Bernal is the best known of the contemporary apostles of Diop's ideas, and he has in a sense amplified the latter's influence. Born in 1937 in Great Britain to a family of intellectuals, Bernal's father was the author of several works on the history of science, while his mother, the daughter of a famous professor of Egyptology at Oxford, was an anthropologist. In 1987, he caused a sensation by publishing *Black Athena: The Afro-Asiatic Roots of Classical Civilization,*[2] in which he claims that Athena, daughter of Zeus and tutelary divinity of Athens, was none other than the goddess Néit, whom the Greeks had borrowed from the Egyptians, and thus from black Africans. His purpose

[1] *Discours Sur le Colonialisme,* [Discourse on Colonialism] Présence Africaine, 1955.
[2] Free Association Books, London, 1987, for the first edition.

is to illustrate the debt classical civilization owes to Africa.

Martin Bernal is not, properly speaking, an Afrocentrist, but his publications have been utilized by the Afrocentrists, and rightly so, as a confirmation of their principal stalking horses — the "negritude" of ancient Egypt.

Does Bernal have the authority to call into question all that is known about the history of Greece and Egypt? Not on the basis of his credentials. Bernal's main field is Chinese studies; he is not in any sense an authority on the Eastern Mediterranean and Greece. His doctoral thesis was about the intellectual exchanges between the West and China in the 1900s, and most of his scientific articles are concerned with the Far East and the war in Vietnam.

At the outset, Bernal's book announces his intention to "revise" [sic.] the historiography of Egypt and Greece. The first volume is entirely devoted to the manner in which the historians of the past two centuries have developed the Indo-European paradigm. Rewriting Egyptian history, Bernal criticizes the vision of a purely white, Mediterranean Egypt, cut off from the south; ie Nubia, which is seen as the country of the Blacks.

In doing so, he is determined to break down a door that had already been open for several years. In fact, Egyptologists had not waited for the work of a Chinese specialist to observe that ancient Egypt was not an eastern Mediterranean creation, but a melting-pot receiving identifiable local influences from the lower and middle Nile valley, on the one hand, and undoubtedly Saharan or Nubian influences, on the other.

Having enjoyed considerable success with *Black Athena,* Bernal published a second volume[1] which appeared in 1991. Wishing to push his demonstrations further, this book imprudently launches into a scientific domain he had not mastered, undermining any credibility for his thesis.

But the book appeared in a receptive climate. Afrocentrism, which was at the height of its influence, derived weighty arguments from it.

In the United States, the impact of Bernal's book was considerable. The African-American community and the Afrocentrist "historical" school threw all their political weight behind it and gave the book an enormous amount of pub-

---

[1] *Black Athena: The Afro-Asiatic Roots of Classical Civilization: Vol. II: The Archeological and Documentary Evidence,* London, 1991.

licity. The controversy in the United States was such that the magazine *Newsweek*, in its issue dated September 23, 1991, even featured the work on its front cover, with the question: "Was Cleopatra Black?"[1] In the inside pages, one finds other bizarre questions like "Was Beethoven Black?" And even, "Was Western Civilization Born in Africa?" The first copies sold out fast.

This second volume contains a large number of references. It re-locates Greece at the periphery of the eastern Mediterranean world and thus at the confluence of currents that ancient historiography sometimes had a tendency to forget, but which the historians of ancient Greece do not deny.

Bernal advances four postulates, some of which he took directly from Diop without having accounted for the refutations mentioned above. In doing so, Bernal's method is scientifically unacceptable because the basis of his thesis pays no attention to the present state of knowledge in African studies.

The first postulate is that, without the human and cultural input of the Semites and the black Africans, Greek civilization would never have been born. Since the Greeks and then white historians of Greece were shocked to learn this, they have all hidden it, interpreting the Greek myths in ways that excluded any outside influence. In other words, there has been a conspiracy against the truth that Bernal takes it upon himself to denounce.

His second postulate is that Hellenic culture was as much indebted to influences of the Semitic world and to Egypt, the latter being assumed to be Black, as it was to those bequeathed by the Indo-Europeans.

A third postulate states that, in contrast to us, the ancient Greeks knew their civilization had been created by the Egyptians, and thus by black Africans, as well as by the Phoenicians, who had introduced their gods and their alphabet into Greece. This is what Bernal defines as the "Ancient Model," according to which Greece had been colonized by the Egyptians and by the Semites from the eighteenth century B.C.

Bernal's fourth and last postulate maintains that, in the 19th century, with European imperialism triumphant, it was not possible for Whites to accept that they owed everything to Blacks, whose colonization they justified on the

---

[1] This was a perfectly ridiculous eye-catcher. Cleopatra VII, the one with the famous nose, reigned in Egypt from 51 to 30 B.C. She was of Greek origin and the documents of the time attest in an irrefutable manner that her skin was white.

grounds that they were bringing civilization to Africa.

In response, let us look at three elements of these postulates. To begin with, the first thesis is not new. It was even dominant in the 17th and 18th centuries, as was the belief during the same period in the Trojan origins of France, for example. Both of these theories were revealed for what they really were, just legends, once modern history and its scientific methods imposed themselves.

Secondly, at no point is Bernal convincing. Despite an avalanche of quotations and references, they do not advance his arguments, and he does not support any of his propositions. But above all, adopting a position that is unacceptable from a scientific point of view, Bernal confuses the two different notions of "influence" and "origin." Even if Semitic and Egyptian influences did exist, displaying them does not prove the Semitic and Egyptian origins of Greek civilization.

Bernal maintained that Athens was 50 percent Indo-European, 25 percent Asiatic (that is, Semitic), and 25 percent Egyptian, or "Black." Except for the assumption that "Egyptian means black," these propositions are worth looking at. No Hellenist would in fact maintain that Greece was born in a vacuum and had not been exposed to outside influences.

The problem lies elsewhere. The percentages Bernal gives are based on cultural traits at the expense of archeological facts, whose discovery he arrogantly ignores. This is strange, to say the least, coming from an academic claiming to be renewing eastern Mediterranean studies.

Because, and this is the great novelty of Volume II compared to Volume I, Bernal deploys himself on the terrain of the history of the eastern Mediterranean and. soon becomes bogged down. His etymological comparisons are erroneous, as are indeed his historical interpretations. In fact, since the book was published, his reasoning has been refuted by Mary Lefkowitz and R. MacLean.[1]

Short of arguments and trapped by his lack of knowledge, Bernal was reduced to accusing the specialists of classical Greece of having discarded everything in their discoveries which would have contradicted the model of the Indo-European origins of Greece and would have confirmed his own model.

---

[1] M. Lefkowitz & R. MacLean, *Black Athena Revisited,* University of North Carolina Press, 1996.

Since then, Bernal has depicted himself as the victim of a "racist" plot.

The Myth of a Return to Africa

A recurrent idea held by the Afrocentrists is that of a cultural community uniting native-born Africans and the descendants of former slaves transplanted to the New World. This is not a new idea. At the end of the 18th and beginning of the 19th centuries, philanthropists debated returning a certain number of these slaves to their continent of origin. It would seem that the oldest of these projects probably dates back to 1713 and to the Quakers, led by George Keith. Reverend Ezra Stiles, and later, Dr. Samuel Hopkins, took up the idea, as did Thomas Jefferson in 1781.

In 1786, the English abolitionists founded the Society for the Abolition of the Slave Trade. Granville Sharp then became head of an organization for the repatriation of former slaves and Black Americans, with the aim of creating a "Province of Freedom" in the future region of Freetown; a base from which liberating Christianity could be spread to the interior of Africa by freed slaves who would be its missionaries. In 1787, the British government agreed.

The people involved were Black Africans living in London who had already undergone extraordinary adventures, as they had been what the British called "loyalists," remaining faithful to the Crown and refusing to join the American insurgents during the War of Independence of 1775-1783. At the end of this war, when the former 13 colonies had become the United States of America, these black "loyalists" decided to follow the British troops in their withdrawal and some embarked for Europe.

In 1787, the philanthropic bodies proposed to these "loyalists" the idea of leaving for Africa in order to form a community of free farmers. One morning in April, 327 Blacks and 87 Whites took to sea. Of these 414 immigrants, 80 died during the journey, but the survivors took possession of a site in Sierra Leone, which posed a great many problems with the indigenous Temne tribe to whom the land belonged. In the weeks following their arrival, fevers killed off another hundred of the pioneers. The settlement developed, nonetheless, and soon both blacks and whites were participating in traffic with passing ships, including those involved with the slave trade.

In 1790, a chartered company was created which would become the Sierra Leone Company. Its goals were both commercial and philanthropic, fighting slavery and promoting Christianity. The colony was then reinforced by Blacks coming from Canada, and more precisely, from Nova Scotia. Once again, these were former Black slaves who had remained loyal to the British and had withdrawn with them from the thirteen former colonies to Canada, which remained British after the victory of the American revolutionaries. Freed and established in Canada, they scraped by without really finding any steady employment. When in 1791 it was proposed that they populate the company's territory, they accepted. On March 28, 1792, 1,200 Nova Scotians disembarked on the beach of this outpost where, five years earlier, the "loyalists" had first set foot. It was these Nova Scotians who baptized the settlement founded in 1787 with the name of "Free Town."

Meanwhile, in the United States, the Negro Union of Newport was born in 1788. This was a black movement that militated in favor of a massive reinstallation of Blacks in Africa. Several attempts to accomplish this took place, but they resulted in tragic failures. This was notably the case for two expeditions that Jefferson sent to Sierra Leone in 1815 and 1820 with the agreement of the British government in London. The expedition of Paul Cuffies, a person of mixed "Afroamerindian" origins, was also a failure.

In 1816, the American Colonization Society was founded by Reverend Robert Finley from New Jersey. Its goal was to organize a vast movement of return to Africa. The idea, however, was far from accepted unanimously by Blacks themselves. Many of them were opposed, notably those in Philadelphia, Boston, and New York. They thought that the principal objective of such a program would be to get rid of them. Soon the idea became more precise and it evolved into a reinstallation, not of all the Black Americans but simply slaves who had been emancipated and captives liberated at sea by ships hunting down slave vessels. On March 3, 1819, Congress voted to authorize the colonization of a territory in West Africa upon which it would be possible to resettle a certain number of these cases.

Throughout the 19th century, two philosophies opposed each other. One defended a mass emigration. The other was embodied a little later by Reverend H.M. Turner, who favored a colonization "of quality," if not to say elitist in nature. In 1903, the Colored Emigration and Commercial Convention was created. It solicited financial support from Congress to organize the transfer to Africa of all those who desired it. Among the most serious attempts, the best known and the most emblematic were those of Sierra Leone[1] and Liberia.

A third wave of black colonists arrived in Sierra Leone in 1800. These were slaves from Jamaica who had rebelled. Originally, they took to the hills but were eventually captured. The repression was severe. The 550 who escaped hanging were deported to Canada, but their presence was not really welcome there. So they, too, became volunteers for the colony.

Other black colonists who would later land at Sierra Leone included former soldiers from the British West Indies regiment, who founded the villages of Waterloo, Hastings, and Wellington. In 1827, the Church Missionary Society (CMS) founded the Fourah Bay College to the east of Freetown, where the resettled African Americans would be educated.

These first pioneers were to a large extent impregnated by Anglo-Saxon culture. That was not the case of the later arrivals, mainly captives liberated at sea when slave ships were boarded. After 1808, the Royal Navy started intercepting all vessels it found engaged in slaving, and the freed slaves were installed at Freetown. From 1820, the "Freedmen" outnumbered the first settlers, and they continued to arrive until about 1850, with a peak between 1830 and 1840.

These newcomers were of all ethnic origins, from Guinea in the north to Angola in the south, but the most numerous contingent were the Yoruba, who had been sold at the time of the wars which marked the decline of the Oyo kingdom.[2] At Freetown, they became domestic servants or soldiers for the "elite" constituted thereafter by the black "Anglo-Saxons."

The governor of the colony, MacCarthy (1814-1824) saw in the numbers of these arriving Yoruba the opportunity to create a Christian core group capable of evangelizing Africa. He envisaged giving them a solid education before sending them back to the Yoruba country, and created a village removed

---

[1] T.C. Maccaskie, "Cultural Encounters: Britain and Africa in the 19th Century," in *The Oxford History of the British Empire,* vol. III, 1999, pp. 665-689.

[2] On this subject, see Chapter I-1, "The Real Nature of the European Slave Trade," in the present book.

from Freetown where Anglican missionaries of the CMS and Protestants of the Wesleyan Missionary Society (WMS) taught them the rudiments of Christianity. The CMS had arrived in 1804, and the WMS in 1811. Several dozen of these Yoruba were indeed sent back to their home country, in the south of present-day Nigeria, where they introduced Christianity and paved the way for the installation of the British in 1861, followed by annexation of the region in 1870.

Sierra Leone was thus a haven for former slaves who had bought their freedom, been liberated, or were deported there. The goal of the white Christian promoters of this settlement was a generous one: the creation, following the evangelical model, of a mixed population merging former slaves and indigenous peoples, bringing the "light of Protestantism" to the native Africans through their "brothers" from across the Atlantic.

It would be an understatement to say that the graft did not take. The former slaves had only contempt for the Africans whom they considered savages. This applied to both the indigenous populations and the new migrants who had been "freed at sea." There were frequent fights between the black colonists and the natives, and even wars, notably with the Temne from 1805 to 1807.

Refusing to mix with the "primitives" the freed slaves constituted a closed, inbred caste. This soon became a veritable apartheid, and they exploited their "brothers" of color like cattle, keeping power to themselves. Having become city dwellers and shopkeepers, some accumulated large fortunes. They regarded themselves, literally, as an aristocracy, giving themselves different names such as Krios (or Crios), and even "White Men." In 1920, the Krio elite regrouped itself within a political association, the National Congress of British West Africa (NCBWA). It demanded elections, then independence, naturally for its own benefit. Since London did not consider the NCBWA representative of the territory's populations, tension arose between the Crown administration and the Krio leaders. An astonishing evolution then began to take place in the latter's minds. To spite the British who did not want to transfer power to them, they started to lay claim to their African origins. Some even abandoned their English names and developed a virulent anti-white racism. In this way, they hoped to prevent London from granting independence to the "native" black majority whom they hated and who would sweep them from power.

Liberia also became a resettlement zone for former slaves. This country was founded in the 18th century as a British commercial outpost where British agents were based. In contrast to Sierra Leone, Liberia was not used initially as a place of colonization for Anglicized and Christianized slaves. It was at first merely a debarkation point for captives freed at sea after the prohibition of the slave trade.

One of the earliest settlements was that of African Americans on Sherbro Island. In 1821, the United States bought a territory in the region, and the following year, a vast resettlement movement took place. This involved the creation of several colonies including Mississippi in Africa, Maryland in Liberty, Providence Island Settlement, and the Bassa Cave Community.

In 1847, Liberia became independent and the resettlement movement continued. In 1851, 7,600 blacks had been resettled there and their numbers grew to 12,000 by 1867.

The British agents who had originally established Liberia, meantime, gave birth to a population of racially mixed descendents who today still bear English names (Caulker, Cleveland, Roger, or Tucker). Living with their eyes turned towards Britain or the United States, whose fashions they copied, they were a small minority, barely two or three percent of the population at most. They nevertheless had an important role within the territory. In order to distinguish themselves from the natives, they gave themselves the title of "Honorable," and it was they who ran the country until 1980.

However, on April 12, 1980, the American Negro graft was ultimately rejected, by the "native Negroes," who reproached the African-American leaders for exploiting them. To put an end to the arrogant domination of this "little African America," Sergeant Samuel Doe, a member of the Krahn ethnic group, took power in an orgy of massacres that started with the execution of the "Honorable" dignitaries of the deposed regime of President William Tolbert.

In the final analysis, the Colonization Movement, still a pet project of Afrocentrists, was a total failure. Some of the reasons include lack of preparation and means on the part of expeditions, difficulties encountered on the coast of Africa, diseases, and the hostility of the natives towards the black colonists. One final reason for these failures was the discord among the new arrivals, notably those who were freed at sea and who, at best, belonged to ethnic groups with nothing in common, and at worst, were enemies.

* * *

In conclusion, neither Egypt nor Greece were black; black Africans did not discover America in their pirogues; and the myth of a black cultural community shared by African Americans and native-born Africans has only led to bloodshed.

Unfortunately, the clear historical facts supporting these positions have not been sufficient to end the ridiculous, and dangerous, debates over these issues. The problem is that the Afrocentrists, notably the American ones, do not reason like historians. It seems that, for them, history is not a science, but a means of affirming self-enhancing visions that permit them to overcome the frustrations of a community that is wounded by its psychological complexes and existential problems. In doing so, the African-American intellectual elites have fallen into a trap similar to that of their third world counterparts in Africa, where the dominant historical school of each country attributes local failures to exogenous causes, usually involving European imperialism.

This phenomenon is by no means isolated. In India "historians" forming the Subaltern Studies Group have effectively renounced history as a science. To justify their postulates, they use sociological, psychological, or philosophical analyses, refusing to recognize the difference between "fact" and "myth." The Subaltern Group asserts that official history is only a form of Western imperialism because it is written with Western historical concepts and that the history of India can only be written by natives and for natives. In that sense, their method is the same as the Afrocentrists, for whom the facts of history have become part of a conspiracy by the white world set on debasing black people.

In these circumstances, only Blacks can write, for Blacks, the history of the Blacks, thus imposing a "counter-history," a revised African past that permits Afrocentrists to teach younger generations that Africa before the arrival of the Whites was a kind of terrestrial paradise. This has been going on since the 1950s.

> Some [i.e., the French-speaking intelligentsia grouped around the review, Présence Africaine] propose an idyllic vision of African civilization based around its cultural unity, in order to show that Africa participated in the general movement of universal history [. . .] Others, like [. . .] Kwame Nkrumah [present] an idealized version of pre-colonial society, denying the heterogeneity of social groups and their antagonisms within an African society which is presumed to have been communitarian and egalitarian.[1]

Any African renaissance must involve the abandonment of these myths.

---

[1] R. Botte, op cit., 2002, p. 159.

Part Two

In Support of an African Renaissance

Until now, this book has dealt with the misinformation concerning slavery and colonization, which, coupled with Afrocentrism, constitutes the basis for a case against Europe, America, and the white world in general. As has been shown, the myths it promotes are false and impose an artificially accusatory and guilt-provoking vision of North-South relations.

It is time now to re-establish the real history of the continent, the one that will permit Africans to view their true past head-on and build a future on a more solid foundation. It is also the one that will allow Europeans and Americans, to know their African partners better, to cease making grave errors in their evaluations, and, henceforth, to provide effective help to a continent on the brink of an abyss.

Chapter V

The Peoples of Africa

African Man is only a concept; he does not exist in reality. In the Africas of the deserts, the savannas, the rivers, the forests, the highlands, the ocean shores, etc., there live many different peoples, separated from each other by their lifestyles, their physiognomies, their cultures, their religions, their skin colors, and their languages.

Over 1,000 languages are spoken in black Africa, just counting the principal ones. Today they are classed in four groups (called "phyla" by linguists), which are in turn divided into principal groups and subgroups.

The history of pre-colonial Africa concerns the locations of linguistic groups and their migrations. When colonization began, "ethnic tectonics"[1] had not begun. It only came into being when the colonizers trapped the native populations within the artificial boundaries they traced at that time.

Ethnic groups often share a linguistic heritage but are made up of an infinite number of tribes and clans, contributing to today's problems.

Tracing the linguistic groups is essential to understanding the history of Africa and its population movements. Two major questions allow one to learn the origins of the population of the continent: how long were language and "race" linked and when did the speakers of the different language groups or proto-groups become separated?

Knowledge of the origins of linguistic families has come about thanks to a number of studies,[2] primarily those based on genetics. The accompanying

---

[1] The placement of ethnic groups can in effect be compared with the great movements of the terrestrial crust and to the telluric shocks that are produced when diverse elements come into contact.

[2] Notably: S.H. Ambrose, "Archeology and Linguistic Reconstructions of History in East Africa," in C. Ehret & M. Posnansky, *The Archeological and Linguistic Reconstruction of African History,* Berkeley, University of California Press, 1982, pp. 104-157. See also: C. Ehret, "Who Were the Rock Painters? Linguistic Evidence for the Holocene Populations of the Sahara," op cit.; and C. Ehret, *African Roots of Egyptian Culture and Language,* Barcelona, 1996.

Linguistic Groups

The Afrasian or Afro-Asiatic

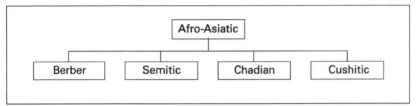

The Nilo-Saharan

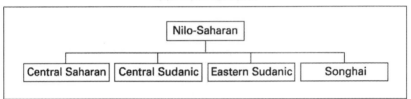

The Niger-Congo

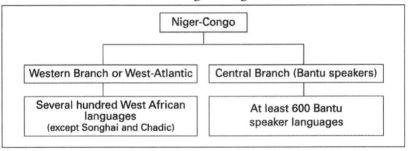

The Khoi-San

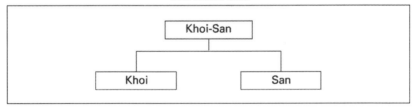

Map XIV: Ethno-linguistic Africa

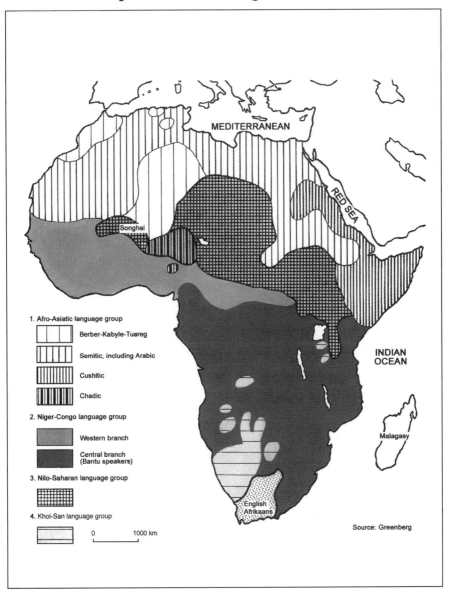

MEDITERRANEAN

RED SEA

Songhai

INDIAN
OCEAN

1. Afro-Asiatic language group

Berber-Kabyle-Tuareg

Semitic, including Arabic

Cushitic

Chadic

2. Niger-Congo language group

Western branch

Central branch
(Bantu speakers)

3. Nilo-Saharan language group

Malagasy

4. Khoi-San language group

English
Afrikaans

0   1000 km

Source: Greenberg

diagram[1] compares the distances separating African populations as a function of genetic markers chosen in the blood groups, the serumal proteins (albumin and immunoglobulins), as well as in the Human Leucocyte Antigen (HLA) system, which is constituted by histocompatibility antigens that are specific to an individual and which intervene in cellular recognition. It shows very clearly the remarkable distance between three populations: the Pygmies, the Khoi-San, and the Tutsis. This indicates that their genetic differentiation is ancient.

The distance separating the Tutsis from other African populations is especially significant. It is evidence of disparities between the Hutus (who belong to the Bantu-speaking Central Branch of the Niger-Congo phylum) and the Tutsis and demonstrates clearly that the differences are genetic, and thus "racial," rather than economic, as Jean-Pierre Chrétien, Jean-Louis Amselle, Catherine Coquery-Vidovitch and other ideologue historians would have us believe. The work of Froment[2] which concerns the differentiations based on cranial analyses confirm these genetic conclusions.

This diagram also shows that, from a genetic point of view, the Afrasians (Berbers, Egyptians, Cushitics, etc.) who are not "Negroes" in the sense used by Cheikh Anta Diop, and are clearly distinguished from the black African populations. The points of overlap between the one and the other are in effect quite peripheral. The Afrasian speakers are thus—except, of course, in cases of interbreeding—genetically different from speakers in the Niger-Congo and Nilo-Saharan phyla, who constitute the immense majority of the populations of Africa south of the Sahara.

Lastly, this diagram demonstrates effectively that originally "race" and language were linked, and that the speakers of the great African proto-languages had different genetic, and thus "racial," characteristics.

Africa Before the Blacks

With the exception of the Khoi-San, who were present in Africa from 30,000 to 40,000 years ago, no other three great ethno-linguistic groups appeared until around 20,000 years ago. The latter groups were the ancestors

---

[1] See p. 147. Taken from Excoffier et al, *Genetics and History of Sub-Saharan Africa: Yearbook of Physical Anthropology*, No. 30, pp. 157-194, 1987; and Froment, A., "The Population of Central Africa: The Contribution of Anthropology and Paleo-Anthrobiology in Central Africa," pp. 13-90, Paris, 1999.

[2] A. Froment, 1999, op cit.

The Differences Between African Populations
According to Genetic Markers

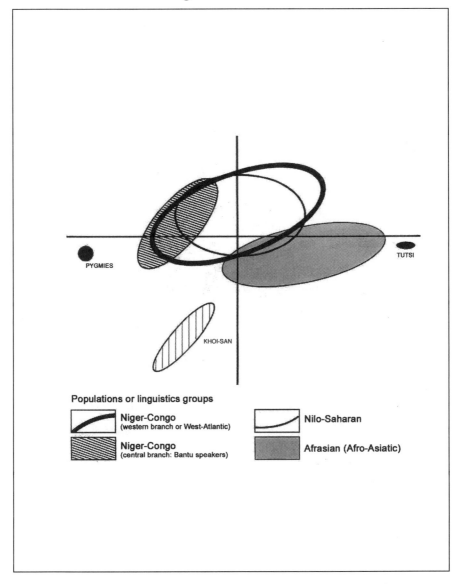

of the contemporary populations of Africa, and apparently their arrival did not occur in uninhabited regions. Everywhere in Africa, residual Negroid populations seem to indicate that, before the present occupiers of the land, there were other men and women living in these spaces.

Documentation of this question is very fragmentary, and it is impossible to form a synthetic overview on the subject given the existing state of research. So let's examine the details.

Among these residual Negroid or paleo-Negritic groups, some are well-known, others less so. They are:

– The Bassari in West Africa

– The Dorobo to the east of the continent, in Kenya and Tanzania

– The Tatog, Hadza, Iraqw and Sandawe tribes also in eastern Africa, which are all residual populations.

– The Renge, in the Interlakes region, notably in Rwanda and Burundi, who are attested to in the oral traditions. This is a different population from the Pygmies and was already settled here when the ancestors of the Hutus and the Tutsis arrived in the region.

– The Khoi-San in southern Africa who are made up of two populations: the San and the Khoi (or Khokhoi), or cattle-raising San. San and Khoi[1] belong to the same linguistic phylum and use a "click" language, replacing consonants with clicks of the tongue against the palate. It is the oldest African linguistic strata. The Khoi-San appeared 30,000 or even 40,000 years ago. They are physically different from the Blacks in whose midst they live:

> *The skull of the Khoi-San is slender and even paedomorphic,[2] and of small dimensions, with weak sexual dimorphism; it is short, wide, and pentagonal, with marked frontal bumps and a proportionately reduced face, triangular in form. They possess (in principle) physical particularities such as: yellowish, wrinkled skin, "peppercorn" hair, narrow and oblique eyes, high cheekbones, unpronounced prognathism, thin lips, lobeless ears, a concave nose with cleanly soldered bones, erasure of the rough line of the femur, steatopygia,[3] short hands, feet, and members,*

---

[1] Formerly known as "Bushmen," as seen in the film, *Les Dieux Sont Tombés Sur la Tête [The Gods Must Be Crazy]*.

[2] That is to say, that it retains childlike features.

[3] That is to say, well-rounded buttocks.

hypertrophied labia minora in the women, penis rectus,[1] in the men, and some genetic frequencies [. . .] of which the most typical are the haplotypes Gm 1,13,17 and GM 1,21 of the serumal gammaglobulins, utilizable to measure the degree of interbreeding with the blacks. This set of traits makes them an extreme example of differentiation in the human species.[2]

The San drew all of their resources from the natural environment. Hunting and gathering could not support large communities, so each group was composed of only about 20 individuals, moving across immense territories in response to the migrations of game, the ripening of tubers and wild grasses, and the drying up of flash-flooded areas. Under the pressure of cattle-raising Khoi, then under that of Bantu-speaking Blacks, they found refuge in the Drakensberg Mountains or in the desert steppes of the Kalahari. Their movement increased in the 18th century, when the Dutch Boer colonists occupied their space and eliminated the San who attacked their cattle.

The San subsist today in small groups, and they constitute a people in danger of extinction. Their space is shrinking, and they only live in some isolated regions of Namibia, Botswana, and perhaps Angola.

While the San groups usually did not exceed a maximum number of a few dozen individuals, the Khoi lived in semi-grouped habitats composed of huts with enclosures for cattle, the "kraals." The first Europeans who visited the region of the Cape of Good Hope designated the Khoi by the name of Hottentots, from the onomatopoeia "Hautitou," which they chanted during their dances. This appellation was attached to them for a long period.

Many Khoi words serving to designate cattle have Nilo-Saharan roots and more precisely are close to the Central Sudanic group. This would have been the result of contact with the speakers of these languages from whom the Khoi could have learned the techniques of cattle-raising. Where did this phenomenon take place? We do not know.

Today, the Khoi[3] have disappeared as an autonomous group and only subsist through the "Cape Coloured" mixed race population. The interbreeding in

---

[1] That is to say, in erectile position, even when in repose.
[2] A. Froment, "Le Peuplement de l'Afrique Centrale: Contribution de l'Anthropobiologie," ["The Population of Central Africa: The Contribution of Anthropology"], op cit.
[3] Formerly called Hottentots.

this case did not concern Bantu-speaking Blacks but was the result of a mix between Khoi women and Dutch colonists.

Before the arrival of the Blacks and Whites, the Khoi-San occupied all of southern Africa. They left thousands of paintings on rock walls in this region. The most ancient of these have been identified in Namibia, and date from 27,500 years ago; the most recent date from the nineteenth century.

What was their origin? Were they the first modern Africans? Some people suppose so, but that theory has not been formally proven.

Nilo-Saharan, Afrasian, and Pastoral Migrations

In chronological terms, the Nilo-Saharan phylum came next and seems to have formed a separate identity about 20,000 years ago. This phenomenon took place in the central region of the present-day Sudan. Some Nilo-Saharan speakers also colonized the southern Sahara roughly 18,000 to 10,000 years ago.[1] The Afro-Asiatic or Afrasian phylum may have emerged roughly between 18,000 and 15,000 years before our times, and its zone of origin may have been situated between the mountains by the Red Sea and the Ethiopian plateaus. Fifteen thousand years ago, it divided into northern and southern branches. The latter gave rise to the Cushite or Cushitic languages. Around 10,000 B.C. the northern branch subdivided into proto-Berber, proto-Egyptian, and proto-Semitic groups.

About 7500 B.C. pastoralism seems to have made an appearance in the Sahara. It was practised both by the white Afrasian Berbers in the north and among the black Nilo-Saharans to the south.

Between 3000 and 2500 B.C., droughts became more severe in the southern part of the Sahara and the black herders left the region. Some went in the direction of Nubia, while the majority headed south towards the Sahel. Another consequence of the droughts was the retreat southwards of the isohyet.[2] This had the effect of drawing away the tsetse fly, thus opening a non-infested corridor stretching from the Atlantic coast of West Africa to the Indian Ocean, passing through the Ethiopian piedmonts. It was by means of this corridor that pastoralism would have been introduced into eastern Africa. At least that is the hypothesis developed by Smith,[3] which we accept.

---

[1] L. Le Quellec, *Art Rupestre et Préhistoire du Sahara*, [*Art Rupestre and Prehistoric Art of the Sahara*] Paris, 1998, p. 490.

[2] The curve on a map connecting points receiving the same amount of rainfall per year.

[3] A.B. Smith, "Origins and Spread of Pastoralism in Africa," *Annual Review of Anthropology*, No. 21 (1992), pp. 125-141.

Map XV: Africa 3,500 Years Ago

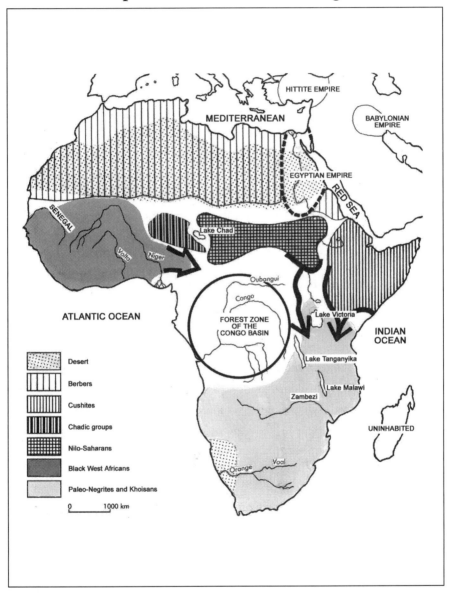

Between 2000 and 1500 B.C. two pastoral waves headed south. One, coming from the Ethiopian highland, was linguistically made up of Southern Cushitics. It migrated towards present-day Kenya.[1] The other, composed linguistically of Southern Nilotic, used the highlands corridor stretching from the south of Ethiopia to Lake Victoria to end up in the Interlakes region. Discoveries by archeologists seem to confirm this schema of north-south progression because, the further south one goes, the more recent the dates of pastoralism become.

It is unclear how pastoralism was introduced in southern Africa although it is generally accepted that it would have been the result of contacts established between the newcomers and the Khoi-San hunter-gatherers.[2] In the present-day South African province of Northern Cape, the remnants of sheep have been traced back to the first century B.C. On the western coast, measurements put this phonemona at A.D. 500. Bovines seem to be unknown in these areas before roughly A.D. 650.

The Expansion of the Bantu-Speaking Peoples

The Bantu languages evolved out of proto-Bantu, which was originally a common language that emerged about 5000 B.C. after the Niger-Congo phylum was separated out.

The term "Bantu" was "invented" in 1862 by the German philologist Wilhelm Bleek. Bleek suggested using this word to express the kinship existing between the spoken languages of the southern third of Africa, which were based on "common proto-prefixes." Bleek had observed that, in all the 600 or so languages of the area he studied, the term ntu or muntu in singular, and bantu in plural form, was used to designate "man" or "men." That's how the notion of a bantu-speaking group originated.

It is important to keep in mind, however, that the only kinship is linguistic. Neither "Bantu Man" or the "Bantu race" exist. Although there was obviously an initial relationship between language and "race," this is no longer the case. Bantu-speakers reside within populations which are "morphotypically" quite

---

[1] R. Robertshaw, *Early Pastoralists of Southwestern Kenya*, Nairobi, British Institute in East Africa (BIAE), 1990.

[2] A.B. Smith, "On Becoming Herders: Khoikhoi and San Ethnicity in Southern Africa," in *Africa Studies,* 49 (2) (1990), pp. 51-73.

Map XVI: The Migrations of the Bantu-Speakers

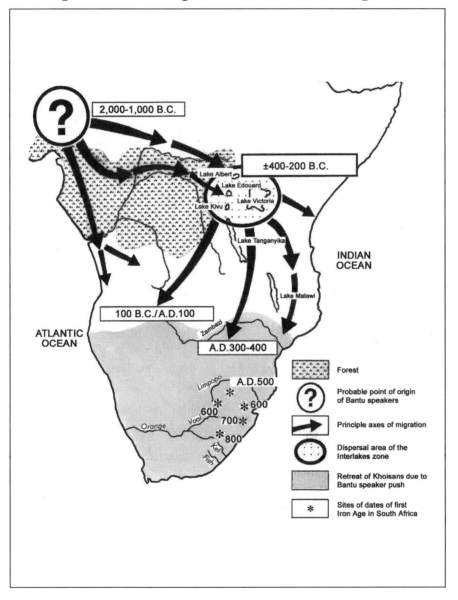

2,000-1,000 B.C.

±400-200 B.C.

Lake Albert

Lake Edouard

Lake Kivu

Lake Victoria

Lake Tanganyika

INDIAN OCEAN

100 B.C./A.D.100

Lake Malawi

ATLANTIC OCEAN

Zambezi

A.D.300-400

Limpopo

A.D.500

600 * * 600

Orange Vaal 700 *

* 800

Forest

? Probable point of origin of Bantu speakers

Principle axes of migration

Dispersal area of the Interlakes zone

Retreat of Khoisans due to Bantu speaker push

* Sites of dates of first Iron Age in South Africa

distinct from one another. Some examples include the Pygmies and the Tutsi in Rwanda and in Burundi (Map XVI).

In 1995, a summary of findings based on a study of 440 of the 600 languages in the Bantu-speaking zone was proposed by Vansina.[1] It drew four principal conclusions:

– The migrations of the Bantu-speakers started in the second millennium B.C.

– The existence of two migratory flows, one along the Atlantic coast and the other towards eastern Africa, was confirmed.

– When the migrations started, the Bantu-speakers were still hunter-gatherers and had no knowledge of iron metallurgy.

– The people who migrated eastward probably crossed the tropical forest by taking the rivers rather than by bypassing them. Their final stopping-point was the Interlakes region.

Between 300 and 100 B.C., leaving behind the mass of groups installed in eastern Africa, certain pioneers once again took up the march. The Bantu-speakers completed their settlement in the zones they now occupy from the fourth to the 18th centuries A.D.

In this way central Africa, and then southern Africa, were populated. The process was lengthy and complex, but we do not know the exact modalities. What is certain is that it was not completed until the end of the 18th century, when the Bantu-speaking pioneers met the Dutch pioneers, who had been present in the Cape region since 1652.

The Interlakes Melting Pot

The Interlakes area of eastern Africa seems to have played such a decisive role in the history of how a great part of the continent was populated that it can be called the "interlacustrine melting pot." In the archeological discipline, the region has provided the oldest dates for the First and Second Iron Ages, suggesting that a number of innovations started, or were introduced, between Lake Victoria and the Kivu region before spreading to all of eastern, central, and southern Africa. Specifically, the ceramics of the Interlakes region are the oldest of all those composing the "Industrial Complex of the First Iron Age" in eastern

[1] J. Vansina, "New Linguistic Evidence and the Bantu Expansion," in *Journal of African History*, 36, 2 (1995), pp. 172-195.

Africa. They would thus belong:

> [. . .] to the industry of the ancient Iron Age which is geographically
> closest to the supposed initial source.[1]

This "supposed initial source" may have been situated northwest of Lake
Albert, within the linguistic zone of the Central Sudanic group, and thus
belonged to the Nilo-Saharan phylum. Archeological digs would permit us to
be more certain, but these have not occurred because this area of the southern
Sudan has been at war since the 1950s.

The same principle applies in the linguistic field. A "J Zone," isolated by
linguists at the Royal Museum of Tervuren in Belgium, corresponds precisely to
the Interlakes region and appears to contain the most "archaic" languages of the
entire eastern Bantu grouping. Within this "J Zone," the Rwanda and Rundi[2]
languages are the most archaic of all. This discovery has led Coupez[3] to say that
everything leads one to believe that the Bantu languages spoken in eastern, central, and southern Africa were derived from these two languages. With them,
we would thus have the primordial point reached by the first migrants two or
three thousand years ago.

How Southern Africa Was Populated

The history of the population of southern Africa presents a perfect illustration of the gap that exists between historical reality and its representation in the
media, which is the fruit of ignorance, or even worse, of an ideologically motivated lie. When the Dutch arrived in the region in 1652, the Blacks had not yet
completed their southward migration nor crossed the Great Kei River contrary to
the postulates laid down by the Afrocentrists and certain European historians.

Even now, there are more Whites than Blacks in a large part of the
Republic of South Africa (RSA). The prevailing idea, however, is that South
Africa was formerly and entirely populated by black peoples who were slowly
chased off their lands by the Dutch colonists. This is far from the truth.

The most advanced point of the Bantu-speakers' migration into southern
Africa was represented by the Nguni linguistic group, which was divided today

---

[1] D. Phillipson, "L'Expansion Bantoue en Afrique Orientale et Méridionale: Les Témoignages
de l'Archéologie et de la Linguistique" [Bantu Expansion in Eastern and Southern Africa: The
Evidence of Archeology and Linguistics], in L'Expansion Bantoue, Actes du Colloque de Viviers, 1977
(published 1980), pp. 649-684.

[2] Burundi.

[3] A. Coupez, "Aspects de Phonologie Historique de Rwanda" [Aspects of Historic Phonology of
Rwanda] in Annales Aequatoria (1980), pp; 575-590.

Map XVII: Blacks and Whites in South Africa

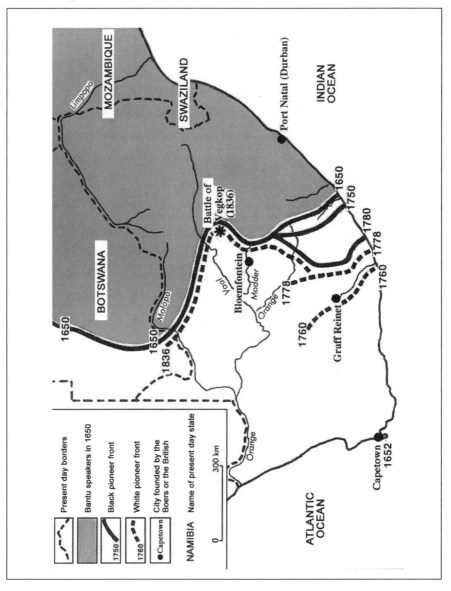

Map XVIII: Bantu-Speakers and Dutch-Speakers in South Africa

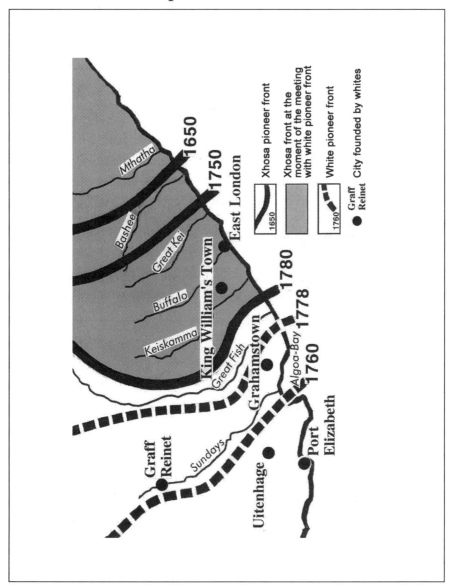

into the Zulu, Ndebele, Swazi, and Xhosa tribes. The southernmost of these tribes were the Xhosa.

Up until 1740, the Xhosa had lived between the Mthatha and Bashee (or Mbashe) rivers. Finding himself hemmed into too narrow a space, one of their chiefs, Langa (1704-1794), decided to look for new pastures. He headed south, crossing the Great Kei and in the direction of the Great Fish river. Ten years later, in 1750, his half-brother, Phalo (1702-1775), also crossed the Great Kei and came to establish his kraal,[1] near the present-day city of King William's Town.

In 1760, the Dutch-speaking Boers, who had left the Cape region a century before, reached Sundays river and founded the city of Graff Reinet. The two pioneer fronts were thus advancing slowly towards one another. In their progression they literally crushed the first occupiers of the land — the small bands of Khoi-San – who were caught in the vise between the two. So Blacks and Whites met 120 years after the settlement of the Dutch at the Cape of Good Hope, and more than 1,000 kilometers (600 miles) away from Capetown. Southwest of the Great Kei river, the Whites had arrived before the Blacks.

The Whites and the Xhosa would fight from 1779 to 1853 in eight different conflicts, known as the "frontier wars," trying to establish a limit between their respective territorial possessions. The Xhosa stopped fighting in 1853. After this, those living to the west of the Great Kei river would be placed under the tutelage of British advisors, whose mission was to assist their chiefs. The British profited from the situation by settling 6,000 colonists in the hinterland of the Port of East London, founded in 1848. In 1866, the Xhosa country would be joined to the Cape Colony.

That moment marked the end in this region of the great migratory movements of the Bantu-speaking people, which had started several millennia previously, and that of the Boers, which had commenced in 1652.

It should be very clear that we are not seeking here to justify any political prolongation of these events (such as apartheid). We merely hope to show why present-day news should not be confused with history and why the latter can only be understood by taking the "long view," and not through the shortcuts postulated by a simplistic ideology.

---

[1] Enclosure.

Chapter VI

The Real Shifts in Africa's Fortunes

The real shifts in Africa's fortunes were not due to the slave trade or to so-called colonial pillage. On a more profound level, they were brought about by several great historical transformations, internal and external to Africa, that intervened during the long span of continental time and provoked fundamental evolutions.

Before reviewing these historical shifts, it is important to note that there were also great climactic changes which would condition the African landscape and affect developments there.

First of all, between 10,000 and 60,000 years ago, Africa grew cold and underwent a hyper-arid phase. The forest in the Congo basin shrank, to the benefit of the savannas, and the Sahara desert spread.

Next, following this cold, dry period there was a hot and humid sequence[1] which lasted from about 6,000 to 9,000 years ago, or from 7000 to 4000 B.C. During this period, the Sahara desert shrank considerably and the Congolese rain forest doubled its surface area, forming a barrier dividing the continent in two. Man then saw his travels restricted by the natural milieu. This African Humid Period or Holocene Climactic Optimum[2] saw the emergence of the first Neolithic cultures and presented profound regional differences.

Finally, the post-Neolithic Arid Period (roughly between 4500 and 1500 B.C.) provoked another break. The Sahara spread once again, but having

---

[1] M. Leroux, "Interprétation Météorologique des Changements Climatiques Observés en Afrique Depuis Dix-Huit Mille Ans," [Meteorological Interpretation of Climatic Changes Observed in Africa Since 1800] in *Géo-Eco-Trop,* 16, (1-4) (1994), pp. 207-258.

[2] The Holocene is the most recent geological epoch of the Quaternary period; it started about 12,000 years ago and extended from 6,000 to 9,000 years before our time.

Map XIX: Africa Between 9,000 and 6,000 Years Ago

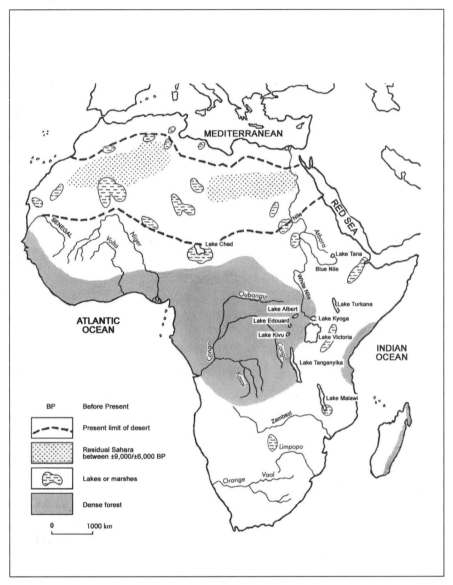

become herders and thus producing their own resources, Africans were no longer condemned to follow the retreat of the wild fauna. The Sahara then became the almost exclusive domain of a white, proto-Berber population, while the black herders who had previously occupied the southern and part of the central Sahara withdrew southwards to the Sahel.

There then began the great Sahelian period, which only ended when the Europeans discovered the coastal regions of the Gulf of Guinea.

"The Victory of Caravels over Caravans"

This first great African historical shift took place with the so-called period of "Great Discoveries," when the Portuguese, followed by the other European maritime powers,[1] established outposts along the Atlantic coast of Africa. In doing so, they tipped the economic and political heart of the continent in the direction of the ocean. Following the arrival of the Portuguese, the north-south commercial axes from the Maghreb to the forest were diverted towards the Gulf of Guinea and Senegambia; the western Saharan trails were largely deserted then, while those of the eastern Sahara continued to be frequented in the direction of Egypt. It was, as the Portuguese historian, Magalhès Goudinho, put it, "the victory of the caravel over the caravan." The limits of this striking formula have been revealed by historical research, but it nevertheless underlines an essential fact: the Atlantic coast of black Africa, which, until then, had been completely marginal in the history of the continent became, in the space of a few decades, the principal economic sphere of all West Africa. This would continue for several centuries and reached a particular height with the slave trade. The kingdoms of the interior declined, while new, powerful ones were born where the Europeans landed and bought slaves from their black suppliers.

Previously, it was above all the Sahel region that had flourished. Starting with the trans-Saharan commerce in the eighth and ninth centuries, great empires and "intermediary" kingdoms successively emerged there. They ranged to the east and west of Lake Chad, and between North Africa, which exported the produce of its craftsmen, and the African forest to the south, which

---

[1] With the notable exception of the Spaniards.

Map XX: The Victory of Caravels Over the Caravans

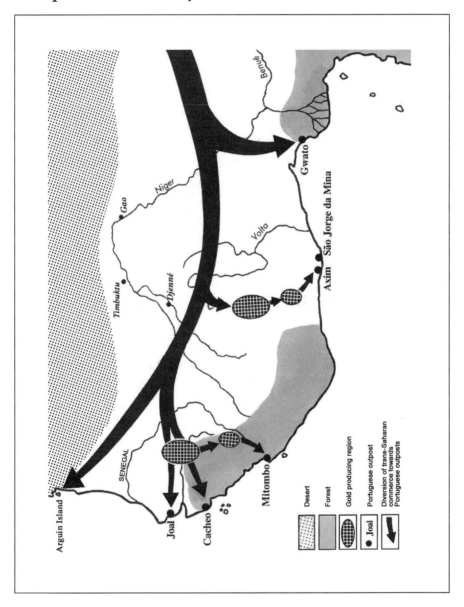

Map XXI: The Great African States at the Beginning of the 19th Century

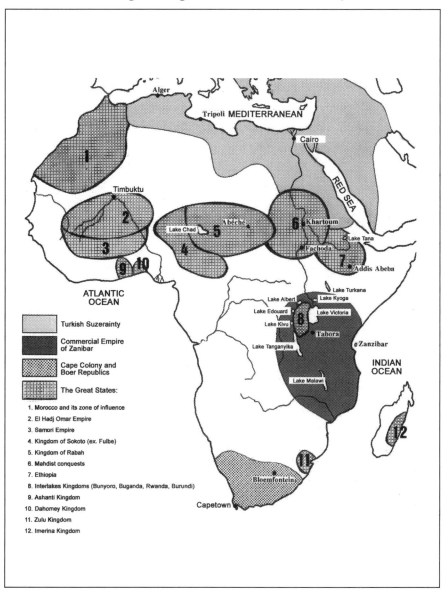

Alger

Tripoli MEDITERRANEAN

Cairo

RED SEA

1

Timbuktu

2

Lake Chad 5 Abéché 6 Khartoum

3 4 Lake Tana

9 10 Fachoda

7 Addis Abeba

ATLANTIC
OCEAN

Lake Turkana

Lake Albert Lake Kyoga

Lake Edouard 8 Lake Victoria

Lake Kivu

Tabora

Lake Tanganyika Zanzibar

INDIAN
OCEAN

Lake Malawi

	Turkish Suzerainty
	Commercial Empire of Zanibar
	Cape Colony and Boer Republics
	The Great States:

1. Morocco and its zone of influence
2. El Hadj Omar Empire
3. Samori Empire
4. Kingdom of Sokoto (ex. Fulbe)
5. Kingdom of Rabah
6. Mahdist conquests
7. Ethiopia
8. Interlakes Kingdoms (Bunyoro, Buganda, Rwanda, Burundi)
9. Ashanti Kingdom
10. Dahomey Kingdom
11. Zulu Kingdom
12. Imerina Kingdom

12

11

Bloemfontein

Capetown

exported gold, spices, and slaves.

In this same Sahelian-Sudanese region, an internal shift took place in the 19th century. It appeared when the jihad served as a smokescreen for the imperialist ambitions of certain northern warrior communities. The latter tried to extend their power at the expense of southern bodies impoverished by the end of the Atlantic slave trade, decided unilaterally by the Europeans. But these expansionist political aims were blocked by colonialism.

At the end of the 19th century, the British colonial push[1] began inwards from the coasts and, with the exception of resistance by the Ashanti kingdom, progressed without difficulty until meeting the Sahel sultanates. The British troops were generally welcomed by the southern populations, who saw in them a protection against the Muslim, slave-trading northerners. A French push, which took place essentially along the Senegal-Niger river axis, also resulted in the destruction of northern Muslim sultanates, including the Empires of Ahmadu, Rabeh, and Samori. This benefited the populations that they held in submission. Colonization thus nipped an attempted revival of the Sahel in the bud, to the advantage of the coastal poles.

The golden age of the Sahel would never return, but throughout the region, the deep sense of northern, Sahelian, Muslim, and continental identity evoke the memories of the empires of Ghana, of Mali, and of Songhaï, in contrast to the southern coasts, which were open to the wide Atlantic and to the cultural and religious influences of Europe. A permanent conflict exists between the two influences which is now being illustrated in Nigeria and Côte d'Ivoire, two countries divided by a north-south cleavage.

The Defense of the Dominated and Downfall of the Dominant

The second great shift occurred at the time of the continent's colonial partition. In the years 1890-1900, colonizers established their power at the expense of the most active peoples in the region's history. The mighty empires that resisted the colonial push were defeated. Their destruction, dismantlement, or submission benefitted the populations they had dominated up until then. The

---

[1] This was examined at greater length in Chapter II.

traditional powers of Africa were shut down, putting the "ethnic tectonics" on hold, so to speak.

Colonialism thus provoked, the transformation of several potential African "Prussias:" Madagascar and the Hova-Merina monarchy, the Empire of Sokoto, the Ashanti Kingdom, Dahomey, and the conquering groups assembled by El Hadj Omar, by Samori, by Rabeh, etc. Up until then, all these political entities had been engaged, more or less forcefully, in regional unification, along the same lines that Prussia succeeded in carrying out in Europe.

Colonial rule also halted the migration of various peoples, as in the case of Côte d'Ivoire, South Africa, and Zimbabwe. It subjugated others, stopping them at a given moment in their history. This was the case, for example, of the Tutsi state of Rwanda, cut off from its natural field of expansion in West Kivu (situated in the Belgian Congo), which had constituted an outlet for its surplus population (as recent events have indeed demonstrated). Restricted to the highlands bordering the Congo-Nile watershed by colonial partition, imperialist Rwanda was reduced to nothing more than a small, landlocked kingdom, embedded in its mountain setting.

Sometimes, colonization reversed existing balances of power by weakening certain ethnic groups and reinforcing others. In Namibia,[1] for example, the Ovambo profited from the elimination of the Herero, who had previous dominated the region, and they still hold power today as a result of this colonial ethnic reversal.

Colonization also carved up states, such as millennial-old Morocco, benefiting others like Algeria and Mauritania which were born of the colonial partition. The present-day problems of Western Sahara are the result.

Reversal of Balances of Power

The third great shift, which has generated many of the present crises in Africa, occurred with independence in the 1960s. At that point, decolonization confirmed the reversal of ethnic balances of power that colonialism had brought about. Populations which were formerly dominated had often become the

---

[1] Former South West Africa.

source of local officials for the colonial powers, and it was they who inherited the artificial states bequeathed by the departing colonizers and were put in charge. Under them, or under others who soon replaced them, the electoral mathematics of democracy would attribute legitimacy. Utlimately power went not to the best, the most competent, or well-trained, but to the most numerous; to the ethnic groups whose principal virtue was their birthrate. The law of numbers, the great leveler of elites previously unheard of within the natural African order, would thus disrupt a social harmony based on natural authority, inherited hierarchies, respect, and submission. One does not vote in Africa for the candidate who is reputed to be the most competent, or the closest to one's own ideas; one votes for the candidate who will best defend the interests of one's own ethnic group.

This explains why the pastoral peoples who were almost always in the minority because they had the ancestral wisdom to limit their demographic growth to that of their flocks, were swept from power or reduced to second-class citizenship by the farmers whose uncontrolled reproduction was by definition superior to the herders. Democracy was, in the end, a bonus to lack of foresight. This was notably the case in eastern Africa, and particularly in Rwanda and the entire Great Lakes region, where the peoples without any state traditions were placed at the head of states they had not created themselves, for the sole reason that their power was mathematically legitimate in the eyes of affluent democrats in Europe and America.

Wherever they had not been totally broken by colonialism, however, the formerly dominant peoples have done everything they could to restore their authority. Because their very survival depends on a shift in power, the troubles, wars, and even massacres, in Nigeria, Rwanda, Madagascar, Chad, Mali, Niger, the Sudan, etc. all stem from their need to agitate.

The Aftermath of the Cold War

The fourth great shift happened in the 1990s and when the Cold War ended and Africa ceased almost overnight to have strategic value. The continent was abandoned by those who, only the previous day, had courted it, and the full extent of the underlying problems was revealed. In the second half of the decade, they took several forms: political crisis, institutional crises, and humanitarian crises.

The governments of the states that resulted from colonial partition rapidly proved to be completely out of touch with African realities. The post-colonial frontiers have often divided peoples, or, on the contrary, condemned populations to live together who never had a common destiny. They thus regularly appear to be artificial overlays and sometimes even "prisons for peoples," from which stem the crises in the Democratic Republic of the Congo (DRC, former Zaire), or the Horn of Africa (Somalia, Ethiopia, Eritrea), to name two examples.

Constructed within these artificial frontiers, the post-colonial states are, in most cases, empty juridical shells that do not coincide with the flesh and blood countries that produce true human roots. Political boundaries prevent different groups from cohabiting in a social harmony that could reconcile the contradictory notions of unity of destiny and respect for ethnic, tribal, or clannish differences.

Moreover, the pure and simple transposition of Western political institutions has provoked an indescribable state of chaos. In Africa, where authority is not traditionally shared, it has been distributed haphazardly, without any prior reflection concerning the creation of countervailing powers and the mode of representation or association to the government of the minority peoples. They are condemned by democratic electoral mathematics to be forever excluded from political power and its advantages.

In the countries of the northern hemisphere, societies are individualistic, and the constitutional bases rest on common convictions or on political programs transcending cultural or social differences. Because of decolonization, individual suffrage now determines political legitimacy. However, such a notion is foreign to Africa, where societies are traditionally communitarian, hierarchical, and based on solidarity. The idea of a nation is thus not the same as in Europe. In the one case, social order rests upon individuals, and in the other, on groups. The principle of "one man, one vote" prevents taking into account the real African political reality that resides in groups: the ethnic groups, tribes, or clans.

Throughout three decades, from 1960 to 1990, priority was given to the constitution or reinforcement of nation-states. As they had to advance by leaps and bounds, the African states born out of decolonization took the "authoritarian shortcut," which is why, as a general rule, the single party became identified with the state that was to be formed. Ethnic particularities were fought as potential ferments of division that would weaken the state edifice still in gestation. But, in reality, one ethnic group, or even a single tribe, would monopolize power, identifying itself with the single party, and thus the state, while those excluded felt alienated by the movement of national fusion and were even opposed to it.

This idea predominated throughout the whole Cold War period, which unfortunately for Africa coincided with the period in which it won independence. The priority of the two blocs was to maintain their positions, and this favored the political status quo. Strong regimes were needed upon which one side or the other could rely.

Then, when the Cold War ended and Africa's political and economic failures were faced, the question of power was raised. Some postulated that the attempts at nation-building and the economic development which was supposed to result from it, had failed due to a deficit of democracy. Africa then began to suffer a "democratic diktat," which brought the downfall of the African single-party regime, or at least its redefinition. The phenomenon expressed itself in a multiplication of crises throughout the entire continent. But, this "democratic ukase" also turned out to be a patent failure. It could not have been otherwise, because the democratic postulate not only did not contain any state yeast to help it rise, but it also carried the germs of anarchy, and a total breakup of existing institutions.

Indeed, no state anywhere in this world has ever been created by democracy. If one thinks carefully about it, it was not democracy that built the constitution of the nation-states of Europe, but force, ruse, will, and time. It was only after their creation that democracy was introduced there. And even then, the movement was not self-evident. The French revolutionary upheavals had to be spread across Europe in order to bring down the old aristocratic order. It was not democratic initiatives that forged Italy, but the French armies sent by Emperor Napoleon III. Nor was it the democratic ideals that brought about German unification but Prussian energy channeled by Chancellor Bismarck and the military victory of 1870 against France. Even the United States of America was not born of democracy or consensus, but out of a war. Originally, the U.S. was in fact a British colony, which forged its destiny through battles fought against the mother country.

Faced with the political upheavals and tragedies that the African continent was experiencing, notably in Somalia, the countries of the North formulated the concept of "humanitarian interference," a neo-colonialism for "nice people." This doctrine rests on the "kind sentiments of well-to-do democrats in the industrialized countries." It was invented by a moribund pro-Third World ideology and recycled by North American agribusiness which saw this as a means of disposing cheaply of its food glut while restoring its tattered public image. It was also imposed on public opinion by a media "bombardment," in which appalling images were shown without the slightest explanation. Lastly, it was accepted by politicians of the industrialized nations, who were afraid of being accused of lacking human feeling.

$$* * *$$

The consequences of this policy are calamitous. Not only has "humanitarian interference" not resolved the deep causes of the crises it was supposed to "treat," it has also amplified others, in Somalia or in Rwanda, for example. Sometimes, it has even provoked shock waves from which the continent is still suffering the consequences, as in Central Africa.

In all cases where this policy—which one can characterize without hesitation as idiotic, or in more diplomatic terms, blind and ill-founded—has been applied, it has resulted in yet more cultural trauma, which is profound and durable. Once again, in the name of a supposedly "universal" morality, the industrialized countries of the North, disarmed by incapacitating myths and a victimization paradigm we have described above, have prevented the situation in Africa from correcting itself.

Chapter VII

Ethnic Groups: The Pivot of African History

With the semantic erosion imposed by "political correctness," the word "tribe" has become a pejorative term. That's why the term "ethnic group," which is regarded as having more positive values, is now employed instead. This is incorrect, and the substitution of one word for another has contributed to confusing the public's understanding. Here is clarification.

Definitions

The concept of "race" refers to a subdivision of the human species that pre-existed that of "ethnic group." With time and migrations, contact among populations occurred. Religious, cultural, linguistic, and technical transfers resulted as well as interbreeding, which has provoked the evolution or breakup of the former "racial" units, upon the ruins of which appeared the "ethnic groups."

The "ethnic group" is a human group defined solely by the cultural particularities that unite its members. It is a linguistic community located in theory in a traditional territory. It is not defined by race or morphotype. This creates problems because ethnic frontiers do not automatically follow "racial" frontiers. For example, in Rwanda and Burundi, the ancestors of the present-day Tutsis were long ago "Bantu-ized" by adopting a Bantu language. But, in becoming Bantu-speakers, they did not become morphotypically transformed into Hutus. Interbreeding occurred frequently between Tutsi masters and their female Hutu servants, but it did not cause either the Tutsis or the Hutus to disappear. That would only have been the case if institutionalized interbreeding took place, from the moment when Hutu "blood" predominated in Tutsi lineages, so that one could speak of mixed "ethnic groups," for both groups.

From Race to Lineage

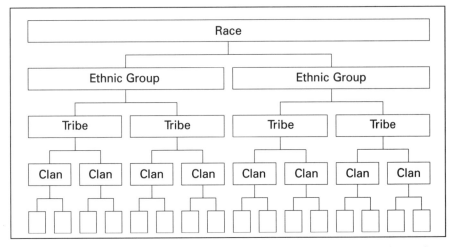

In general, "ethnic groups" are composed of tribes which can have close links or conflicting relations. The "tribe" is a grouping of clans or families under the authority of the same chief. The "clan" is the sociological unit designating blood relatives descended from a common ancestor. Each tribe is composed of several "clans" and a great number of lineages.

Since these groupings are related culturally, they can easily constitute enlarged units. The best example is that of the Zulu. Originally, the Zulus were one of many small tribes within the northern fraction of the Nguni ethnic group (Bantu-speakers). In the 18th century, they conquered several other tribes within this group, which proved easy because they all spoke the same language and adhered to the same system of values. The kingdom that was later constituted took the name of the federating tribe, but not all of the Nguni tribes were integrated into it.

These simplified definitions apply to social realities that pre-existed colonial Africa. The ancient history of the continent is that of its peoples, and thus of its ethnic groups. In pre-colonial African history, all of the state-like institutions had an ethnic base. Furthermore, when these entities resulted in multi-ethnic groupings, they generally didn't last.[1]

Colonization's Role in Ethnic Evolution

As the daily news shows, the contemporary history of Africa also revolves around ethnic groups, from Liberia and Côte d'Ivoire to Somalia. Yet, American Afrocentrists, and the "paradigm historians"[2] claim instead that it was colonialism that created the African ethnic groups. The debate is deformed and biased by linguistic abuses of observers who confuse, as we have said, "ethnic group" and "tribe."

Can one seriously maintain that the African ethnic groups and tribes did not exist when the colonizers occupied the continent at the end of the 19th century? How can scientists write that it was colonialism that created the Tutsi and the Hutu in Rwanda, the Darod and the Saab in Somalia, the Zulu and the Xhosa in South Africa, the Ovimbundu and the Kimbundu in Angola, the Kru and the Mano in Liberia, the Temne and the Mende in Sierra Leone, or the Baoule and the Bete in Côte d'Ivoire?

Afrocentrists claim the reason for this is that they support Afrocentrist positions. To begin with, they allow African Americans to claim a mythic membership in a "Black People" which was supposed to have existed in the "Paradise Lost" that was Africa before the Whites arrived. This is also the ideological basis of the Pan-Africanism advocated by many African politicians, who thus hope to surmount the divisions of their continent.

The Pan-African ideal began in 1885, in Jamaica, with Marcus Garvey and the Rastifarians.[3] It took form with the American, William Edward Burghardt DuBois (1868-1963) who founded the National Association for the Advancement of Colored People (NAACP) in 1908. In 1919, DuBois assembled 57 delegates from the French and British colonies, the United States, and

---

[1] There are some counter-examples, but they are rare: the Toucouleur entity; and in a different spirit, the Muslim empires, born of the jihads, which were sometimes ethnic "agglomerators."

[2] Implying, in the context of this present work, the "victimization paradigm" of European guilt. This "school," which tries to lend credit to the idea of a European culpability for the contemporary ills of Africa, does not self-proclaim itself as the "paradigm historians," the label being our own invention.

[3] A mystical Jamaican current that, in addition to its later musical successes with Bob Marley and reggae, enjoyed great political success in the United States during the 1920s, when Marcus Garvey emigrated there. The movement, which mixes politics and Biblical imprecations, preaches the return to Africa of all the descendants of the slaves disseminated across the American continent, and locates the promised land of the blacks...in Ethiopia!

the Caribbean at the first Pan-African Congress in Paris. At the second Congress held in London in 1921, the Pan-Africans demanded equality between Blacks and Whites. But it was not until the fifth, at Manchester in 1945, that Pan-Africanism took a truly political direction.

Dominated by the West Indian Fritz Fanon, the Ghanaian Kwame Nkrumah (both Marxists), and the Kenyan Jomo Kenyatta (a nationalist), the final declarations insisted for the first time on the necessity for independence and the end of "colonial exploitation." Pan-Africanism then adopted a more militant form with the demand for unity of the future states, marked by the independence of Ghana (1957) and the foundation of the Organization of African Unity (OAU) at the Congress of Addis-Ababa in 1963. The medium-term goal of the OAU was the end of colonialism, cooperation between member states, and the will to resolve eventual conflicts by negotiation.

In the longer term, Pan-Africanism envisioned a constitution of the United States of Africa, which would also integrate the West Indies and the African American community. However, the unitary aspirations of the Pan-Africans did not withstand the Cold War and the creation of the East-West blocs for long, as the OAU members would align themselves with one or the other of the two opposing camps, generating conflicts.

The ideal of Pan-Africanism is a beautiful utopia but does not rest on any historical reality or any social reality, even from a Marxist point of view. If one takes the example of the French West Indies, one observes that beyond official "politically correct" rhetoric about the unity of the black West Indian community, the great reality is the opposite—fragmentation. There is no class struggle, but there are plenty of "racial" barriers which maintain the social impermeability constituted by the real or supposed importance of "white blood" in the veins of various people. Numerous colorful creole terms permit distinctions among individuals, from the "lightest" to the "dark:" Sauté barrière [Barrier Jumper], Négre blond [Blond Negro], Bien sorti [Turned Out Well], etc. According to the Pan-Africans, there was an original and common cultural unity, just as Cheikh Anta Diop postulated and the American Afrocentrists claim. However, in the West Indies as elsewhere, there is no indivisible "black people" but, a mosaic of different peoples.

Secondly, the "paradigm historians" wish to impose the idea that all African problems have a colonial cause. Yet, the news is full of ethnic tragedies that have bloodied the continent. Since the terrible images on TV news reports obviously cannot be denied, their argument consists in maintaining that such tragedies did not exist in Africa before the Whites.

In France, where these "paradigm historians" have, for all practical purposes, swallowed up African studies, the publications dealing with the ethnic phenomenon argue that ethnicity is an amplification or an invention of the first European travelers. Jean-Pierre Chrétien, research director at the Centre National de la recherche scientifique (CNRS) is one of the leaders of this curious historical "school." And he is completely clear on this subject:

Ethnicity refers less to local traditions than it does to the fantasies over-laid by Western ethnography on the so-called world of customs.[1]

Claiming that, in Rwanda and Burundi, the Tutsi and the Hutu are largely colonial creations, the same researcher does not hesitate to write that:

The neo-ethnic consciousness, forged in the shadows of the priests and the territorial agents, is not far removed from the Bantu policy developed in the South African context of apartheid.[2]

Paradigm historians insist that the argument in favor of ethnic groups is specious, anyone who advocates it is automatically labeled a "supporter of apartheid" and effectively dismissed. These kinds of arguments have nurtured a kind of "left-wing McCarthyism" in the field of African studies.

In sub-Saharan Africa, not only were the ethnic groups not created by colonization, they are the basis of all political and social life today. Founded, as it is, on the principle of "one man, man vote," democracy loses sight of the importance of these ethnic affiliations. The obvious consequence is that it favors the smallest common denominator — the tribe, or even the clan. In short, the "democratic diktat" imposed upon the African states by the Americans and the Europeans is in the process of breaking up the ethnic groups, the only federating element of tribal or clannish identities, in favor of the tribe, which is a divisive element.

---

[1] J.P. Chrétien, "Hutu et Tutsi au Rwanda et au Burundi," [Hutu and Tutsi in Rwanda and Burundi] in J.L. Amselle & E. Mbokolo (eds.), *Au Coeur de l'Ethnie. Ethnies, Tribalisme et Etats en Afrique, [In the Heart of Ethnicity: Ethnicity, Tribalism, and the African States],* Paris, 1985, pp. 129-165.

[2] J.P. Chrétien, "L'Alibi Ethnique dans la Politique Africaine," [The Ethnic Alibi in African Politics], *Esprit,* Nos. 7-8 (July-Aug. 1981), p. 111.

The Ethnic Clash of West Africa

West Africa is predominantly characterized by a vast reality of ethnic migrations that had not yet settled down when colonization created borders. Moreover, the large ethnic groups "overlapped" several states whose frontiers had been artificially traced by the colonizers, resulting in contagion and regional implications when internal conflicts arose.

The first case is that of Côte d'Ivoire. In this territory, several large ethnic groups of West Africa came into contact. In answer to the question, "What is the Côte d'Ivoire?" President Félix Houphouët-Boigny once wrote:

> Sixty tribes who don't know one another, who do not have the same dialects, who don't have the same manner of organizing their societies. The villages, every 25 kilometers, were as far away from one another as Portugal or Russia. These men, thanks to colonization, constituted the embryo of a nation.

France originally created the "Colony of Côte d'Ivoire" in 1895-1896. The region was then the point where three peoples in migration had met: the Akan/Baoule (Kwa) coming from the east; the Mande/Malinke arrived from the north, and the Kru/Bete in the west. Colonization "froze" their territorial occupation by the outline of the frontiers. This situation was remarkably described, almost 40 years ago by Gabriel Rougerie:

> At the turn of the century, foreign minds had conceived the definition of a quadrilateral at the edge of the West African bloc. Its limits insinuated themselves among the elements of the relief, embracing by pure chance a disparate sampling. In this net, too, were caught groups of men, each of them living its particularism, each having reached a different moment in its history, its migration, its evolution.[1]

After independence, President Houphouët-Boigny succeeded in putting ethnic demands to sleep, even if his own people, the Baoule and those associated with them were particularly well-favored. His successor, Henri Konan Bédié, also a Baoule, did not manage to maintain the ethnic alchemy elaborated by his predecessor, and opposition groups began to assert themselves.

---

[1] G. Rougerie, *La Côte d'Ivoire, [The Ivory Coast]*, Presses Universitaires de France, Paris, 1964, p. 63.

Map XXII: The Ethnic Clash of West Africa

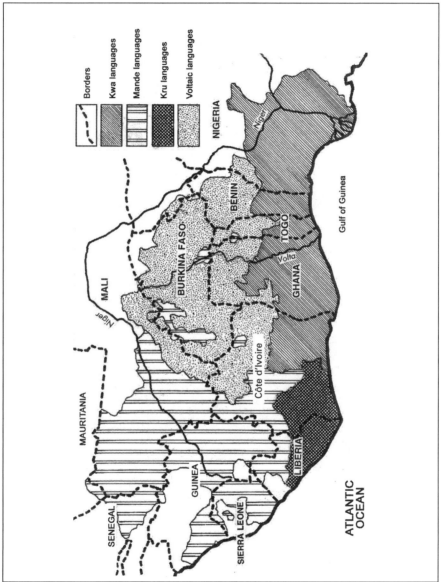

Map XXIII: The Ethnic Groups of Côte d'Ivoire

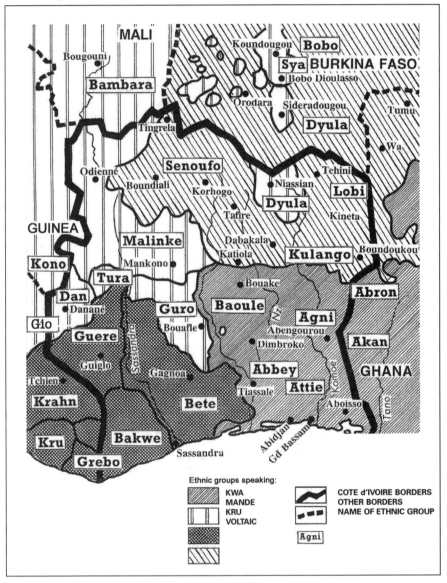

The 14 million (or 16 million according to the census) native-born Ivorians[1] are distributed into ethnic groups as follows:

Ethnic Distribution of Côte d'Ivoire

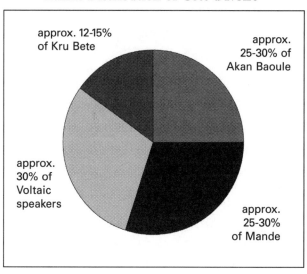

approx. 12-15% of Kru Bete

approx. 25-30% of Akan Baoule

approx. 30% of Voltaic speakers

approx. 25-30% of Mande

To these ethnic divisions must be added the religious divide between Islam in the north and Christianity in the south. On December 24, 1999, the coup d'état of General Robert Guei ended the power of the Baoule. The general belonged to the Yacouba/Dan, a tribe within the southern Mande ethno-linguistic group which totaled, with its cousins the Guro, about 10 percent of the Ivorian population.

In order to organize a tailor-made election for himself, the general excluded Alassan Ouattara, a member of the Malinke, one of the tribes from the northern Mande ethno-linguistic group, and president of the Rassemblement des Républicains (RDR), a northern and predominantly Muslim, political party. He did the same with the representative of the Baoule. Then, as his official contender, he dubbed an adversary more to his liking, Laurent Gbagbo, a Bete whose "ethnic weight" was only about 12 percent of the electorate.

---

[1] To this native-born population must be added three to four million immigrants, of which two million from Burkina Faso, 800,000 Malians, and at least 200,000 Guineans.

Côte d'Ivoire: A Territory of Conquest (16th – 19th Centuries)

The current events in Côte d'Ivoire can only be explained by the history of the establishment of its great ethnic groups. Yet, we continue to hear that it is only a construction "of the priests."

What we are seeing today is the resumption of a movement put on hold during the colonial era. From the 16th to the 19th century, Côte d'Ivoire was in fact a territory of conquest for three great peoples of West Africa, whose expansion took place at the expense of the area's indigenous inhabitants.

Coming from the west, forest peoples belonging to the Kru ethnic group pushed back the members of the southern Mande group, whose split gave birth to the Dan Yacouba and the Guro. Continuing their progress eastwards, the Kru later would come up against the Baoule, who made them retreat back to the west bank of the Bandama river.

Coming from the former Ashanti kingdom in what is now Ghana, the Baoule and their relations (Agni, Abe, Aki, etc.), who are all Akan and belong to the great Kwa group, conquered all central and southeastern parts of the present-day Ivory Coast, pushing back the Kulango to the north, and blocking the push by the Kru at the Bandama.

Originating in the Sahel and the Sudanese savannas to the north, the Malinke, who belong to the northern branch of the Mande (or Mandingo), exerted a double pressure. To the south, they threatened the Dan and the Guro, caught between them and the Kru. To the east, their push was at the expense of the Senufo.

Contrary to what some affirm, here as elsewhere, the ethnic groups have proven to be neither "inventions" nor "creations" of colonialism.

Map XXIV: Côte d'Ivoire: A Territory of Conquest (16th – 19th Centuries)

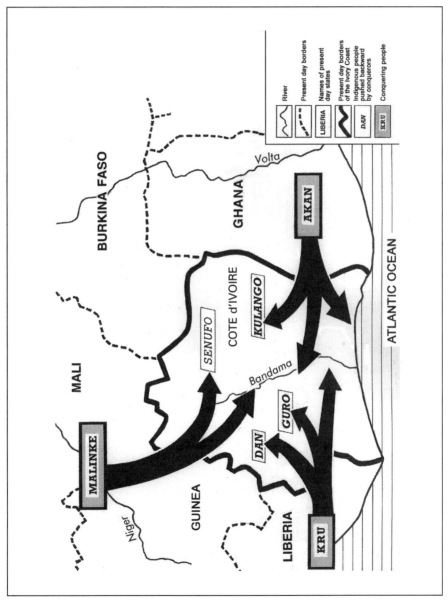

Gbagbo would serve as both a guarantor of democratic fair play and an easy sparring partner.

The presidential ballot of October 22, 2000 was thus devoid of any significance. Ouattara represented at least 45 percent of the votes: those of the Voltaic peoples (about 30 percent of the Ivorian population) and the northern Mande (about 17 percent). President Bédié, or any other official Baoule candidate, would have been assured of a good portion of the 25-30 percent of Akan/Baoule and related peoples. Between them, those two candidates would have thus carried at least 70 percent of the vote, which just about equaled the number of abstentions. In the "pro-Ouattara" and "pro-Bédié" ethnic zones, abstention was high, while in the west of Côte d'Ivoire, the Dan zones of General Guei, and the Kru/Bete areas of Laurent Gbagbo, participation reached almost 100 percent. Ethnicity was clearly a key factor.

With only 60 percent of the votes cast Laurent Gbagbo won these elections by default, although barely 30 percent of those registered actually voted. The ethnic count of these votes was easy to calculate: 10 percent of Yacouba/Dan/Guro who voted for General Guei and 12 to 15 percent of Kru/Bete. To the latter should be added about 5 percent of Socialist voters, who were members of other ethnic groups but gave their votes to Laurent Gbagbo anyway. The latter's election was hailed by the French Socialist government of Prime Minister Lionel Jospin. The new president was installed in power, but his legitimacy was entirely "relative." Is this really democracy?

At the end of September 2002, a military rebellion seized half of the country. Côte d'Ivoire was cut in two. The partition had already been a reality in peoples' minds for several months. No federating potential existed any longer because all the great political forces in the country are ethnic and regional, and to a lesser degree, religious in nature. Today, the great traditional north-south cleavage between the Sahelian world and the coastal or forest world is more present than ever. The news thus confirms geography and history.

Because of its ethnic diversity, this crisis will leave traces despite any superficial, temporary fixes.

There are four solutions, which would account for these facts:

– The creation of an artificial government of national unity, which would not resolve the crisis in depth, but would act as a temporary fix.

– The imposition of strong ethnic-regional power on the other ethnic-regional components, a solution that ignores the "democratic diktat."

– The acceptance of a reality: Côte d'Ivoire has ceased to exist and partition has become a necessity. (Even though it must also account for an ancient southern fracture between the Kru/Bete and the Akan/Baoule)

– Lastly, a regional reorganization involving the breakup of the frontiers of Côte d'Ivoire, Burkina Faso and Liberia, which would allow the birth of three new states: a Kru grouping, a Baoule grouping, and a "northern" entity.

A second example is that of Liberia, where three great ethnic groups are present: the Kru, the Mande, and the Mel, whose population distribution we do not know with certainty. (Map XXV) The Kru live in the south and east of the country. They are divided into six tribes: the Krahn, the Grebo, the Kru, the Bassa, the De, and the Kwa. The Krahn (four to six percent of Liberia's population) were in power during the presidency of Samuel Doe (1980-1990). He took control from the descendants of black colonizers, the freed slaves who came from the United States in the early and mid-nineteenth century.

The Mande belong to one of the principal West African groups, spreading across Senegal, Guinea, Mali, and Côte d'Ivoire. In Liberia, the Mande occupy the north. They are divided into northern and southern branches, as well as seven tribes: the Loma, the Gbandi, the Bandi, the Kpelle, the Mano, the Gio, and the Vai. The current president, Charles Taylor,[1] is a Gio and his party, the National Patriotic Front of Liberia (NPFL) recruits essentially from his tribe as well as from the Mano (southern Mande). The Mano and the Gio are related to the Yacouba/Dan.[2] And lastly, the Mel live astride the frontiers of Guinea, Sierra Leone, and Liberia.

An ethnic war broke out in Liberia on December 24, 1989 between the Krahn (Kru group), and the Mano, who were allied with the Gio (both belonging to the Mande group). The regional contagion was immediate

---

[1] Ousted since this text was written.

[2] The ethnic group of General Guei, the ephemeral head of state (by putsch) of the Côte d'Ivoire, assassinated at the end of September 2002. In December 2002, Gio and Mano combatants from Liberia came to the aid of their cousins, the Yacouba/Dan in the Côte d'Ivoire, thus internationalizing even more the Ivorian ethnic war.

Map XXV: Languages and Peoples of Liberia

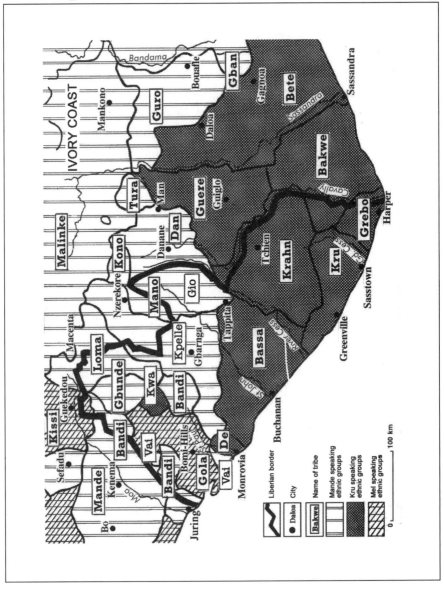

because the Krahn are related to the Bete in Côte d'Ivoire, where they currently hold power through Laurent Gbagbo. At the time, however, Côte d'Ivoire was directed by the Baoule, who supported the Mano and the Gio to weaken the Kru/Bete, who were opposed to President Houphouët-Boigny.

Since 1997, when Charles Taylor became president, a Gio (Mande group) has been in power, but the conflict hasn't ceased. The Liberian war has caused over 200,000 deaths to date in a population of only two and a half million inhabitants and exiled over a million refugees. The departure of Charles Taylor in 2003 did not end the conflict.

In Guinea, three great ethnic groups make up 89 percent of the population:

Ethnic Distribution of Guinea

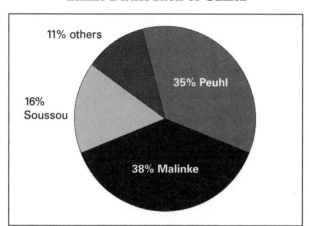

Since the 1950s, the Peuhl and the Malinke, who are nearly equal in size have competed for power, leaving the Soussou in the role of onlookers.

Independence in 1958 was obtained by Sekou Touré, a Malinke. It permitted his group to monopolize power for their own benefit, while persecuting the Peuhl to the point of "ethnocide." In 1984, the death of the dictator created an immense political vacuum. Guinea was on the brink of civil war and of breaking up into homogeneous ethnic zones.

While the potential successors to Sekou Touré were tearing one another apart, power slipped away from the Malinke. In order to fill the void, a putsch brought Colonel Lansana Conté, the country's highest-ranking officer, to power. This member of the Soussou group was acceptable to both factions. The Malinke understood that they needed to allow time for the excesses of the previous regime to be forgotten. The Peuhl, broken by three decades of persecution, needed time to rebuild their strength. For the Malinke Peuhl, Lansana Conté, was no more than an interim president. But he managed to get promoted to general, hung on to power and even succeeded in keeping his powerful ethnic adversaries divided.

At the end of 1999, the contagion of the conflicts in Liberia and Sierra Leone touched Guinea. War broke out in the east, where related populations live on both sides of the artificial frontiers inherited from colonization.

Nigeria

Nigeria is another ethnic mosaic. Its 923,000 sq kilometers (356,000 sq. miles) make it a giant of a country and its demographic weight is such that its very existence unbalances the entire western part of the continent. With 120 million people, one in five Africans living south of the Sahara is Nigerian.

On paper, Nigeria seems homogeneous. However, it constitutes an incred-

Ethnic Distribution of Nigeria

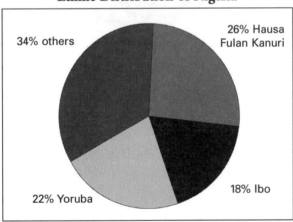

34% others

26% Hausa Fulan Kanuri

22% Yoruba

18% Ibo

ible human puzzle. It is composed of dozens of different peoples who have never shared an ounce of common destiny. Nature and history have combined to merge three great areas, each dominated by a large population group:

– In the north is a group comprising the Hausa, the Fulani, and the Kanuri. It is Muslim and has a strong warrior tradition. The Hausa/Fulani/Kanuri constitute a vast grouping, even if they are linguistically different. Prior to colonization, they were organized in powerful empires, and their traditional chiefs, including the Emir of Kano and the Sultan of Sokoto, are still very influential. The Hausa/Fulani/Kanuri control the Nigerian army, and thus power, even if they happen to "delegate" it to southerners, as is currently the case with President Obansanjo, a Yoruba.

– In the southeast, the Ibo are mostly Christian. Following their attempted secession from the rest of Nigeria in 1967-1970 the terrible Biafran war took place. The victory of the northerners left Biafra defeated, and the Ibo lost any political role. Thereafter northerners monopolized power.

– In the southwest are the Yoruba.

Besides these north-south ethnic divisions there is a significant religious question between Muslims and Christians, which has exacerbated regional tensions tragically illustrated recently on the occasion of the election of "Miss World 2002."

In each of these regions, the three principal confederations of ethnic groups,[1] have imposed their power on multiple "small" ethnic groups comprising in all between 30 and 40 percent of the population. Prior to independence in 1960, these "small" ethnic groups were worried. Local autonomy, guaranteed by British "indirect rule," was going to be taken away by the three internal groups as the main groups sought to establish power over the country.

The constitutional demands being made at the time were contradictory. The "Big Three" wanted a maximum decentralization of power in order to exercise tight control in their respective zones of influence. But the "small" ethnic groups preferred reinforcement of federal power in the hopes of finding a counterweight to the regional hegemony of the dominant ethnic groups. When they failed to obtain satisfaction, they were excluded from a political game that from

---

[1] The "Big Three" as they are called by the Nigerian press.

Map XXVI: The Three Great
Ethnic Groups of Nigeria

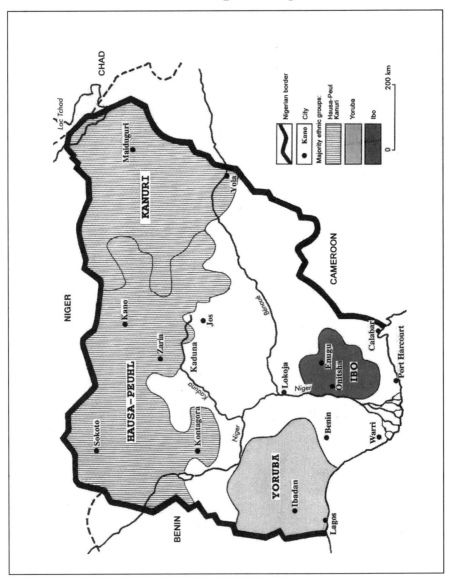

then on would have only three players.

Today, northerners hunt down southerners, while the latter expel northerners from their regions. Each day sees an ethnic regrouping in Nigeria. This may foreshadow great regional tragedies and perhaps even a territorial partition.

The Kongo Bloc

The peripheries of the so-called "Kongo Bloc," are also a real powder keg. Angola, the Democratic Republic of the Congo (DRC), and Congo (Brazzaville) have interlinked population problems. The regional stakes there are complicated by the fact that this region is a major producer of oil.

The Angolan nation does not exist. A Portuguese colonial creation, Angola brings together in an immense area of peoples divided by language, culture, and history. Its ethnic regions are not integrated by the national administrative overlay.

The majority of the population is linked to three great ethnic groups:

– In the north, the Bakongo are part of the Congo bloc which spills over into the DRC and Congo (Brazzaville).

– On the coast and in the center, the Kimbundu are in power in Luanda, associated with a mixed race group.

– In the south, the Ovimbundu, led by Jonas Savimbi and UNITA, were engaged in a "thirty years war," against the central government from 1975 to 2002. The death of Savimbi in 2002 and the military defeat of UNITA that followed have changed the balance of power, but the ethnic reality that was at the root of the conflict remains.

In Congo (Brazzaville), democracy had naturally benefited the most numerous group. That was how, in 1992, the Ngbaka, whose tribes constitute 48 percent of the population, gained the upper hand over the M'Bochi who only make up 13 percent. In October 1997, however, the M'Bochi under General Sassou Nguesso retook by force the power they had lost five years earlier in the election.

The Kingdoms of the Cow and the Spear

Throughout the Interlakes region of eastern Africa, the cow and the spear dominated over the hoe and the granaries. Here, cattle were regarded as sacred.

Map XXVII: The Three Principal
Ethnic Groups of Angola

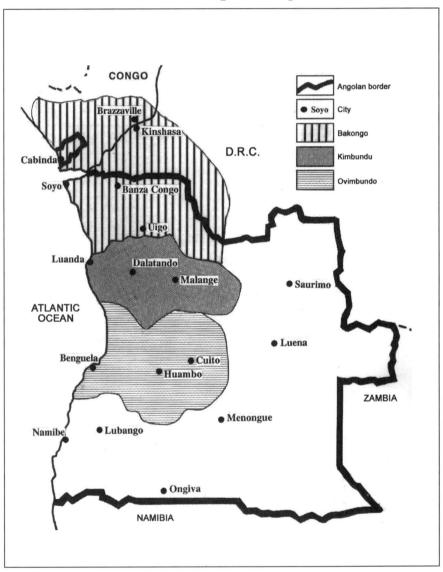

Politically, the kings did not reign over men but over herds; in Rwanda, even over "bovine armies." In the royal enclosure, a cowpat fire burned symbolizing the life of the monarch. When the king died, the fire was left to die before it was proclaimed that the "milk had been spilled."

In the pre-colonial period, this region was organized into several states. From north to south, the principal ones were Bunyoro, Toro, Ankole, Buhaya, Karagwe, Rwanda, Burundi, and lastly, Buha. All these kingdoms were led by tall herdsmen observing the same aristocratic, pastoral, and warlike values.[1]

Rwanda constituted an exception because it is a centuries-old nation-state not divided into ethnic groups. Its two populations, the Tutsi (about 20 percent of the population) and the Hutu (about 80 percent) speak the same language and are conscious of belonging to a single, unique nation. As has been noted above, their differences are not ethnic but "racial."

These two different populations have preserved their morphotypical characteristics. The idealized version of the Tutsi can be seen in artistic portrayals, with slim waists, fine features, and elongated heads.

The ideology at the root of the social, political, economic and military domination of the Tutsi is based on "racial" values. Even if the boundaries between rich Hutu, owners of cattle, and the poorer Tutsi, without cattle, are sometimes blurred, membership in one group or the other is irreversible, and the separation of the two populations is as definite as sex. The genetic differences revealed by Excoffier,[2] already mentioned, underline this social reality. Can one seriously claim, as Jean-Pierre Chrétien does, that these social, historical, and genetic differences were introduced by colonization?

At the same time, they melted together with the Hutu into one political and national mold created by the Tutsi monarchy. For this kingdom, independence in 1962 was traumatic. The minority Tutsi elite had to abandon power to the Hutu because they were outnumbered. Massacres of Tutsi by the new Hutu government occurred periodically in 1961, 1963, and 1973. In 1994, a genocide took place. Having no chance of returning to power democratically, the Tutsi took it by force the same year.

---

[1] For further information, see Lugan, B., *History of Rwanda from Prehistoric Times to the Present*, Paris, 1997.
[2] Op cit., 1987.

Burundi, Rwanda's fraternal twin, is another of the states in the Interlakes region created by the Tutsi pastoral minority. As in Rwanda, the "cow and the spear" dictated their law over the "hoe and the soil," that is to say, the Hutu majority. Pre-colonial Burundi was, however, different from Rwanda in several ways. The kingdom of Burundi was never as centralized. Perhaps this was because the Tutsi are divided into two distinct and often opposing groups here. One might characterize some as "great Tutsi." They are similar to those in Rwanda and created the Urundi state. They live mainly in the north of the country. The Hima or "little Tutsi" are installed in the south, mainly in Bututsi (the Bururi area), and they represent the last Nilotic migratory wave to arrive in the region around the 15th and 16th centuries. The northern Tutsi consider them somewhat rustic "cousins."

The kingdom of Urundi took the name Burundi on November 28, 1966. The mwami,[1] Ntare V was deposed by Colonel Micombero. Micombero was a Hima (southern Tutsi) who established a republican regime and tried to avoid an imminent Hutu revolution. However, at the beginning of 1972, a violent Hutu uprising took place in southern Burundi. The army restored order by instituting severe reprisals. In 1988 and in 1993, new massacres of Tutsi occurred in the north and center of the country, the survivors retreated to Bujumbura, which became a city with a Tutsi majority.

On August 28, 2000, a peace agreement sponsored by Presidents Clinton and Mandela, was signed at Arusha in Tanzania. It was supposed to conclude the civil war, but it did not end the fighting. Since then, new power-sharing agreements between Tutsi and Hutu have been signed. In Rwanda, similar pacts were concluded a few months before the genocide of 1994.

Today, the deadlock is total. The Tutsi army cannot hold Burundi alone, while the Hutu are unable to defeat them. Trapped in its dogma of democratic power-sharing, the international community is demanding that the Burundi army become "bi-ethnic." This leaves no alternative for the Tutsi but to be massacred or to partition Burundi. Democratic power-sharing is an idle fancy, and the only option seems to be the constitution of a Hutuland and a Tutsiland. In other words, either partition or genocide.

[1] King.

Map XXVIII: Ethiopia and Its Peripheries

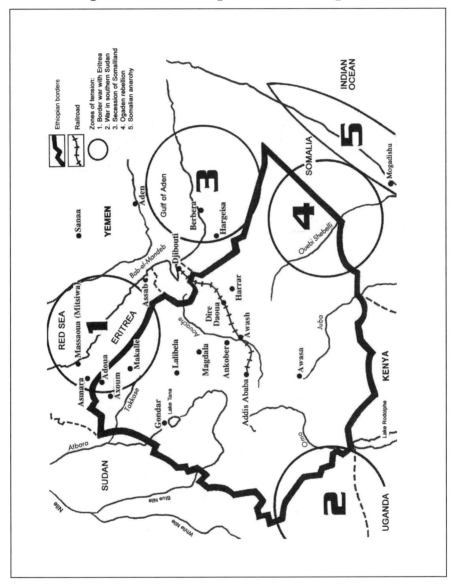

193

The Peoples of the Horn

Ethiopia is another mosaic nation composed of more than 70 ethnic groups. The entire history of the country flows from this reality, swinging between the desire to maintain the cohesion of the whole entity and the aspirations of the peripheries to win autonomy. (See Map XXVIII) Geographically, the country has always been unstable also. It has either expanded into the peripheral regions in the direction of the Red Sea and present-day Somalia (the Ogaden region), or it has ended up retreating to the central Amhara plateau, which constitutes the heart of the country.

Ethiopia is the dominant power in the Horn of Africa region. Or at least when it is strong and "united." Since the Negus[1] Haile Selassie I was deposed in 1974, it no longer plays the role of regional "policeman." Moreover, the country, already dismembered by Eritrean independence, is now threatening to break up completely. An important result of Eritrea's independence has been the loss of Ethiopia's sole access to the sea.

Somalia's situation is different from that of Ethiopia, because the opposition there is not ethnic but tribal and even clannish. With the exception of several thousand descendants of black slaves, all the inhabitants belong to the Somali ethnic group. They are divided into tribes, clans, and sub-clans, and occupy a vast part of the Horn of Africa. The Somali tribes can be classified into three groups. The colonial frontiers overlaid on the nomadic zones of these groups forced many Somalis to live outside the frontiers of Somalia. They were distributed among five territorial units: British Somaliland, the Northern District attached to Kenya, Ethiopian- and then Italian-ruled Ogaden, Italian Somalia, and French Somaliland. There, traditionally, their members had practiced a nomadic pastoralism.

After World War II, the British contemplated the idea of reuniting the Somali population within a single state. The so-called "Bevin plan," would have allowed the constitution of a "Great Somalia" assembling British Somaliland, former Italian Somalia, and the Ogaden. But the project was aborted due to the opposition of Ethiopia, and only British Somaliland and Somalia were merged creating the present-day borders of Somalia. But the idea of a "Great Somalia"

---

[1] Emperor.

The Somali Tribes

```
                          ┌─────────┐
                          │  Darod  │
                          └─────────┘
   ┌──────────┬──────────────┼──────────────┬──────────┐
┌────────┐ ┌───────────┐ ┌─────────────┐ ┌──────────┐ ┌────────────┐
│Ogadeni │ │Warsangali │ │ Dhulbahante │ │ Maheran  │ │ Majertein  │
└────────┘ └───────────┘ └─────────────┘ └──────────┘ └────────────┘

                      ┌─────────┐
                      │  Saab   │
                      └─────────┘
               ┌──────────┴──────────┐
          ┌───────────┐         ┌──────────┐
          │ Rahawein  │         │  Dighil  │
          └───────────┘         └──────────┘

                   ┌─────────┐
                   │  Irir   │
                   └─────────┘
        ┌──────────────┼──────────────┐
   ┌──────────┐  ┌──────────┐   ┌──────────┐
   │ Hawlyé   │  │  Issak   │   │   Dir    │
   └──────────┘  └──────────┘   └──────────┘
                           ┌──────────┴──────────┐
                      ┌──────────┐         ┌─────────────┐
                      │  Issa    │         │ Gadaboursi  │
                      └──────────┘         └─────────────┘
```

would haunt Somali nationalists who saw it as the means of escape from tribal demons (Map XXIX).

Independent Somalia was soon torn by tribalism, and its parliamentary regime amplified the divisions; each tribe, each clan, and every sub-clan had its own political party. For less than five million inhabitants, 90 parties were registered.

The first president, Aden Abdullah Osman, was succeeded by Ali Shermake, who was assassinated on October 15, 1969. The head of the army, General Siyad Barre then took power. He was a Darod-born member of the Marehan tribe. Aware of the country's divisions, he undertook a vigorous policy of de-tribalization. To put an end to what he considered a scourge, he found a remedy in Somali nationalism. The country's flag was given a star with five branches that symbolized the aspiration to regroup all Somalis, both those living in Somalia and those in Ethiopian Ogaden, Kenya, and Djibouti.

Map XXIX: The Somali Tribes

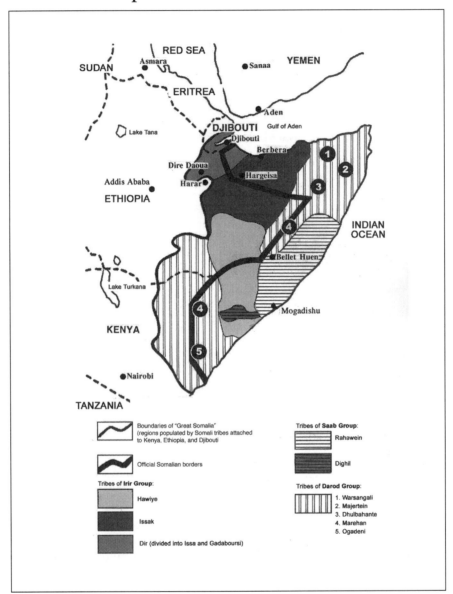

Boundaries of "Great Somalia"
(regions populated by Somali tribes attached
to Kenya, Ethiopia, and Djibouti

Official Somalian borders

Tribes of **Irir Group**:

Hawiye

Issak

Dir (divided into Issa and Gadaboursi)

Tribes of **Saab Group**:

Rahawein

Dighil

Tribes of **Darod Group**:

1. Warsangali
2. Majertein
3. Dhulbahante
4. Marehan
5. Ogadeni

Under Siyad Barre, Somalia, previously pro-Western, turned towards the Soviet bloc, which wanted to gain a foothold in this geographically strategic zone. In exchange, Somalia received sizable quantities of arms allowing Barre to launch the Ogaden war.

In the meantime, the Ethiopian revolution had brought down the monarchy there, replacing it with a socialist regime. For Siyad Barre's regime, fortune had turned. The USSR chose to anchor its regional presence in an old state, Ethiopia, rather than in the nascent Somalia. It reversed its alliances, abandoning Mogadishu in favor of Addis Ababa. The offensive by the Somali army in Ogaden was blocked by the Ethiopian forces of Colonel Megistu, thanks to the support of his new Soviet ally. "Great Somalia" would never come into being. Moreover, once this myth vanished, tribal realities reasserted themselves with even greater force than before.

More and more challenged, the president saw his power slipping away, and he was now forced to seek support from tribalism. Soon, the government was designated as MOD, signifying Marehan, Ogadeni, and Dhulbahante, the three Darod tribes at the center of power. All the posts in the government, the military, and the police force were given to members of these three tribes, which led to a military rebellion by disgruntled Majertein officers. The repression was severe, and the Darod tribes began a merciless war among themselves.

At the end of a generalized conflict, which saw the breakup of ancient tribal coalitions, the powerful tribe of the Hawiye (Irir family) allied with the Majertein and Ogadeni (Darod family) defeated the Marehan, the regime's last defenders. President Siyad Barre was overthrown on January 27, 1991, and two Hawiye clans, the Abgal and the Habar Gedir (or Habr Gedir) clashed.

Ali Mahdi Mohammed, chief of the Abgal clan undertook, first of all, to clear Mogadishu of his former Majertein and Ogadeni allies. Then he entered into a war against the Habar Gedir clan, led by "General" Mohamed Farah Aidid. A famine that was devastating Somalia at this time served as a pretext for the unfortunate American intervention that took place in December 1992.

The Somali civil war continued to rage and on August 1, 1996, Aidid was killed in the fighting, only to be succeeded by his son Hussein Aidid. At the end of 1996, the chiefs of 26 Somali factions agreed to a transitional government. In December 1997, they also agreed to a conference of all the Somali clans elements but, after several delays, that project was abandoned. Since then, a number of other attempts at an accord have failed, and the fighting has never ceased.

With a surface area of 2.6 million square kilometers (one million square miles), the Sudan is theoretically one vast African state, but the geography, history, and settlement of its peoples distinguish two Sudans:

– Geographically, North Sudan is a desert, and life there is a "gift from the Nile." It faces the Arabian Peninsula and the Mediterranean, and shelters 21 of the 28 million Sudanese in an area of 1.9 million square kilometers (730,000 square miles). Politically and religiously, northern Sudan belongs to the Islamic world and is attempting to impose its law in the south, which refuses this imposition.

– South Sudan has shrubby or semi-luxuriant vegetation, because water is present. Its populations are "African" and not Arab. They are Nilotics related to those of Uganda and the whole pastoral world of East Africa. There are seven million inhabitants, of which 40 percent are Christians, 2/3 of them Catholics.

Not only is the Sudan cut in two geographically, it is also divided between the "white Islamic" and the black world, as one moves south. In the Sudan, the question is not ethnic, but racial, and pits white Muslim Arabs against black Christian or animist Nilotics. The British colonizers had recognized the peculiarity of South Sudan which it placed under a special administration in order to protect the populations against Muslim expansionism. However, after independence was awarded in 1956, British protection vanished, and the pre-colonial Arab Islamic push south resumed. Since 1963, the southerners have been at war with the northern government over Islamization.

This resistance of the south has weakened the Sudanese state, since Islam is the nation's only unifying factor. For years now, peace accords are regularly signed, but they have not been respected in practice, and partition seems the only solution. But the Sudanese government cannot envisage that because oil reserves have been found in the south.

The Truth About the Creation of the Merinas

The "Big Island" of Madagascar presents great geographical diversity between the eastern coast, with its tropical luxuriance, the desert-like savannas of the west, and the central highlands, the heart of the Malagasy state. It was there that men from distant Asia, beginning in the eighth century AD, transplanted the civilization. The current population resulted from this meeting of two peoples, one coming from Indonesia, and the other from Africa.

At the end of the 16th century the Merina (or Imerina) kingdom emerged, from the union of various ethnically related small principalities whose populations descended from Indonesian migrants. At the beginning of the 19th century, the kingdom extended its authority beyond the original zone of the central plateau. In the 1890s, it controlled about 2/3 of the island of Madagascar.

This imperialist policy provoked opponents, including the Sakalave. As we saw earlier, several of their chiefs placed themselves under the protection of France in the 1840s to escape from Merina rule. Madagascar as a whole became a French protectorate in 1896. The monarchy was abolished, and the Merina state destroyed. Colonization was not responsible for creating ethnic groups here. However, it did change the balance of forces that managed them.

In 1956, the French Loi-cadre, or Framing Law, instituted universal suffrage. This changed the political situation of the island because the more numerous Cotiers (meaning people of the coast), gained power. The 1958 elections were won by the Parti Social Démocrate de Madagascar, whose leader was Philibert Tsiranana, a Cotier schoolteacher from the northwest, who belonged to the Tsimihety ethnic group. The Merina party, the Parti du Congrès de l'Indépendance (AFKM in the indigenous language) was beaten. It was a revolution. The formerly dominant Merina came under the authority of the Cotiers. In Madagascar, as in many other regions of Africa, colonization gave the advantage to the former losers, thus provoking profound upheavals.

Madagascar obtained its independence on June 26, 1960, and Philibert Tsirinana became President of the Malagasy Republic. However, the Merina were only waiting to retake power. The occasion to do so arrived in May 1972, at the time of the "student revolt" in the capital, Tananarive (now called Antananarivo). Urged on by the Merina elites, the students destabilized President Tsirinana, who turned power over to the army's chief of staff, General Gabriel Ramanantsoa, a Merina born of a Tananarive aristocratic family and a former colonel in the French army. Order was restored, but Madagascar chose a revolutionary nationalist path from then on.

The balance of power thus tilted back in favor of the Merina. This exasperated the Cotiers. A schism began in the army, whose higher-ranking officers were Merinas. A military mutiny took place on December 31, 1974 in a camp at the capital. Although it was suppressed, the divisions within the army forced General Ramanantsoa to transfer power on February 5, 1972 to his Minister of the Interior, Colonel Richard Ratsimandrava, a Tananarive Merina of servile origin. He was assassinated on February 11. On June 15, the Provisional Military Directorate, which had taken control, designated as president a naval commander, Didier Ratsiraka, a Cotier from the Tamatave (present-day Toamasina) region and a member of the Betsimisaraka ethnic group.

Re-elected as head of state in 1982 and 1989, Didier Ratsiraka committed Madagascar to a socialist path and ruined his country. But having returned to power by the ballot box again, he was driven out in 2002, following a turbulent electoral campaign. His challenger, Marc Ravalomanana, a Merina and the mayor of Antananarivo, proclaimed himself the winner before the end of the official count. Today, there is still considerable agitation and renewed exacerbation of ethnic tensions between the Cotiers and the Merinas.

* * *

Based on the cases we have just seen, it is impossible to claim that the ethnic differences in Africa are the result of colonialism. Yet that is precisely what Jean-Louis Amselle, research director at the French École des Hautes Études en Sciences Sociales [EHESS - School of Advanced Studies in Social Sciences], Editor in Chief of the review, *Cahiers d'Études Africaines,* and one of the leading figures in the school of "paradigm historians," persists in doing. He was not afraid to write in 2002 that:

> [. . .] one is justified in wondering if the tribal characteristics imputed to Africa are not veritable projections of Europe upon exotic societies, a projection destined to comfort, by purification or elimination, its own identity. This projection of Europe, carried out at the time of colonization, has indeed had an impact because it contributed in the shaping of the ethnic groups of this continent, hardening them, so that once the colonizer withdrew, these new tribal forms were launched in an assault against the African state apparatuses. This colonial tribalism [. . .] thus constituted [. . .] a time bomb whose effects are still being felt in Liberia, Sierra Leone, the Sudan, Ethiopia and Eritrea, Rwanda, and in the two Congos.[1]

As long as the human reality of Africa is denied with such blindness by ideologues, it will obviously be impossible to propose concrete solutions to the Africans. In the face of glaringly obvious ethnic phenomena, the manipulators of history show themselves to be the worthy heirs of Jean-Jacques Rousseau, who, at the beginning of his *Discourse on the Origin of Inequality* wrote:

> Let us begin then by laying facts aside, as they do not affect the question.

---

[1] J.L. Amselle, "L'Afrique, un Parc à Thèmes" [Africa: A Theme Park], in *Les Temps Modernes, [Modern Times]*, Nos. 620-621 (Aug.-Nov. 2002), p. 49.

Chapter VIII

False Answers to the Africa Question

Europeans, Africans, and Americans all approach the question of Africa with an accumulation of complexes. They are blocked from taking into account the realities of sub-Saharan Africa that are dragging it into the abyss.

European Anxiety, African Schizophrenia, and American Neuroses

Because Europeans have a guilty conscience, they have let themselves be persuaded that they depopulated Africa with the slave trade, then plundered it during the colonial period. They are thus convinced that they must repair their wrongdoings. In seeking forgiveness, they have condemned themselves to carrying the continent's burdens. The first people who are responsible for this false analysis are the researchers and academics, the "paradigm historians," who monopolize African studies in a number of countries, and particularly in France, both within the CNRS and in EHESS, where recruitment takes place through a sort of doctrinal endogamy.

At the risk of repetition, it is important to note that "Westernized" Africans have fully understood all the benefits they can derive from victimization, and they have set up business using the incapacitating myths that prevent the white world from looking reality in the face. They are past masters in the art of turning the guilt complexes of Europeans, the political naivety of white Americans, and the frustrations of African Americans to their own advantage.

Thus, they have persuaded themselves, before persuading the naive elsewhere, that, if Africa remains underdeveloped it is because the Atlantic slave trade emptied it of its substance, because Europe built its industrial revolution on the profits from that trade (thus enriching itself at Africa's expense), and because colonization plundered the continent.

Americans, although born in the dominant nation of the world today, also find it impossible to adopt a realistic approach to Africa. The electoral weight of their African-American population is too heavy, and its political influence is too great. African Americans have an idealized vision of the continent "of their roots," and a perception of the white world that is founded on resentment.

The reality is that African Americans are descended from black men and women who were sold long ago to European slave traders by other Blacks. However, they continue to reject this reality in favor of the myths promoted by Afrocentrists like Cheikh Anta Diop or of Martin Bernal. They seek refuge in a "counter-history" which exascerbates their frustrations and allows them to avoid addressing the real problems.

In doing so, they demonstrate eloquently that they have remained "true" Africans. Like their brothers and sisters who remained behind on the ancestral lands, they deny problems and refuse to look reality in the face. They produce African-American versions of those masks and dances that permit Africans to find release from the real world, such as gospel music and rap. But also, and more frequently, they take refuge in the writings of those who have forged a fictitious history aimed at them, with its frequent references to the "Golden Age" of a pre-colonial Africa, before its harmony was broken by the Whites.

The behavior of the white American elite with respect to African problems seems to stem mainly for a need for moral and philosophical conformity. But it also reveals a deeper sentiment, one that has not yet been really admitted in public, even if a number of leaders no longer fear to address it in private. It concerns a desire to keep the ideal of the "melting pot" alive despite evidence that points to its passing.

To many observers, it seems that the unity of the American nation is crumbling a little more each day. A proliferation of phenomena indicates that the United States is fragmenting into communities of different racial, ethnic, and linguistic groups. These groups have little in common and they function outside the federal system, except where social welfare benefits are concerned.

The only common denominators are philosophical — the concepts of God and "universal democracy." It is doubtful that this fragile cement can hold together such an ethnic and racial mix much longer.

The fragmentation of the U.S. is occurring at a rapid rate. While the Civil Rights movement at the beginning of the 1960s was based on a positive desire for integration of the whole, its later evolution, in the form of "affirmative action," dealt a blow to the founding values of America. Introduced by President Lyndon B. Johnson in 1965, this notion has led to minorities placing their pre-occupations, their preferences, and their choices in ethnic, religious, and sexual matters above national needs and, ultimately, above the very concept of the nation itself. A system that had worked from 1820 to 1960, when 85 percent of immigrants were Europeans originating from the same basic matrix in terms of ethnicity and civilization, became impossible as soon as the country began to receive bigger and bigger waves of immigrants from Latin America and Asia, on top of the existing African-American population. Since the 1960s, the newest immigrants are actually 50 percent Latin American and almost 40 percent Asian.

Neither African Americans nor more recent immigrants are demanding fusion but instead want to maintain identities based on ethnic roots. This ethnic shift and the rise of diverse communities have turned the United States from a "melting pot" into a "salad bowl," a kind of mixed vegetable dish in which the mayonnaise won't set.[1] In this way, they have created ghettos for themselves in which they can watch "black" television, go to "black" schools and universities, seek a professional future in "black" companies," be buried in "black" cemeteries.

With great lucidity, President Clinton indeed recognized this new situation, when, on June 13, 1998, before students at the University of Portland, he declared:

In a little more than 50 years from now, there will no longer be a [white] racial majority in the United States.

---

[1] Translator's note: A "typically French" mixed culinary metaphor!

Moreover, the founding values of the United States, which were built on the importance of the individual, regardless of origin or color, have died because of affirmative action. The European immigrants who disembarked at New York wanted to forget their past misery and be absorbed, through their work and their sense of enterprise, into the new nation. Individual success was proposed as a model confirmed by religion. But values that suited Europeans could only offend a black community, separated by their history and their resentments towards Whites.

As they became aware of their electoral strength in the context of the American two-party system, African Americans gradually transformed their demands for integration into a philosophy of separation. The latter resulted in affirmative action and political correctness.

The appearance of these sentiments, although invented in the name of equality, are profoundly anti-egalitarian. They recognize an obvious fact: that people are different, even in the United States of America, and grand speeches will not change human nature.

This was a mental revolution whose consequences still have not been measured fully but which has led to a result that is both surprising and strange. At first, so that certain groups might elevate themselves, its members were favored by facilitating their access to levels of education or training that they would not have reached by merit alone. Then, when that proved insufficient, it became necessary to slow, and thus to penalize, the individual careers of those from communities reputed to be "favored" or "not in danger." Egalitarianism, pushed to a paroxysm, thus resulted in a profoundly inegalitarian philosophy, in the name of good intentions, of social justice, and of anti-segregation.

It led to a major shift in the American educational system. Historically, American society has been pulled upwards by its best performing sectors — elites being created in part through its academic institutions. With affirmative action, a choice had to be made:

– On the one hand, the level of the best institutions could have been lowered so that all the new "communities" would have access to them through the policy of racial quotas. But this risked ruining the motor of research, and in the short term, the country's economy.

– Or, on the other hand, the competitiveness of elitist education could be maintained, while allowing the development, outside the competitive circuit, of universities adapted to the communities finding it difficult to integrate upwards.

It is the second solution that was chosen. As a result, many second- and third-rate universities were abandoned by Americans of European and Asian origins to their black fellow citizens. These are the intellectual "ghettos" where many black "historians" have undertaken to rewrite the past. And it was here, too, that Afrocentrism was born. Terrorized and disarmed by the idea of being treated as "racists," WASP's have allowed these myths to become reality.

The New American Awareness

Despite occasional realism, the global American approach refuses to take into account the specifics of the African situation. For the United States, in Africa as elsewhere, the liberal economic model is the universal solution.

Present in certain parts of the continent during the Cold War era, notably in the former Zaire,[1] in Angola and in the region of the Horn, the United States neglected the rest of sub-Saharan Africa for a long time. It was only at the end of the 1980s that the Americans seemed to "rediscover" the black continent, and their diplomacy then had some brilliant successes, essentially in southern Africa where it was directly involved in the origin of the "global settlement" of the Namibian question. Washington was effectively the "godfather" of the regional accord that led to both the retreat of South Africa from Southwest Africa (present-day Namibia) and thus to its independence in 1990 and the withdrawal of Cuban troops from Angola.[2]

The Africa that the Americans approached then was a rather quaint world in which classic diplomatic definitions could still be applied. Their partners in discussions were South African or Soviet diplomats who spoke their language and reasoned the same way they did. The situation would be different in Somalia, as they learned at their own expense.

---

[1] Today the Democratic Republic of the Congo (DRC).
[2] Quadripartite accords of New York in 1988 between the USA, USSR, Cuba, and South Africa.

In that country, the wars of tribal or clannish militias, mentioned above, had provoked an atrocious famine, and American public opinion, urged on by the media, became aroused. The cause was judged important by the White House, which engaged in some humanitarian overbidding.

In blind ignorance of local realities, President Bush Sr. decided that intervention was necessary to "return hope" to the Somali populations. There were warnings, but all of them useless, as no one managed to persuade the American president to renounce his philanthropic crusade, not even his Kenyan ambassador, who, being an expert on the region, declared in the form of a sally directed at his own country's leaders: *"If you liked Vietnam, you'll love Mogadishu."*

However, the ambassador was reprimanded. Nothing was supposed to tarnish the media show.

In December 1992, the United States, having wrested reluctant approval from the UN, intervened militarily in Somalia. Bush named his operation "Restore Hope." A new doctrine was even invented for these circumstances, called the "right of humanitarian interference."

An American expeditionary corps disembarked in a scene which, if even if not purely theatrical, received a blaze of media attention. A few weeks later, the "boys" had to open fire on those they were supposed to be helping and the first soldiers were killed. An American helicopter pilot was even lynched. For American public opinion, which, up until then, had been basking in the glow of good intentions, it was incomprehensible. The "Restore Hope" operation had turned into a nightmare, and a bloodbath, hissed at and spat upon by the people it was meant to save. The "Good Samaritans" had discovered, a little late in the day, that Somalia was a disconcerting place.

On May 4, 1993, the UN came to the United States' rescue by landing an additional 28,000 soldiers from other countries. On June 5, 23 Pakistani "blue helmets" were killed by "General" Aidid's militias. On June 12, an American commando failed in an attempt at reprisals against this Somali warlord. And finally, on October 3, 18 American soldiers were killed, and President Clinton, followed by the other Western governments, announced a military withdrawal.

In March 1994, in Nairobi, a reconciliation agreement was signed between the two Hawiye leaders, Aidid and Ali Mahdi Mohammed. But it resolved nothing. As of August, the state of anarchy was nearly total, with Ali Mahdi Mohammed's men controlling the north of Mogadishu, while Aidid's held the south. On August 22, seven Indian UN troops were killed.

The Americans had just become aware of their impotence. They had re-embarked their own troops, leaving behind in the Somali mess, replacements, that is, a UN contingent of Pakistani and Bengali soldiers whom the Somali militias transformed into live targets. It was a total fiasco.

On February 28, 1995, a new landing was required to extract those unfortunate troops who had been taken hostage. It was baptized Operation "Unified Shield." The UN thus left Somalia having suffered a stinging political and military defeat which had cost it 136 dead and 423 wounded troops. The Somali clans found themselves alone again and fought one another even harder.

For the United States, the Somali experience served as a lesson. From then on, there would be no question of direct military engagement, and any eventual intervention would have to be carried out by its allies: Nigeria and South Africa. Washington thought these two countries could provide the local partners to whom it could "subcontract" the continent's problems.

In this respect, it is important to see that the current desire for a pax americana stems from a well-understood principle of realpolitik. Profiting from Europe's effacement and the serious incompetence of French diplomacy undermined by 20 years of procrastination, the United States is trying to breathe life into a peace dynamic within the major zones of conflict in Africa, notably in the eastern Horn and in the DRC. Its status as the only remaining superpower favors this voluntarism because none of the belligerents can afford to go against the Americans' will. All of them thus agree to participate in negotiations, knowing perfectly well that the discussions will resolve none of the real underlying problems, and that in the end, they serve only to save face and win time.

Be that as it may, the American strategy is in conflict with its official moral and democratic principles which are nevertheless constantly reaffirmed. Thus, we find Washington supporting some quite undemocratic regimes (such as Museveni in Uganda, Kagame in Rwanda, and the archaic Dos Santos in Angola), because all these countries hold keys to regional conflicts. In the case of Angola, the interest of the United States is increased by the attraction of oil. By relying on these countries, the American goal is only to establish peace. Democracy will come after.

Regarding this point, one measures the great difference in method between Paris and Washington. For Paris, hamstrung by its principles, the prerequisite is still democracy, or in current jargon, "good governance." But for its part, Washington has not hesitated to show itself to be more realistic. Which explains its recent inroads on the continent.

To concretize its policy, the United States needs countries willing to act as deputies. South Africa was chosen because of the infrastructures inherited from the pre-1994 regime and the presence of white managers. As for Nigeria, it was retained for reason of its demographic size. For Washington, this latter country was intended to become the African counterpart of Turkey, and like Turkey, it was foreseen that Nigeria would play the role of regional or even continental policeman with proper supervision by American advisors. Illustrating this choice, American aid to Nigeria increased from $7 million in 1998, at the time of the military dictatorship, to $109 million in 2000. In August 2000, during his African tour, President Clinton stayed in Nigeria, where he obtained from his counterpart Olesungu Obasanjo, the rapid creation of a military force composed of five mechanized battalions. These eight to ten thousand men would be totally funded, equipped, and trained by Washington but placed at the disposal of the UN, which could intervene in place of the United States. The blood of American boys was too precious to be spilled in Africa. The Somali lesson had been retained.

Two great problems, however, limited this plan considerably: first was the weaknesses of South Africa, whose political, economic, and social situation has not ceased to deteriorate, growing closer to that of Third World countries each passing day. The country has also suffered from the emigration of its white population. To the extent that this has become a hemorrhage it has reduced the interest it represents for America.

Secondly, the chaotic situation in Nigeria has made any policy based on that country seem like an illusion. As was noted above, Nigeria is a profoundly divided and disintegrating country, on the brink of civil and religious war. This was masked in 2000 by the shared religious sentiments uniting Presidents Clinton and Obasanjo, both of whom are Baptists, but it remains the case.

The American "Liberal" Solution: "Trade Not Aid"

Aid to Africa has failed. To increase it even more would not provide any answers because it does not attack the root causes of the disease. The communist "models" have gone bankrupt and ruined those countries that tried them. The only apparent solutions left to potential donors are free-market liberal ones. And these have indeed been chosen by the United States with "Trade Not Aid" and by the Africans themselves with NEPAD. But they are still programs giving first priority to economic questions, and therefore doomed in advance to failure.

In 1976, in an effort to bolster U.S. trade with the Third World, the Generalized System of Preference (GSP) was adopted. It was accorded without reciprocity to all underdeveloped nations. With respect to the volumes of trade, however, this system was very restrictive, since it only applied to $1.6 billion worth of goods before customs duties, out of total imports worth more than $14 billion in 1999. In addition, this system was quite hypocritical because out of these $14 billion, $8 billion consisted of oil, $1.5 billion of various mineral ores, and only $580 million concerned African textiles.

In June 1997, under the direction of President Clinton, the U.S. defined a policy specially aimed at the black continent, called "Partnership for Growth in Africa." Its goal was to try to get the countries situated to the south of the Sahara to participate more fully in the world economy. To this end, it was thought advisable, first of all, to create a commercial partnership between the United States and this part of the continent—in order to escape from the impasse of the one-sided relations between donors and assisted. The solution that was devised involved stimulating African exports artificially. In the end, this method was similar to that applied to African-American students in order to facilitate their access to educational establishments. The African economies would, in their turn, benefit from a form of affirmative action.

In 1998, President Clinton made the first of his two visits to Africa. During this highly symbolic journey, he expressed the extent of Washington's interest in the continent. And in fact, the Americans did seem at that point to be paying closer attention to Africa.

It was about time since, Africa as a whole represented barely one percent of America's total foreign trade in 1998. Moreover, 2/3 of this one percent was oil alone. That same year, the principal exporters to the United States in sub-Saharan Africa were (in order of importance): Nigeria (oil), the Republic of South Africa (mining products), Angola, Gabon, and Congo; oil in all three cases. Two years later, unfortunately, the situation had hardly changed; 80 percent of American imports from Africa still consisted of oil, with diamonds and platinum comprising most of the rest.

With the exception of two or three countries, Africa south of the Sahara was absent from American economic preoccupations, an impression confirmed when we look at Aid to Developing Countries (ADC) allocated by the U.S. In 1999, American ADC was equivalent to one percent of the federal budget, or $13.3 billion. This was about the same as Japan's ADC and only half the amount given by France. Of this sum, $5 billion was allocated to Israel and Egypt. Sub-Saharan Africa as a whole received only $1 billion, barely six percent of the U.S. ADC. In 2000-2001, American ADC to Africa remained at the same level and reached just 6.2 percent of all U.S. ADC. And yet, all the members of the OCDE committed themselves to transfer each year ADC worth 0.7 percent of their GNP. In 1998, the United States gave only 0.1 percent compared to 0.9 percent for Norway, 0.8 percent for the Netherlands, 0.7 percent for Sweden, and 0.4 percent for France.

In May 2000, the fifth summit meeting of African and African-American leaders was held. It was jointly presided over by President Obasanjo of Nigeria and Reverend Leon Sullivan, an American civil rights activist. At the same time, the U.S. presidential elections were approaching and the pressure of 30 million African Americans was directed at the White House. The great majority of them are Democrats. To please them, the American government had already adopted, with an enthusiasm worthy of an adept in self-hypnosis, the concept of an "African Renaissance," which had already been outlined several years earlier by Nelson Mandela and his vice-president in the RSA, Thabo Mbeki.

Following this, the Clinton Administration also popularized the idea of "Trade Not Aid," accompanying this slogan with proposals to exempt from customs duties, under certain conditions, African textiles entering the American market. This was opposed by right-wing Republicans, including Senator Jesse Helms, who made himself their spokesman by declaring:

> *I don't think the commercial vocation of our country is to favor the economies of emerging countries to the detriment of American workers.*

The fear in certain American circles was that flooding the American market with products that had only transited through Africa could spell ruin for the American textile industry. On the other hand, the African-American leaders spoke up in favor of this measure, notably through the voice of Reverend Jesse Jackson, who affirmed:

> *[. . .] we do not see Africa as a continent in debt, but as a guarantee of America's future, and we should seize the chance to establish a real and lasting partnership.*

"The Trade not Aid" scheme rests on the Trade and Development Act, whose first section is the Africa Growth and Opportunity Act (AGOA),[1] according preferential treatment for textile and agricultural imports from sub-Saharan Africa; adopted by the Senate on May 11, 2000.

This legislation quickly revealed its hypocritical aspects. The reasons for this hypocrisy involve its mode of application. With the new system, the U.S. offered certain African states a commercial status of tariff preference for a period of eight years, during which they would benefit from fiscal exemptions for certain goods. The first among these was textiles but only on the condition

---

[1] Law dealing with trade and economic opportunity in Africa.

that they were produced from American thread and cloth. Moreover, products that entered into direct competition with American goods could be excluded from the accord.

In the case of particularly poor countries (those whose annual per capita GNP was less than $1,500), the law permitted imports from them of clothing, even if they were made with non-American cloth, for a trial period of four years. But the restrictive conditions were particularly severe. Firstly, if these imports rose too much, the law provided for a return to quotas; next, the origin of these products had to be clearly readable; thirdly, American customs inspectors were authorized to go to the countries concerned to inspect the factories where they were made; and finally, any fraud would bring a five-year suspension of the preferential regime.

In any case, the United States was hardly risking anything. In 1999, out of $60 billion worth of American textile imports, less than $600 million came from Africa, and in the years 2000-2010, African textiles will only represent two to three percent of all textiles imported by the United States.

The African "Liberal" Solution: NEPAD

Presented as demonstrating a new awareness on the part of Africans themselves of the need to take charge of their own development, the New Partnership for Africa's Development (NEPAD) was above all a strategy designed to make financial sponsors and lenders aware of the need not to abandon Africa. At the root of NEPAD was an acknowledgement of failure on the part of many African heads of state.

The situation was judged so critical that three of them proposed different programs:

– The South African president, Mbeki, was the author of a plan known as "African Renaissance."

– The Algerian president, Bouteflika, invented a "Millennium Africa Plan."

– The Senegalese head of state, Wade, advocated a "Plan Omega."

These three proposals had sufficient points in common that a synthesis was obviously needed. This took place in March 2001 at the OAU summit. Out of the fusion of the three plans was born the New African Initiative (NAI).

NAI was adopted in July 2001 at the summit of OAU heads of state in Lusaka. In October, it received its definitive name — the celebrated NEPAD.

At first glance, NEPAD is an initiative based on the idea of a revival of foreign investments in the African economies combined with structural reforms and "good governance." Its goal is the eventual deliverance of the continent from dependence on international aid. The creation of NEPAD seemed to imply that Africa had decided to renounce accusations in favor of a realistic examination of the causes of its economic failure and that it had finally resolved to take charge and cease making demands on the outside world.

The reality of the situation, however, is different as the following key points show:

– The first great ambiguity of NEPAD lies in the fact that the funds Africa will use to launch its development plan come once again from the industrialized countries. As in the past, Africa wants to count on itself but with the money of others. And its needs are colossal, since it is necessary to inject $64 billion each year in order to launch NEPAD, and that assumes an unrealistic annual growth rate of seven percent over 15 years.

– Secondly, there is a big question regarding the modalities of investment. NEPAD assumes private companies will risk considerable capital in countries where the infrastructure is run down or still needs to be created. Without roads, rail, or reliable airports, however, it is unlikely that private investors will be attracted. How can Africa be made into a continent that draws in private capital when corruption completely distorts economic reality? And how can risk-taking be encouraged in an unstable political environment and with judicial practices suffering the gangrene of corruption?

–A third problem is the direction of NEPAD, which has been put in the hands of a working group, baptized the Management Committee, which has been assigned to establish norms and rules of good conduct. In the words of Senegal's Vice President, it will be:

...put into practice starting with the NEPAD's priority sectors, regrouped in domains and divided among the initiating countries in the following manner:

South Africa: good political governance, peace, security, democracy.
Algeria: human development.
Nigeria: good private economic governance and capital flows.
Senegal: infrastructures, environment, NTIC, energy.
Egypt: access to markets, diversification of products.[1]

The net effects are that:

– South Africa, the most crime-ridden country in the world and one in which the state apparatus has been confiscated by an ethnic party, the ANC Xhosa, will be put in charge of the security and democracy of the continent.

– Algeria, a disintegrated society led by a despotic nomenklatura stuffed with its embezzlements and in which at least 30 percent of the active population is unemployed, will manage Africa's human development.

– Nigeria, a state with countless mafia-like structures whose specialties are the fraudulent export of capital, an archetype of state bankruptcy and the diversion of national riches (oil), is to take charge of "good private economic governance" and "capital flows."

– Senegal, where the destruction of the environment is in a phase of acceleration and which disposes of no energy sources at all, will guide NEPAD in these areas.

What's more, it will be these countries that will be charged with dividing up the colossal sums that are to be poured into Africa. When it is these very same countries that are among the most corrupt on the continent, even though the norm in this area is difficult to establish.

Finally, NEPAD's founders reveal themselves to be at odds with their own project in the preamble by outlining the need to cease seeking outside causes for African problems.

Readers may now be better able to evaluate the document published by the Vice-President of Senegal, whose text constitutes a perfect summary of the

---

[1] Vice-Presidency of Senegal, *Le NEPAD Expliqué [NEPAD Explained]*. One notes in passing that agriculture, which nevertheless supports 800 million Africans and represents an important part of the national wealth of the continent is strangely absent from these headings. And the same concerning AIDS.

"paradigm of victimization:"

> *Africa [. . .] considers that it has been marginalized by historical evolution*
> *[. . .]. Its impoverishment stems from the cumulative effects of three hundred*
> *years of slavery, of one hundred years of colonization, and since independ-*
> *ence, from the economic domination that has taken the form of the exploita-*
> *tion of its resources and the labor of its population via the perpetual*
> *historical tendency of prices to fall.*[1]

In short, he continues to attribute the sad state of African affairs to slavery, colonization, and exploitation of its resources. If readers wonder why any African leader would take such a step backward and resort to incantation, it is because they need to condition the affluent people of the industrialized countries. It is understood that if the latter feel themselves to be responsible and guilty, they will be more inclined to be generous.

In the final analysis, the essential difference between previous aid policies for Africa and the new ones can be summed up in a single sentence. Since 1960, the industrialized nations have been giving to Africa at a pure loss; with NEPAD, they are being asked to invest at a pure loss.

The experts in the industrialized countries are not duped by such propositions, however. In private, critics are already at work because they are aware that they are in the presence of a another strategy on the parts of the African countries to try to engineer the return of their sponsors, who have already had their fingers badly burned in the past. All the more so since the idea of a partnership with the private sector in the industrialized countries is not really new. Great hopes were based on this idea in the 1990s, and all of them were dashed. But the decisions are not theirs to make, and the political leaders of the G8 appear to have already agreed to support NEPAD.

NEPAD depends above all on the support given to it by the industrialized countries at the G8 summit. The countries in question do feel guilty about the failures of the "Structural Adjustment Plan," the great reform imposed by the World Bank and the International Monetary Fund (IMF). As a result, they have decided

---

[1] *Le NEPAD Expliqué, [NEPAD Explained]*, Op. Cit.

to back NEPAD in order not to appear as if they were abandoning Africa.

NEPAD is the economic part of a program of African union that supporters believe is based on a new idea, full of hope and historical realism—Pan-Africanism. However, it was this same "new" idea that provided the foundation for the Organization of African Unity (OAU), born on May 25, 1963 in Addis Ababa. During forty years of existence, the OAU never resolved any of the continent's problems. Having proved its ineffectiveness, it was scuttled at Durban on July 8, 2002, and subsequently transformed into the African Union (AU).

Taking note of the impotence of the late OAU, the African states represented in the AU have decided to give the new organization real means of action on three points: political, with the creation of an African parliament; economic, with the foundation of an African bank; and military, with the raising of an African army made necessary by the integration of the "right of interference" decided by the signatories.

The objective of the new organization is ambitious: to put the integration and development of the continent back on track, following the example of what the Europeans have accomplished. To achieve this, Africa has been divided into several great regions within which processes of regional union will be put into effect. These will constitute steps leading up to the creation of a United States of Africa, full of peace and love, the ultimate aim of Pan-Africanism, the ultimate aim of the AU.

Two differences in method, however, distinguish the construction of the AU from what was done with the European Union. Where the Europeans have acted with patience and only at the end of a long process, the African initiators of the AU have chosen to hurry. This seems to carry the mark of the project's chief instigator, Colonel Kadhafi. Also, where the Europeans have demanded that candidate members to the Union meet both economic and political criteria, the AU is open to all unconditionally, as long as they are Africans. This reflects the same old myth of the "African People."

Still in its infancy, the AU has already shown itself incapable of dealing with its first three major problems. First of all, it is experiencing difficulties getting funded. How will countries with their economies in tatters meet the enormous needs engendered by such an institution? Moreover, will the richest African countries commit themselves to aiding the less well-off? This is unlikely, because even their "black gold" has not allowed development to take place. If such wealth has not even been distributed equitably at the national level, how can one imagine that it could be on an international level?

Secondly, there is a problem with leadership. Above all, it is clear that two of the principal African leaders, Presidents Kadhafi of Libya and Mbeki of South Africa, have completely divergent views on the subject of the AU. Furthermore, the AU charter is in conflict with the "Kadhafi case" since the Libyan "Guide of the Great Revolution" refuses to submit his power to a test of election, arguing his legitimacy to be derived precisely from that said revolution.

Last comes the question of local realities. Three large crises, which the late OAU was incapable of treating, are making the African continent tremble. They are:

– The question of Western Sahara, which caused the division of African countries between the supporters of Morocco and the advocates of a "Sahrawi state." Morocco withdrew from the OAU, in 1984, when the Sahrawi Arab Democratic Republic (SADR) was admitted. But among the five heads of state that gave speeches at the official ceremony launching the AU at the Durban stadium in South Africa, the one speaking in the name of North Africa was the "President" of the RASD, Mohamed Abdelaziz. A real provocation in the eyes of Morocco.

– The conflict of the "Kongo bloc" in which 10 countries, all members of the AU, were directly implicated at the moment of its birth.

– The question of Zimbabwe whose dictator Mugabe has received support from many African leaders, who, at the same time, adopted with NEPAD the AU charter concerning democracy and "good governance."

To all these diverse problems, one should also add, at the risk of making this "Raft of the Medusa" sink altogether, the questions of AIDS, the famine spreading in southern and eastern Africa, and the waste of natural resources. There are just so many major difficulties that the AU is incapable of managing under the conditions existing today.

In the end, all the solutions proposed are once again economic ones, even though the principal obstacles to an African renewal are not economic, but political, cultural, historical, etc. Solutions will only come through recognition of an obvious fact obstinately denied by the ideologues, which is that Africans are not poor Europeans with dark skins. To save Africa, it is therefore urgent to overturn all the universalist dogmas that are stifling it and preventing it from redefining itself.

---

[1] Translator's Note: The "Raft of the Medusa" is a reference to a famous shipwreck that occurred off the coast of Africa in 1816. After the ship Medusa ran aground and sank, a makeshift raft was built, initially holding afloat 149 persons, but, after 12 days at sea, only 15 survived, the others having been thrown overboard or even devoured by their companions.

Conclusion

Steps to a True Resolution

Americans and Europeans take the same globalizing approach to Africa. Even if the word is fashionable, this vision of the continent does not correspond to any African reality. It is directly born of the ideological movements of the 1950s, 1960s, and 1970s; it is the result of a guilt-provoking Pan-Africanism forcing down our throats and the myth of a "Black People" victim of a white world. But the differences between a Wolof and a Tutsi are at least as numerous as those between a New York stockbroker and a Russian metalworker. Or perhaps greater, since the New Yorker may be the descendant of a Muscovite immigrant, but it is a certainty that the inhabitant of Dakar and the one from Kigali do not have any ancestors in common.

America and France also share a messianic approach to Africa. There is nothing surprising about this since the two countries are governed in the name of the same revolutionary principles. For the French and American ruling elites, nourished at the breast of their 18th century revolutions, men are the same everywhere even if they live under different skies. The French idea of assimilation through culture and adhesion to the principles inherited from the revolution of 1789 is a close relative of the more down-to-earth American version called the American Way of Life.

The British approach the issue quite differently. That is why one never saw the schoolteachers of His Gracious Majesty trying to make little Hausa children learn that they were descended from William the Conqueror, even though their French counterparts, seriously and with dedication, were making Algerian pupils recite the famous lines, "Our ancestors the Gauls".

Léon Blum, Secretary-General of the Section française de l'Internationale ouvrière (SFIO)[1] and future Prime Minister of the Popular Front government that came to power in France in 1936, declared on July 9, 1925 to the French Chamber of Deputies:

We admit the right and even the duty of the superior races to attract to themselves those that have not reached the same degree of culture.

Marshal Hubert Lyautey, the first Resident-Minister of France in Morocco, which he supervised from 1912 to 1925, and the very model of a colonizer respectful of colonized peoples, for his part wrote a sentence that still has considerable force. In the context of a triumphant imperialism and of colonial superiority in the 1920s it was even more significant:

Africans are not inferior, they are other from us.

Everything is said in quotations. On the one hand, Léon Blum, the great political leader of the Left, a socialist, humanist, and universalist, impregnated with French revolutionary culture, molded by the ideals of 1789, believes himself invested with a mission to impose all that on others, in total ignorance of what they are and the most profound contempt for what they think. On the other, a monarchist army officer, serving France and not the Republic (the difference is huge) and who, because of his education and his experiences out in the field, refuses leveling universalism and becomes the defender of the cultures and civilizations of those he is colonizing.[2]

In the debate between Blum and Lyautey, it is obvious Lyautey is right: Africans are "other" from us in at least three essential ways:

To begin with, Africans maintain a different relationship with their community. What characterizes African thought are complex networks of mutual support and dependency linking relatives through lineage, clan, tribe, and ethnic group. In the end, Africans are "prisoners" of this protective pyramid. In contrast,

---

[1] Ancestor of the present-day French Socialist Party.
[2] His Moroccan achievements attest to this. One can read further on this subject in: B. Lugan, *Histoire du Maroc des origines à nos jours [History of Morocco from Its Origins to the Present]*, Librairie Académique Perrin, Paris, 2000.

Americans and Europeans share an extreme individualism, which leads them to an entirely different manner of perceiving their milieu and situating themselves within it. This difference is an abyss.

Next, the perception of time is radically different. African Man does not have the same notion of tomorrow, or the future, as an American, European, or Asian. To the casual observer, he often seems lacking in foresight, but this is a false impression. It is the very idea of the future that is strange to him. Tomorrow does not exist for him; only the present counts. The form of "fatalism" that stems from this vision is difficult to understand for civilizations where the agenda is king.

And lastly, there is the relationship to the sacred in the cosmogony of the black man. African Man is constantly being crushed by hostile forces that he must appease by rites, sacrifices, and dances. From this fact stems the importance of ritual in all African cultures. Thus, masks, which are generally intermediaries between men and these forces, reflect the harmony of the surrounding world: often troubling and grimacing for the forest peoples crushed by their sylvan environment; more smiling, even kindly for those living in the savanna.

These three differences lead to another observation: African Man, both the one in the bush as well the one in the township, tends to deny the problems that Europe and America pose for him. Because he is a prisoner as of the group, of time, and the forces beyond his control, innovation, which is the creed of the Western world, is perceived by the African as a betrayal of customs, that is to say, of his ancestors. And one must above all avoid provoking the ire of one's ancestors against oneself, because then it will be the group (whether one calls it the extended family, clan, tribe, or ethnic group) which will suffer because they will come prowling around the living to reproach them for their betrayal.

In short, African Man is strongly inclined not to innovate. He must, in analogous situations, repeat the same gestures with the same tools, and reproduce the same codified social relations. His culture is characterized by immutability, and this has made sub-Saharan Africa a receiver rather than a conceiver in terms of technology. It has received from outside, through the

Arabs or the Europeans, all the elements of technological modernity. This philosophy of the group, based on technical immutability and social immobility, moreover, can only result in the failure of all attempts to reconcile the African with the European "Promethean" vision, in its lay or religious versions.

Genetically, linguistically, historically, there does not exist a "Black People" in the sense that the Afrocentrists understand it, but the African populations nevertheless do share common mentalities. Whether these be social, political, or religious responses, African Man reacts, in general, differently from European Man.

The European approach is the opposite of the African philosophy: individualism is opposed to the group, doubt to custom, questioning to tradition. European Man seeks to understand nature in order to explain it and try to tame it. Western civilization is based on individualist notions that are perfectly bizarre, and even incomprehensible, to Africans. So it has been with Christianity, an individualist religion that is impermeable to African communitarian perceptions that propose, for example, saintliness as an ultimate goal, with all the consequences that stem from that. A saintliness that, in Christian civilization, may take the "commonplace" exterior form of chastity, poverty, and humility. But these traits are strange and even traumatic concepts for the "average" African, who adulates the strong, despises the weak, and constructs societies that see in polygamy proof of the generative power of their rulers, in wealth the possibility of supporting a numerous clientele, and in sumptuousness and appearance the means of imposing respect.

The New York stockbroker, even of Russian origin, who goes home every evening to his apartment on Long Island is perfectly incapable of understanding how, for the Pygmy returning home from the hunt, his home is the forest itself. In a sense, the Pygmy had just gone out to open the collective refrigerator. And it is also for this reason (the community rather than the individual) that "evangelized" Africans tend to favor external forms of expression that allow group participation; including in the churches of Atlanta with their gospel music and "interactive preaching." Strong, lively, and colorful, Christian celebrations in Africa abandon the individual aspect, although it is the essence of Christianity, and find in the collective rites a substitute for their incomprehension of a religion that proposes the search for personal salvation.

To try to save Africa, it is therefore essential to account for the idea of difference; Africans are "other". Awareness of this will permit a modification of the approach "Whites" take with respect to the continent and help them understand that on the one hand it is futile to want to harvest plums from a palm tree. And on the other hand, it will allow them to understand that Africans do have a culture of their own to develop, an evolution of their own to pursue, against the democratic ukase, and this may force "right-thinking" people, of whatever color, to find themselves saying that perhaps their way of thinking is not, after all, the "sole" path forward.

The problem is that the "victimization paradigm" has installed in people's perception of African questions a schizophrenia between obvious facts and fantasy. The obvious facts are those that all observe, but forbid themselves from taking into account because they contradict the dogmas to which they have submitted. And the fantasy is one that constantly keeps slipping away, yet is proclaimed as universal and intangible truth: the famous "African People" who are soluble in the universal Humanity of the Enlightenment.

* * *

Because the claims of Europeans, Africans, and American Afrocentrists alike are false, their propagation has had the result of interfering with the possibility of resolving Africa's underlying problems. Only taking the true realities into account will allow it to escape from the present chaos.

The suggestions that follow will only appear to be iconoclastic to those who have a superficial or ideological vision of the various Africas. They are not in any sense "miracle" remedies. Their originality lies simply in a different, realistic, and concrete approach to the continent.

We propose a seven-part program for resolving Africa's problems:

1) The most urgent need is a temporary return to ethnic bases. For, while

ethnicity is not an end in itself, it is an obligatory passage for any African reconstruction. In the midst of generalized disintegration and rampant anarchy, it is critical to restore the smallest common denominator around which men can be assembled in order to then proceed to rebuild by enlarging. This return to ethnic realities should involve two great steps:

– First of all, the reconstitution of a territorial and social order accepted by all thanks to a general ethnic withdrawal

– Next, moving beyond this withdrawal by means of territorial contracts of free association, whether these be federations, confederations, or other models. The essential condition for their success is that they not be based on the individualist representation of the "democratic diktat," with its murderous corollary of "one man, one vote," that has destroyed internal African balances.

2) In the longer term, the only answer is to rectify certain frontiers, or even redefine them completely when this is historically and humanly legitimate. Here is a project for the African Union that is a truly new: to put all of the details on the table and redraw the natural dividing lines of the continent.

These new frontiers should be based on the ethnic groups that most often do have territorial bases, the real flesh and blood homelands of their members. It is upon these homelands that the new African constitutional organization should be based because it is the only basis that would not represent a break with the continent's philosophical and cultural roots. The international institutions should thus no longer systematically oppose attempts to call into question the existing frontiers.

3) Africans must also come to understand that "Western" democracy cannot be imported in its existing state. Any political system has in fact a great deal of historical relativity. In no country of Europe, with the exception perhaps of Switzerland, has democracy existed for more than two centuries. But Europeans have a history that extends back much further than the 18th and 19th centuries. The birth of the nation-states on the Old Continent owes nothing to them. France, Germany, Italy, England, Russia, Spain, etc. existed before them and were not forged by democracy.

African societies were born neither with colonization nor with decolonization and even less with the democratic diktat. Africa should re-establish the real links that bind it to its long history, links that have been cut off by the universalist ideologies that have been artificially imposed upon it. A solution might be found in a system where representation is based upon groups, and no longer on individuals. But even so, the Western system of "one man, one vote" would have to be forgotten once and for all. It would thus be a veritable intellectual revolution for the Americans and the Europeans as well as for those Africans who believed they would receive dividends for eternity owing to the dominant demographics of their ethnic group.

4) Next, one should cease to believe that economics can solve everything. We have shown that the principal African crises are structural, and that they have historical, political, and cultural roots.

African behavior itself does not give priority to economics. Here is one example. In Zimbabwe, President Mugabe knows that the white farmers assured 95 percent of industrial exports and 80 percent of food production. He was never unaware of the fact that by confiscating their lands, he was going to ruin his country and provoke the current famine. The Westerners who reason as economists have simply not understood that the president's priorities were on a symbolic level rather than in terms of commercial profitability. By re-appropriating the land, he acted as an African "liberator" chief and is adulated by the entire continent. That he pushed his country into the famine is secondary, both to him and to Africans.

By the same token, the key to the African crises does not consist in an increase in aid programs. To date, the results of these have been worthless. Nor does it lie in the selective and hypocritical "Trade not Aid." Instead, it must take into account the continent's specificities, in the forefront of which is the ethnic factor, a major, even determinant, social reality south of the Sahara. As long as the approach to Africa's problems continues to be primarily economic, they have no chance of being solved

5) Africans should be distrustful of the "magic" formulas that the economic development professionals want to impose upon them. They should be aware

that these are only passing Western fashions that have arisen after decades of intellectual neo-colonialism that took the names of "Marxism," "socialism," "liberalism," "Third Worldism," or "transfer of technologies." The two terms currently in vogue are "good governance" and "local appropriation of policies," notions that have succeeded "structural adjustment" and "conditionality of aid," which for a while replaced "self-centered endogenous development," "training of trainers," "industrializing industries," or even "small projects." And we can expect new variations to emerge that once again will be imposed as just so many provisionally definitive creeds.

6) It is also important to prohibit "humanitarian interference," this neo-colonialism of pity, from blocking the regional re-compositions now taking place, in eastern Africa as in southern or western Africa. Caught between the liberal sharks who exploit them and the naive staff of the NGOs who treat them like children, sub-Saharan Africans are too often abandoned and left to feel excluded from the countries of the north who have come to aid those who are more miserable than they. Similarly, the American Peace Corps, the European Volunteers for Progress and all these "supervisors" too often come looking in Africa for answers to their own existential problems. Village wells, home improvements, small mills, small dams, small farms, village gardens. These "small whites" in reality are stifling Africans with their thousands of "small" projects whose "small" capacities are the result of "small" ambitions, all of it backed by "small" means with a total absence of any perspective.

7) Lastly, it is time that the political leaders of the north understand and admit that, before being "French-speaking" or "English-speaking," "Christians," or "Muslims," the inhabitants of Africa are above all Africans who speak African languages and who have their own beliefs. More generally, and as the Ivorian novelist, Ahmadou Kourouma,[1] put it:

"Africa is inhabited by animists, some tinged by Christianity, others by Islam."

In this respect, the promotion of the French language ("francophonie") by "activists" and institutions presents considerable dangers for the future of the African continent. Its first great defect is that it keeps the French-speaking

---

[1] Of whom one can cite the excellent novel, *En attendant le Vote des Bêtes Sauvages [Waiting for the Vote of Savage Beasts]*, Le Seuil, Paris, 1998.

African elites rooted in a history and a culture which is foreign to them. A phenomenon of acculturation is produced with a worrying tendency: a bigger and bigger divide is in effect opening up between the people and the French-speaking nomenklatura. The latter, which has been encouraged to pursue studies abroad are less and less at ease in their "home" countries, and often end up settling in France or Quebec. For Africa, this represents a total loss.

In France, the laws concerning foreign residents prevent making these economic migrants understand that they are indispensable in their country of origin and that they are nothing but deserters. In Quebec, the situation is even worse. The linguistic obsession there is such that, in order to resist the oppressive environment of the English language, the authorities encourage immigration by French-speaking African graduates. Literally "bought" on the continent where they are recruited by means of ads, they are then transplanted to Canada's "Belle province" whose women no longer produce enough French-speaking children, so that they will produce battalions of linguistic auxiliaries that will permit the Anglo-Saxon "invaders" to be contained. It is thanks to this new "slave trade" in Blacks and North Africans that local statistics of the French-speaking population have been artificially inflated. Proudly standing on its fields of snow, Quebec's French-speaking rooster can thus continue to crow, albeit strangely, thanks to this new "Black Force." It is not irresponsible to say that this policy is literally criminal. Idiotically promoted by the institutions charged with defending the French language, it contributes to killing Africa by emptying it a little more each day of its most educated children.

Nevertheless, in France, criticism from certain circles rains down whenever the sacred principle of francophonie is questioned; it has become the new Maginot Line to which right-minded people cling like mussels to a rock.

This is not to say that Africa should be deprived of one of the great international languages that facilitates exchanges and is vital to its development. Nor should the importance of a common history be ignored. However, it must be agreed that Africans are not firstly English-speakers or French-speakers.

To attempt to approach contemporary African realities on the basis of these linguistic criteria is to advance blindfolded into the complex terrain of African political relations. To give one example, take the "Great Lakes" region of Africa. An error the French made here was to believe that, because the populations here were French-speaking for a few decades, countries like Rwanda or Burundi would gravitate towards French-speaking West Africa. Quite to the contrary, a myriad of factors has led them to look to the east, which by accident of history is English-speaking.

* * *

If it does not want to die, sub-Saharan Africa must ultimately become its true self. It must start by asserting its African identity. Faced with the multiple challenges to the continent, how would chiefs like Samori, El Hadj Omar, Shaka Zulu and Moulay Ismael have reacted? Today's Africa lacks leaders like these, with roots in its soil, in its long history.

Crushed by the victimization paradigm and the "good intentions" of affluent people in the countries of the North, Africa must make its counter-revolution. The reconstruction of Africa will only be carried out by a return to the natural African order.

At the same time, Africans must accept the fact that it is impossible to return the continent to the condition it was in back in 1850. It will only be when Africans have found innovative solutions to their political, ethnic, and constitutional questions and when they have delimited new entities within which they can govern themselves according to their own systems, that the economic solutions can be searched for and proposed. Not before.

While it may be true that rivers never return to their source, the sick can still aspire to recovering their health. Africa is gravely ill, and to save it, one has to stop first of all administering ideological potions which not only do not agree with it, but are actually killing it slowly. The African counter-revolution will consist in a return to its traditions, upon which can then, and only then, be introduced other political and economic elements imported or adapted from the outside.

The error is in continuing to give priority to economics as all the development projects propose, when the true emergency is a political. Everything must thus be restructured starting from the real, that is to say, from the ethnic groups which are the African variant of nationalism and the federating element of tribalism.

African societies being intrinsically inegalitarian, the return to the natural African order will necessarily pass by the domination of some and the submission of others. Stuck in their universalisms, are the affluent people of Europe and America ready to accept that and renounce their egalitarian dogmas? In the end, that is the real question.

Africa is not Disneyland, and the rains do not wash away the leopard's spots, any more than they do the zebra's stripes.